I0165882

WHAT DID YOU DO IN THE GREAT WAR GRANDPA?

THE STORY OF THE 749TH TANK BATTALION,
AND ITS' ASSIGNED INFANTRY REGIMENTS
IN WORLD WAR II

VOLUME TWO

B. J. BRYAN

Beautiful Wrinkles Press

CREDITS

ISBN 13   978-0692472378
ISBN 10   0692472371
Beautiful Wrinkles Press
Copyright © 2015 by Bonnie J. Bryan (B.J. Bryan)

This book was produced in the United States of America.

Dedicated to the memory of
Ernest Humphries
1917 - 2000
and
George A. Baker
1913 – 2007
who lived through it
and to those who gave all.

ACKNOWLEDGEMENTS

I owe a million thanks and respect to Nadine Servant, Mayor of Cameret, France.

In addition to her duties to her community and to her family at home, she never failed to send me correct spelling of names and countries that my brother-in-law mentioned in his journals. She has always been courteous and friendly in her emails.

It would be remiss on my part if I did not mention my manuscript consultant, Author T. E. Watson. He has been working with me for several years, including my three books thus far, and has never failed to answer any of my questions.

It has been a pleasure working with him; I hope we get to continue this for years to come. He can be contacted for consultation at; tew@tewatsononline.com

My dear family and precious friends who have given me encouragement and belief in my writing efforts should also be thanked. All the feedback I have received has been nothing but wonderful.

Table of Contents

Table of Contents cont.

1 MARCH TO
31 MARCH 1945

1 Mar. 1945

The 70th Inf Div was attached to the XXI Corps, 7th US Army. The enemy front lines were located 200 yards north and northwest of Morsbach and on the southwestern edge of Forbach on the road between Rosbach and Forbach. They were also on the northern edge of Forbach in the woods 1,000 yards east of Forbach, 1,500 yards east of Stiring-Wendel, 1,000 yards north of Spicheren, at the northern edge of the woods southwest of Saint Arnual, 1,000 yards east of Gudingen, and 100 yards north of Bebling.

The enemy units in contact were the 347th VGD of the 860th Volks-Grendier Regt (VGR) elements of the 861st VGR, 1st and 2nd Bns of the 880th VGR, the 347th Div Artillery Regt, the 347th Engineer Bn minus one company, elements of the 347th Fusilage Bn, elements of the 486th TD Bn (Infantry), an Assault Bn Of the GHQ, 1st Army, the 347th BG Zweibrücken (BGZ), Volksturm), the 719th Infantry Div, 2nd Bn of the 723rd Regt of the 559th VGD, 1st Bn Of the 1126 VGR, 1st and 2nd Bns of the 1127th VGR, 2nd Mountain Div of the 67th Mountain Recon Bn, and miscellaneous 17th SS PGD and two companies of the Assault Gun Bn.

Enemy action was limited to patrols, artillery, mortar, and scattered small arms fire. Artillery fire increased during the period. The bulk of the fire fell in the Forbach area with an increase in fire noted at each meal hour. Twenty-five (25) light caliber rounds fell at 1130 and 25 medium caliber at 1600 on le Creutzberg. Several airbursts were reported in Forbach. Four enemy were killed of a 9-man group in a paper mill by our Recon Troop patrol at 0600 An enemy counter-patrol from the woods was dispersed at 0705 by our infantry Cannon Co fire. Mortar fire was active in the Forbach area and in Bois de Saint Arnual.

Heavy vehicular traffic was heard in the vicinity of Stiring-Wendel at 1145. The enemy was reported moving lumber by wagon to the bank of the Saar River south of the bridge at 0240 hours. A train was reported seen leaving Sankt Johann in the direction of Neuscheidt at 2240. A train of 34 cars, 8 tank cars, 6 guns on flat cars were observed moving at 0800. The train was heard moving into Sankt Johann at 1835, but the direction of movement was undetermined.

The 274th Inf Regt continued to hold and improve defensive positions and aggressive patrolling. They continued to regroup and reorganize. Co C relieved Co G on the line and then G Co assembled in the vicinity of Etzling and Kerbachen. Cos A and D assembled in Kerbach. Enemy activity was confined to scattered small arms and artillery fire. Relief of Co A by Co K of the 275th Inf had not yet been completed. Co

F was relieved from its attachment to the 274th Inf and reverted to regimental control in the vicinity of Cocheren. Harassing artillery and mortar fire was received during the period.

The 275th Inf Regt continued to organize and improve positions for defense. Patrols continued to operate to the front. Cos A and I interchanged positions.

The 276th Inf Regt continued to hold and improve their defensive positions in Forbach. Patrols operated in the town throughout the period. The 70th Div Artillery continued its harassing and counter-battery missions.

The 749th Tank Bn released Co A to the 63rd Inf Div. Co D was relieved from Div Res and one platoon was attached to each regiment.

Results of Operations: The companies continued to hold and improve their defensive positions, to reorganize and regroup, and maintained constant aggressive patrolling. Enemy activity was confined to harassing small arms, artillery, and mortar fire. No enemy armor or tanks were destroyed.

Location of the 749th Tank Bn Troops revealed the forward Bn CP was at Saint Jean Rohrbach while the rear CP was in Vittersbourg.

The 1st and 2nd Plts of A Co withdrew to Gros Bliedersdorf after having been released from the attachment to the 275th Inf Regt of the 70th Div as of 1500 and attached then to the 63rd Inf Div for an impending mission.

B Co. was in Kerbach was attached to the 274th Inf Regt and remained in defensive positions. Sections of tanks were rotated to defensive positions at 1,000 yards east of Stiring-Wendel. There was no contact with the enemy. One section of the 3rd Plt was in the assembly area in Beneren. The company received 9 tanks with 76mm guns. Seventeen (17) tanks were now in operation. Two light tanks and crews from D Co were attached to this battalion for a combat mission.

Except as noted below C Co was in Oeting after it had been attached to the 276th Inf Regt. The 2nd Plt remained in Forbach guarding the road junctions and railroad underpasses. Maintenance and radio repair work continued.

D Co was in Cocheren and one platoon was attached to each regiment. One platoon was at Forbach and continued to patrol the town. One other platoon was at Alsting. The CP left Cocheren at 1400 for Spicheren and arrived at 1630, with a distance of travel approximately 12 miles. The 1st Plt was attached to the 275th Inf Regt upon arrival in Spicheren. No enemy action occurred and there were no casualties sustained. The Svc Co was in Monskirsch.

The weather was clear and cool. Visibility was fair to good. Combat efficiency was excellent and the morale of the troops high.

2 Mar. 1945

The 70th Inf Div general situation revealed there had been no change in either the enemy front lines or the enemy units in contact. Artillery fire increased during the period. A friendly patrol action precipitated a 2-hour firefight with the enemy including mortar and artillery. The enemy remained otherwise inactive.

Some AA fire was received from the vicinity of Stiring-Wendel at 1405 and 1611. The artillery was estimated to be 400 rounds, one-half light and one-half medium caliber, fell in the division's sector. However, the bulk of the fire fell in the Forbach area where 18 rockets were also reported. 50-rounds of concentrations fell in Spicheren, Etzling and Kerbachen, and Lasting. The enemy fired propaganda leaflets in the center of the division's zone at 1600. Small arms fire was sporadic. Harassing mortar fire was reported in the Forbach area, le Creutzberg, le Giferwald and Bois de Saint Arnual. A 50-round mortar concentration fell at 1200 and a 40-round in Bois de Saint Arnual at 0940.

A patrol clash at 1700 precipitated a 2-hour firefight including hostile mortar and artillery fire. The firefight had died out by 1915. A train was reported moving northwest from Sankt Johann at 0630. Another train was observed standing in the Sankt Johann vicinity at the same hour.

The 274th Inf Regt continued to hold and improve defensive positions. Co C relieved Co G and Co B on the front lines. Co G assembled in Etzling and Kerbachen. Co B assembled in Kerbach and then moved to Behren. Enemy patrol activity was reported in the vicinity of Co L and Co E of the 276th Inf at 1730. Scattered artillery and mortar fire was received during the period. Co A was in the process of relieving Co E of the 276th Inf on the front line so that Co E could move to Cocheren.

The 275th Inf Regt continued to organize and improve its defensive position. Co I occupied the position formerly held by Co A of the 274th Inf. New limiting point with the 274th Inf was established and continued aggressive patrolling. Enemy activity was confined to occasional mortar and artillery fire.

The 276th Inf Regt continued to hold and improve its present position in Forbach. At the close of the period Co E was closing into the assembly area in the vicinity of Cocheren. They continued day and night patrolling. Scattered artillery fire was received in Forbach. Div Artillery fired harassing and interdiction fire against enemy lines of communications. Neutralization fires on enemy gun emplacements continued.

Results of Operations: All units continued to hold and improve their defensive positions. The 275th Inf was organized for defense. Co I of the 275th Inf relieved Co A of the 274th Inf at 1730. Scattered small arms, artillery and mortar fire was received during the period.

The 749th Tank Bn, minus Cos and B attached to the 274th Inf and Co C attached to the 276th Inf; one platoon of light tanks was attached to each regiment. They continued maintenance and repair of equipment.

The 749th Tank Bn situation revealed Co A in the forward position was the location of the Bn CP at St Jean Rohrbach. The rear Bn CP was in Vittersbourg with Co A attached to the 276th Inf Regt in Forbach. D Co's CP was in Spicheren with one platoon attached to the 2nd Bn of the 276th Inf Regt, also in Forbach. One platoon was attached to the 274th Inf Regt in Spicheren and one platoon was attached to the 275th Inf Regt was in reserve, also at Spicheren. The Svc Co was still in Monskirsch.

Co A continued recon routes of advance in the zone of the 253rd Inf Regt of the 63rd Div. The Co CO and platoon leaders made aerial recon in cub plane for possible location of AT positions of the enemy. Tanks moved forward to the zone of the 63d Div. One assault gun of Hqs Co joined the assault gun of Co A.

In Co B the platoons were being rotated in defensive positions in the le Giferwald Forest. One section of tanks was in the assembly area at Behren. There as no contact with the enemy. One platoon was attached to each battalion of the regiment.

One platoon of D Co was attached to the 274th Inf in a reserve status. hey saw no enemy activity during the period.

Plans were made for combat mission that is impending to gain the final division's objective.

Co C's 2nd Plt remained in position in Forbach guarding vital road junctions and underpasses. Recon continued of routes to attack position. One platoon was attached to the 3rd Bn, one to the 1st Bn and one in regimental reserve.

One platoon of light tanks from Co D was attached to the 2nd Bn.

The following was a commendation by Col S.G. Conley given to the CO of Co D, 749th Tank Bn: "Infantry, commanding dated 2 Mar 1945: 'I wish to commend the officers and men of Co D, 749th Tank Bn f or the splendid display of cooperation, courage, and devotion to duty during the recent bitter fighting. In the advance, which has brought us to the frontiers of Nazi Germany, both unfavorable terrain and fanatic enemy have faced us. The superb cooperation of all personnel of Co D, 749th Tank

Bn, has made this advance possible. I am looking forward to our continued successful association and certain that we are ready and competent to storm the frontier of Germany and to destroy the armed forces opposing us.'"

Weather was cool with scattered snow flurries but visibility was good. Combat efficiency was still excellent and morale of the troops high.

3 Mar. 1945

The enemy front lines were as follows: Emmersweiler – 1,000 yards north of Morsbach, north of Marienau, southeastern edge of Fort de Forbach, southern part of Stiring-Wendel, 1,200 yards east of Stiring-Wendel, 1,200 yards north of Spicheren, northern edge of Fort de St Arnual, 1,000 yards southwest of Gudingen, and north of Bublingen. Enemy units in contact were the 374th VGD of the 860th VGR, 14 companies of the 861st VGR, two companies of the 880th VGR, 347th Div Artillery, one company of the 347th VGR Bn, the Assault Bn of the GHQ, 1st Army, the 347th BG (Zweibrücken, Volksturm), the 559th VGD, 1st Bn Of the 1125th VGR, 1st Bn of the 1126th VGR, 1st Bn of the 1127th VGR, 1st Bn of the 1127th VGR, 7 or 8 batteries of the 1559th AR with miscellaneous soldiers of the 116th SS PGD, two companies from the Assault Gun Bn, 1st Bn of the 1125th VGR.

A POW from one of the three companies of the 1125th VGR stated the 1125th VGR is a one-battalion regiment. It was to relieve the 1st Bn of the 1126th VGR but during the day it suffered heavy losses and was now attached to the 1126th VGR.

The enemy resisted our attack with artillery, mortar, and small arms fire. He was driven from pillboxes and mined defensive positions in the woods east and southeast of Stiring-Wendel. In the left attack zone, the enemy was forced from fortified positions in houses west of Forbach. Action prior to the attack was limited to artillery, intermittent small arms fire that was an increase over the preceding period that included mortar and rocket fire. The artillery increased in response to our attack. An estimated 500 rounds of light caliber shells fell during the period although the concentrations were small and scattered. In the Forbach area, the woods east and southeast of Stiring-Wendel and le Giferwald were hit. Twenty-four (24) known rockets fell in the Forbach area, believed to be Nebelwerfer.

Small arms and MG fire from the enemy in pillboxes and entrenchments in the woods east and southeast of Stiring-Wendel and subsequently from the town. Small arms and MG fire came from fortified houses and entrenchments west of Forbach and Bois de Forbach. There was increased mortar fire prior to and during the attack continuing at the end of the period.

The 274th Inf Regt continued the attack to the northeast and Stiring-Wendel against moderate enemy small arms and artillery fire, pillboxes and mines. At the close of the period, the front line was generally along the road. Contact was established with the 275th and 276th Infs.

The 275th Inf Regt continued to occupy and improve their defensive positions and assisted the 274th and 253rd Infs in their attack by supporting fires. They established and maintained contact with them.

The 276th Inf Regt continued their attack to the northwest through Forbach. Heavy artillery and mortar fire was encountered. Enemy mines and pillboxes slowed the attack. Co I moved into Marienau. Elements of the 1st and 3rd Bns were 100 meters beyond the creek in the northwestern section of Forbach. Contact remained intact with adjacent infantry units. The 749th Tank Bn, minus Co A sustained close support for the infantry. Co C knocked out four pillboxes in Forbach. Co B assisted in the capture of 25 POWs in Stiring-Wendel.

Results of Operations: The 275th and 276th Infs launched a coordinated attack at 1817. The enemy's resistance consisted of moderate to heavy small arms and artillery fire. Enemy pillboxes and mines slowed down the attacking units. The 274th Inf was fighting in Stiring-Wendel and the 276th Inf was fighting on the northwestern edge of Forbach. Three friendly tanks were reported lost. One hundred twenty-one (121) POWs were captured during the period.

The 63rd Inf Div's general situation showed the 253rd Inf was attached to the 1st Bn of the 255th Inf, Co A of the 749th Tank Bn; the 1st Bn crossed the line of demarcation at 1410 following the tanks. Upon reaching the open, six tanks were knocked out and they withdrew to reorganize and later returned to form a base of fire to support the infantry attack. Having advanced 400 yards, Co C, on the right, was held up by heavy automatic and 88mm fire. At 1735 all elements had moved into position at the edge of the woods 1,000 yards northeast of Bublingen and reorganized. At the same time Co C of the 253rd Inf was clearing out quarry against enemy resistance. The quarry was finally cleared at 2100 and was reorganized for defense at the close of the period.

At 2200 the 1st Bn of the 255th Inf resumed the attack; however, Co B was held up in the woods 1,000 yards northeast of Bublingen. Co A had cleared out of the woods 1,000 yards north of the same town but was held up in the woods northeast of there. The company had cleaned out the woods 1,000 yards north of the town at 2145 and cleaned out the houses along the main road. They were held up by enemy MGs at the close of the period in the vicinity of the woods north of the town.

After dark Co A of the 749th Tank Bn withdrew to Kleinblittersdorf to refuel and rearm. The attack to reach the final objective was still progressing at the close of the period. The remainder of the regiment continued to defend and improve its present position. The 254th Inf of Co C with one section of assault guns from Co A of the 749th Tank Bn raided Hartungshof and the adjoining woods at 1305 meeting medium resistance of small arms and light mortar as well as artillery fire.

The 1st Bn continued as regimental reserve. The 2nd and 3rd Bns continued to defend and improve their present positions. Recon patrols were active and the 3rd Bn assisted Co C in a raid by fire from the defensive position. Sections of assault guns of Co A of the 749th Tank Bn was released from attachment to the 254th Inf and reverted to control of the parent company unit at 1930.

The 255th Inf reported the 2nd Bn conducted a raid on Habkirchheim at 1430. They encountered heavy enemy small arms and MG fire. They were unable to enter the town. Regimental control continued to defend and improve its present position.

Results of Operations: The 253rd Inf attacked during the period meeting heavy small arms, mortar and artillery fire. They seized the initial objective 1,000 yards northeast of Bublingen and were progressing slowly toward the final objective at the end of the period.

The 254th Inf conducted a raid on Habkirchheim but was driven off by heavy enemy resistance. The division continued to defend and improve positions with recon patrols active in the sectors of the 254th and 255th Infs.

The 749th Tank Bn situation had the location of our troops as follows: The forward Bn CP was St Jean Rohrbach while the rear Bn CP was located at Vittersbourg. Co A was in Auersmacher, attached to the 63rd Inf Div, 253rd Inf Regt. Co B was in Kerbach and attached to the 274th Inf Regt plus one platoon of Co D. Co C was in Spicheren and the Svc Co in Honskirch.

Co A plus one assault gun from Hqs Co attached to the 63rd Inf Div of the 253rd Regt reported their tanks moved out at 0600 from Gros Bliesderstroff south approximately 3 miles to cross the Saar River on a 40-ton pontoon bridge and then moved into Auersmacher. Tanks then moved off at 1405 from Kleinblittersdorf while the infantry jumped off from the front line in the vicinity of Bublingen. They passed friendly infantry in their advance to the objective that was the Hähn Woods and the ground generally to the north.

An air mission was successfully completed on Gudingen, Fechingen, and Bois de

Fechingen. During the air assault six enemy tanks or assault guns were reported moving west from Eschringen and P-47s reported that they destroyed all six tanks or assault guns. As the tanks reached Hinterwald Woods and the ground to the west of the woods, smoke was placed on Hahnsbusch and the small woods further to the north, and other locations as planned. Wind blew smoke to the south leaving the tanks in a smoke screen as tanks moved out from the woods, leaving them in the open. AT guns of the enemy held the advantage as the smoke cleared their position first and as the tanks moved out to attack in wedge formation, two tanks were hit by AT fire simultaneously. The company had advanced 500 yards when they were fired on by 3 enemy AT guns. Enemy locations were not spotted due to smoke.

One tank broke a clutch as a cable tangled around the track. Six Co A tanks were hit by AT fire and three were known to have burned. The remaining three might be recovered. Two complete crews were MIA: Sgt Price, Cpl Mace, T/5 Faust, Pfc Caldwell, Pfc E.E. Cox, and Pfc Leitwein. One other crewmember was KIA: Sgt R.B. Jackson. Slightly wounded were S/Sgt McLemore, Cpl Lang (both evacuated), Pfc Wilkening, Pfc Lopez, Pfc Cherno, and Pfc Bader (none of whom were evacuated). Also wounded slightly and evacuated were Cpl Addis, S/Sgt Mosca, Cpl Osso, and T/5 Dujaleski. The company withdrew to hull defilade position at the attack position. The infantry continued the assault to wipe out AT weapons and were supported by company fire. Nine (9) enemy MG nests were wiped out.

The company and headquarters assault guns, attached to the 274th Inf, for diversionary attack on the right flank was accomplished. The company assembled at 1900 in Kleinsliederstroff and orders were received relieving Co A from the control of the 63rd Div at 2000 and attached to the 101st Cav Grp. They were to move to St Avold reporting not later than 2400. At 2000 orders were received that the company would not be relieved from the 63rd Div until 0730 at which time the company proceed to Saint Avold. At 2200 these orders were cancelled and orders issued that the company would continue to attack against the objective that had not been overrun. The company assembled at Auersmacher and remained there for the night. They then moved to the 101st Cav sector in the vicinity of St Avold per orders.

Co B, plus one platoon of Co D, attached to the 276th Inf Regt moved from Spicheren at 1800 to Neueglassbutten in defense to support A and D Cos. The 274th Regt's 2nd Plt moved from Spicheren at 1600 to a new assembly area in Stiring-Wendel in defensive support of F and G Cos and knocked out 10 pillboxes and 10 MG strong points, taking 50-60 prisoners. The platoon received heavy artillery fire during the move with one officer, St Eck, slightly wounded, and was not evacuated. The 3ʳᵈ Plt moved from Behren to a new assembly area at Forbach at 0800. One tank was detached at 1100 and was given the mission to knock out an occupied pillbox that was holding up the advance of the infantry and to be accompanied by a half squad of infantry attacking a pillbox in the woods 2,000 yards west of Spicheren. The tank advanced to the objective, fired two shots of 76mm destroying the pillbox and enabled the infantry to take 25 POWs in the vicinity of le Sangewald, east of Stiring-Wendel. The mission was accomplished at 1230. Two enemy were slightly wounded and one killed. The tank returned to the platoon assembly area at Forbach at 1300.

At 2100 a platoon moved to support one platoon of I Co at Neueglassbutten. They knocked out 7 pillboxes and 6 MG emplacements, taking 50 POWs. The platoon remained in the town in defensive support.

Co C's 1ˢᵗ Plt attacked with the 3ʳᵈ Bn of the 276ᵗʰ Inf Regt to capture a portion of Forbach north of the railroad. Tanks supported the infantry in their advance across the railroad to west Forbach. They destroyed at least 10 MG nests, demolished many buildings, and destroyed at least four bazookas. Mines knocked one of our tanks out before it could cross the railroad. The remaining three tanks fired on buildings, gun emplacements, and MGs. The 2ⁿᵈ Plt attacked with the 1ˢᵗ Bn of the 276ᵗʰ Inf Regt and with one company of the Free French Forces. In this engagement, one tank was knocked out by artillery and one by mines.

Buildings and gun emplacements were also destroyed by this platoon. One enlisted man, Fairchild (no rank given), was evacuated due to combat exhaustion and one enlisted man, Cook (no rank given), was evacuated from shock and shrapnel.

One light tank of Co D, attached to Co B, hit a mine at the vicinity of a crossroad west of Stiring-Wendel, while running supplies to the infantry.

Weather was excellent to good but was cold and clear with scattered flurries of snow. Visibility was good. Combat efficiency was good and the morale excellent.

4 Mar. 1945

The 70ᵗʰ Inf Div showed the enemy front lines remained generally the same and there was no change in enemy units other than the following additional new units were identified: Remnants of one company of the 347ᵗʰ Engineer Bn, the 3ʳᵈ Co of the 347ᵗʰ Field Replacement Bn and 7 companies of the 2ⁿᵈ Bn of the 1126ᵗʰ Regt of the 559ᵗʰ VGD. The enemy continued to defend with increased mortar and artillery fire when compared to the previous period. In Fort de Forbach the enemy was driven back approximately 1,000 yards. House-to-house fighting continued in Stiring-Wendel and as our troops reinforced, the enemy slowly gave ground. Resistance continued in the military barracks in the area northwest of Forbach and in Marienau.

The enemy was inactive in the right portion of the division's zone. Two ME 109s were reported in the right division's zone at 0725. They did not strafe or bomb. Artillery of light and medium caliber increased to an estimated 700 rounds. The bulk of the fire fell in the Forbach and Stiring-Wendel areas. Twenty (20) rounds were reported in Etzling and Kerbach and Resting between 0115 and 0200 hours.

Harassing fire fell on le Creutzberg, le Gifterwald, and Bois de Saint Arnual. Automatic weapons and small arms fire was active in the building areas of Stiring-Wendel, in an area west of Forbach, and Marienau where house-to-house fighting continued. Mortar fire was scattered and active throughout the period. 50 rounds of heavy mortar fell in Bois de St Arnual from 1525 and 1600. Shu-mines were encountered and were reported to be around bunkers in the Stiring-Wendel area. A train was heard in the vicinity of Sarrebrucken at 0545 hours.

The 274th Inf Regt continued their attack on Stiring-Wendel. One-quarter of the town was occupied by elements of the 2nd and 3rd Bns.

The 275th Inf Regt continued to occupy and improve defensive positions. They maintained contact with adjacent units and aggressive patrolling.

The 276th Inf Regt continued to attack to the northwest. At the close of the period they had elements in Marienau, the northwest sector of Forbach and the southeast sector of Fort de Forbach along the railroad tracks. The units in Forbach continued receiving heavy small arms and artillery fire. Division artillery continued to support the attack.

The 749th Tank Bn, less Co A, with one platoon of Co D and B attached to the 274th, one platoon of Co D and Co C attached to the 276th, and one platoon of Co D attached to the 275th Infs. They assisted in the attack.

Results of Operations: The 275th Inf continued to occupy and improve defensive positions while the 274th and 276th Infs resumed the attack toward the division's objective. The 274th Inf occupied one-quarter of Stiring-Wendel. The 276th Inf secured Marienau and the southeast portion of Fort de Forbach. Artillery, small arms, and automatic weapons fire continued to slow the attacking units. They encountered enemy mines and pillboxes.

The situation of the 749th Tank Bn had the location of troops as follows: A Co plus one assault gun of Hqs Co was attached to the 101st Cav Grp at St Avold.

Co B plus one platoon of D Co was attached to the 274th Inf at Kerbach. Co C plus one platoon of Co D was attached to the 276th Inf at Oeting. One platoon of D Co was attached to the 275th Inf at Spicheren. There were no other changes in locations.

A Co moved into position at 0515 hours to support the infantry. They received numerous orders during the morning concerning being relieved and an attachment from the 63rd Div to the 101st Cav Grp with each being cancelled in due course of time. At 1045 orders were received to the effect that the company would withdraw from the support position by infiltration into an assembly area at Kleinbliedersdorf and would proceed from that point to Saint Avold at 1200. The company was detached from the 63rd Div and attached to the 101st Cav Grp for a combat mission. The company moved at 1200 from Auersmacher to St Avold. The company arrived at that new location at 1615 and a liaison was established with the Cav Grp. They did maintenance work in preparation for the attack mission with the Cav Grp.

Six tanks lost as reported in the previous period was corrected to read as five tanks. One tank crew was found; the tank gun would not function and was moved into the woods. The total was 9 enlisted men had been MIA that was corrected.

The 1st Plt of Co B left the assembly area of Neueglassbutten near the vicinity of Forbach (1,000 yards north) at 0630 in support of Cos L and K of the 274th Regt to attack an enemy position in and around Stiring-Wendel. The mission was accomplished at 1810. Destroyed were one enemy pillbox, three MG nests and three POWs were taken. Several buildings were destroyed by tank fire. The platoon received very heavy artillery fire throughout the day. One section of the 2nd Plt was in support of F Co and one section in support of G Co of the 274th Regt and attacked Stiring-Wendel. The objective was taken at 1700. Six MG nests were destroyed and 18 POWs taken. The platoon remained with the infantry in defensive support. Enemy casualties were unknown. The 3rd Plt left the assembly area at Forbach at 1400 to assist one platoon of I Co in knocking out two pillboxes and that mission was accomplished at 1830. Destroyed were both pillboxes and two snipers were killed. The platoon returned to the assembly area at Forbach.

The 1st and 3rd Plts with the 3rd Bn knocked out 8 pillboxes and took 20 POWs and one enlisted man, Sgt. Whistler, was slightly wounded and evacuated.

The 1st Plt of C Co continued the attack with the 276th Inf Regt. The 3rd Bn moved east from Forbach and captured Marienau. The 2nd and 3rd Plts, with the 1st Bn of the 276th Inf Regt, continued mopping up the section of Forbach northwest of the railroad. Three sections of tanks were used to support the infantry in their attempt to advance west of Forbach. After stubborn resistance by the enemy, our infantry pulled back to their original jump-off east of the railroad. Artillery (8-inch shells) impeded their advance, and the infantry pushed on approximately 500 yards west of Forbach. Five enlisted me were slightly wounded: Pfc Davis, T/4 Galbreath, Pfc DiCarlo, Cpl T.J. Cook, and Sgt Harting, none of whom were evacuated.

Weather was cold, overcast and slight snow flurries throughout the period. Visibility was poor. Combat efficiency was good and the morale of the troops was excellent.

5 Mar. 1945

The situation of the 70th Inf Div showed the enemy front lines to be 1,000 yards north of Emmersweiler-Urselsbach in the vicinity of Petite Rosselle in the woods, 2,000 northwest of Forbach, 500 yards west of Stiring-Wendel and at the northeastern edge of Stiring-Wendel, 1,600 yards east of Stiring-Wendel, 1,000 yards northwest of Spicheren and at the northern edges of the woods at Bois de Sarrebruck, 1,000 yards southwest of Gudingen and 500 yards south of the same town.

Enemy units in contact were remnants of the 347th VGD were remnants of the 860th VGR, six companies of the 861st VGR, remnants of the 880th VGR, 347th Div Artillery Regt, remnants of the 347th Fusilier Bn, remnants of the 347th Engineer Bn, one company of the 347th AT Bn, three companies of the 347th Field Replacement Bn, 347th BG (BG Zweibrücken Volkssturm), also the 559th VGD of the 1st Bn of the 1125th VGR, 1st Bn of the 1126th VGR, seven companies of the 2nd Bn 1126th VGR, 1st Bn of the 1127th VGR, 559th Fusilier Co, elements of the Marsch[1] Bn IX-559, 3rd Bn of the 1159th Div Artillery Regt, and miscellaneous 17th SS PGD of two companies of the Assault Gun Bn, four companies of the Landesschuetzen Bn #12 (regional defense troops).

Resistance was the strongest in Stiring-Wendel area where the enemy was forced from Neueglasshutten and Stiring-Wendel southeast of the railroad and continued to defend in house-to-house fighting northwest of the railroad. The enemy was cleared from Bois de la Reserve (woods), Umbruch and the southeastern two-thirds of Fort de Forbach. Artillery increased to an estimated 1,000 rounds, largely in the Stiring-Wendel-Neueglasshutten area but showed an increase also in the right portion of the division's zone. Enemy artillery increase was largely light caliber.

Our searchlights drew 88mm and 105mm fire in Stiring-Wendel area at 0200 hours, without damage. 75 rounds of heavy caliber fire in the Forbach area fell at 1720.

---

1   The German word for Replacement.

Two 24-rounds of concentrations of light caliber fire fell at 1120 and 1125, 48 rounds of light and medium caliber fell at 1545 and another 120 rounds of undetermined caliber in Stiring-Wendel at 1550.

Enemy infantry resistance continued strongest in the Neueglasshutten-Stiring-Wendel area where the enemy defended with small arms, assault guns, and mortar fire in the house-to-house fighting. Initial determined resistance in the vicinity of Umbruch and the western part of Forbach lessened as the enemy was forced back into Bois de la Reserve and Fort de Forbach. Mortar fire was scattered and active. Enemy flares (white, yellow, and green) were active from 2000 to 0200 hours.

The 276th Inf radios were jammed by a "tone" preventing successful transmission from 0530 to 0630 hours and at 0845 to 0945. Release of POWs held by the enemy were approximately 900 Russian, Yugoslav, Polish, Italian, French, Greek, Serb, and Croat that had been held by the enemy in a prison camp at Stiring-Wendel. The prisoners broke from their captors and entered the nearby American lines during the day. It was reported that the camp, which remained in enemy hands, contained 200 hospitalized POWs.

The CCA of the 12th Armored Div occupied and secured Forbach and Stiring-Wendel south of the railroad.

The 274th Inf Regt continued to attack to the north. The 1st Bn maintained positions along the highway. The 2nd and 3rd Bns cleared Stiring-Wendel to the railroad tracks. Fighting continued north of the tracks.

The 275th Inf Regt continued to occupy and improve defensive positions. The maintained contact with the adjacent units and assisted the 274th Inf in their attack by fire.

The 276th Inf Regt resumed the attack at 0700. The 3rd Bn attacked along the Petite Rosselle Road. At 1800 Bois de la Reserve was cleared of all enemy. The 1st Bn cleared the university area and advanced to a new line. Co B was attached to the 2nd Bn and they consolidated positions. Division artillery fired supporting missions for the infantry and continued harassing and neutralizing fire missions.

The 749th Tank Bn, less Co A, with Co B's assist of the 274th Inf in destroying 4 MG nests and three pillboxes. Co C supported the attack of the 2767th Inf by fire.

Results of Operations: The 275th Inf continued to occupy and improve defensive positions. The 274th and 276th Infs continued to attack at 0700 and cleared the entire enemy from all of Stiring-Wendel south of the railroad tracks, Forbach and Boise de la Reserve. At the close of the period Cos I and L of the 275th Inf, moved to the assembly area. Artillery and mortar fire was heavy in Stiring-Wendel and the 2nd Bn's 276th sector. Little resistance was in the Bois de la Reserve.

The 749th Tank Bn had the tanks located as follows: A Co plus one assault gun of Hqs Co attached to the 101st Cav Grp at St Avold for an impending attack which was coordinated with the advance of the 70th Inf Div. Recon continued for routes of the advance. The company performed usual maintenance duties. Three enlisted men, Cpl Carver, Cpl Lutz, Cpl Richards, suffered from combat exhaustion. Notes do not state if they were evacuated.

B Co plus one platoon of D Co was attached to the 274th Inf with the CP at Kerbach. The 1st Plt took up defensive positions supporting K Co of the 274th Regt and supported the infantry by fire in their advance. The infantry jumped off approximately at 1400 and the infantry was in Stiring-Wendel. The platoon received heavy artillery fire throughout the day. 2nd Plt tanks supported Cos E, F and G of the 2nd Bn in their advance. The tanks took defensive positions and supported the infantry by fire destroying many buildings in Stiring-Wendel. One tank from the 2nd Plt was detached to support one platoon from E Co at 0900. Their mission was to destroy two MG nests so that the infantry could advance. Mission was accomplished at 1800 and the tank returned to the platoon assembly area at Stiring-Wendel. The 3rd Plt jumped off in support of L Co. At 0730 the 274th Inf Regt began attacking enemy positions in and around Stiring-Wendel and ten (10) POWs were taken. The mission was accomplished at 1100. The platoon returned to the assembly area in Neueglasshuten. There were no losses of personnel or tanks during the period.

C Co plus one platoon of D Co was attached to the 276th Inf with the CP at Oeting. Tanks jumped off at 0700 in support of the infantry advance and met varied to light resistance but made good progress. The 1st Plt assisted Co K of the 276th Inf Regt in their advance to Umbruch, approximately 2,000 yards west of Forbach. The tanks did not have to fire, as resistance was very light. The 2nd Plt with Co F of the 276th Inf entered Fort de Forbach, north of Forbach, and advanced to the road junction approximately 1,000 yards west of Stiring-Wendel. No resistance was encountered. The 3rd Plt assisted Co A of the 276th Inf Regt in their advance to the barracks approximately 700 yards west of Forbach and also in the advance to Umbruch. They finished mopping up of barracks area of Forbach cleaning out three MG nests and two pillboxes and moved to Umbruch with the infantry. Very little resistance was met in these sectors. All the tanks of Co C returned to Forbach for the night except for one section of tanks of the 1st Plt which remained at Umbruch with D Co. Light tanks attached to each regiment were not committed.

D Co had one platoon attached to the 275th Inf Regt in reserve at Spicheren. There were no other changes.

The weather was cold, overcast with poor visibility. Combat efficiency was excellent and the morale high.

6 Mar. 1945

The 70th Inf Div general situation revealed the enemy front lines remained generally the same as in the previous period. There was no significant change in contact with enemy units. The enemy continued to defend and conducted active patrolling in Fort de Forbach during the night and followed this with a counterattack by their infantry and two tanks or SP guns after daylight, at 0845. Although fighting continued throughout most of the day, the enemy gained no ground. He was driven from the woods south and southeast of Simon Mines where fighting continued for the mine area.

House-to-house fighting continued in the Stiring-Wendel area. Mortar fire increased during the period to an estimated combined total of 1,400 mortar and light artillery rounds. Rocket fire also increased. The bulk of the fire fell in Fort de Forbach and the Stiring-Wendel area. The enemy in the right portion of our division's zone was quiet.

Two armored vehicles were observed at 0830. The two armored vehicles that supported the counterattack were believed to be from this group. Eighty-six (86) rockets were reported. 107 known rounds of 76 rockets fell in Forbach; 325 known rounds and 50 rockets in Stiring-Wendel. Infiltration by enemy patrols preceding the counterattack was noted in Fort de Forbach. Fire fighting that began at 1845 continued to the end of the period.

The 275th Inf Regt continued to occupy and improve defensive positions. They assisted the 274th Inf by fire. A new limiting point was coordinated with the 63rd Div and continued patrolling.

The 276th Inf Regt's Cos I and L had assembled in the vicinity of the university area and were relieved by the 165th Engineers at 0600. Co K attacked through the 2nd Bn. The 2nd and 3rd Bns met heavy resistance from well-entrenched enemy along the railroad tracks. Patrols were sent into Petite Roselle. The division artillery supported the attacks by the 274th and 276th Inf Regts.

The 749th Tank Bn, less A Co, assisted the 274th and 276th Infs by fire. They destroyed two MG nests and fired on snipers in the woods.

Results of Operations: The 275ᵗʰ Inf continued to occupy and improve defensive positions. The new limiting point was coordinated with the 63ʳᵈ Div and assisted the 274ᵗʰ Inf by fire. The 274ᵗʰ Inf continued mopping up in Stiring-Wendel and resumed their attack on the university area.

The 276ᵗʰ Inf completed its relief by the 165ᵗʰ Engineers and resumed to attack. Ditches, mines, artillery, mortars, and rockets slowed the attacking units.

The 749ᵗʰ Tank Bn situation had their location of troops as follows: A Co plus one assault gun of Hqs Co, attached to the 101ˢᵗ Cav Grp, were in St Avold. They continued maintenance of tanks and recon routes of advance in preparation for an impending attack of a limited objective. The company remained alert for a mission.

D Co, plus one platoon of D Co, was attached to the 274ᵗʰ Inf Regt with its CP at Kerbach and was on alert for a possible counterattack. The 1ˢᵗ Plt remained in the assembly area of Neueglasshutten in general support of the regiment. One section of the 3ʳᵈ Plt left the assembly area at 1220 in support of L Co's 3ʳᵈ Bn to attack MG positions 3,000 yards west of Soucht. The mission was completed at 1400.

C Co plus the 2ⁿᵈ Plt of D Co was attached to the 276ᵗʰ Inf Regt were 800 yards northwest of Forbach and at 1300, they destroyed three enemy sniper positions and completed a second mission of firing on trenches and emplacements along the railroad in the woods northeast of Forbach, knocking out two MGs. This mission was also accomplished in addition to several buildings being destroyed by tank fire. They then returned to the 2ⁿᵈ Bn control in Forbach. The CP moved from Oeting to the college, approximately 800 yards west of Forbach. One platoon of Co D was in reserve at Spicheren with the 275ᵗʰ Inf Regt.

The weather was cold and cloudy with poor visibility. Combat efficiency was excellent with high morale of the troops.

7 Mar. 1945

There were no changes in the enemy's front lines. The 347ᵗʰ VGD of the 880ᵗʰ VGR (remnants), the six companies of the 861ˢᵗ VGR, 1ˢᵗ Bn Res of the 861ˢᵗ VGR, the 347ᵗʰ Div Artillery Regt, remnants of the 347ᵗʰ Fusilier Bn, remnants of the 347ᵗʰ Engineer Bn, one company of the 347ᵗʰ AT Bn, three companies of the 347ᵗʰ Replacement Bn, the "Hesse" Alarm Co, and from the 559ᵗʰ VGD, the 1ˢᵗ Bn of the 1125ᵗʰ VGR, 1ˢᵗ Bn of the 1126ᵗʰ VGR, minus one company, and one company of the 7ᵗʰ Replacement Bn.

The enemy continued to defend without loss of ground. Determined resistance was encountered from dug-in positions along the railroad line in Fort de Forbach. They were generally quiet in the right portion of the division's zone. Artillery fire increased over the previous period. Two enemy armored vehicles were in the vicinity of Simon Mines, fired several bursts and returned to Simon Mines at 0940. One armored vehicle was reported firing at our troops at 1618. Enemy artillery increased to 1,053 known rounds, mostly light caliber. The heaviest concentrations were 60 rounds of heavy caliber from 0530 to 0557 hours; 100 rounds light caliber in the vicinity of Stiring-Wendel from 1025 to 1050; 90 rounds of 88mm at 1400, 100 rounds light caliber from 1600 to 1700; 100 rounds 88mm and 105mm fell at Petite Roselle beginning at 1930 and continued to the end of the period. Enemy snipers continued to be active in Stiring-Wendel. An enemy patrol of undetermined strength withdrew after having a hand grenade thrown at 0315 hours.

The CCA of the 12th Armored Div moved its CP to Forbach and continued occupying cleared areas. They sent patrols into Petite Roselle.

The 274th Inf Regt encountered stiff enemy resistance in factory area northwest of Stiring-Wendel. The 1st and 3rd Bns held in their present positions.

The 1st Bn established outposts and the 3rd Bn continued mopping up. They reorganized along the railroad and prepared to continue the attack. Enemy fire was heavy in the 2nd and 3rd Bn sectors.

The 275th Inf Regt continued to occupy and improve defensive positions. They maintained contact with the 63rd Inf Div and patrolling to the north.

The 276th Inf Regt continued to hold and improve positions with active patrolling to probe enemy lines for unoccupied positions. Attacking units were hampered by artillery, mortar, and intensive small arms fire. Co K relieved Co B at 0715. Co B relieved Co E on the front line. Co E protected the regimental right flank along the road. Division artillery fired TOT on enemy strong points.

In the late afternoon 73 missions with 901 rounds were expended. The 749th Tank Bn, less A Co, provided close support for the infantry. There was no change in disposition.

Results of Operations: Units continued to hold and improve defensive positions along the present front lines. Active patrolling was maintained along the entire front. Units reorganized and regrouped in preparation for continued attack. Enemy resistance was heavy along the 274th and 276th Infs' sectors with artillery, mortar, and automatic weapons fire. No enemy armor was destroyed.

The following info from OIs dated 7 Mar 1945 was as follows:

"The 70th Inf Div will defend in the present position, reorganize, and be prepared to resume attack upon order;

Minute adjustments of present positions to gain more favorable defense terrain was authorized; defensive emplacements would be constructed with overhead cover, and with the view of holding positions with minimum of strength; and continue pressure upon enemy and conduct active patrolling to determine weak spots in enemy's defense."

The 749th Tank Bn situation showed there was no change in location of the troops.

Co A remained alerted for probable attack with the 101st Cav Grp. They continued recon of routes for the attack scheduled for 8 Mar, depending on coordinated plans of the 12th Armored Div and the 70th Inf Div.

Co B tanks supported the infantry who had encountered stiff enemy opposition in the factory area northwest of Stiring-Wendel. The 1st Plt moved from Stiring-Wendel in support of A Co's 1st Bn mission to secure the right flank of the regiment and moved into position at 1745. The platoon leader, S/Sgt Bush, dismounted from his tank to locate the company CP. The area was being shelled and shrapnel killed S/Sgt Bush. The 2nd Plt remained in the assembly area at Stiring-Wendel. The 3rd Plt was in the assembly area at Neueglasshutten. All tanks remained in defensive positions.

Co C remained in Forbach retaining the position held during the previous period.

Co D continued to be held in a reserve position.

Weather was cloudy with rain. Visibility was poor. Combat efficiency was excellent with high morale of the troops.

8 Mar. 1945

The 75th Infantry Division reported the enemy front lines had broken contact as the enemy withdrew from our defensive positions with the result that there is no definite line but enemy artillery fire was heavy. Two tanks were reported in the vicinity 1,500 yards east of Camp de Bitche at 1230. Other reports stated a general withdrawal to the northeast. The 5th Inf with Co A from the 749th Tank Bn attached reported during the early part of the period they continued their mission in the right sector of the company's zone. Infantry action was limited to patrols and scattered small arms fire. One armed vehicle was seen at 1214 hours. An estimated 1200 rounds, mostly light caliber fell during the period. Harassing fire fell in Stiring-Wendel. An enemy patrol of four men was observed in the rear of our position at 2235 but withdrew before contact could be made. One enemy patrol set off two trip flares and withdrew when subjected to mortar fire. A squad of enemy riflemen was observed with an armed vehicle at 1214 hours. Considerable flare activity was reported.

The 63rd Inf Div continued to occupy and improve defensive positions. A raiding party was sent into Gudingen. The 274th Inf Regt maintained the present front line position with the regiment regrouping and reorganizing. They continued active patrolling to determine enemy weak spot and maintained contact with the 63rd Inf Div.

The 276th Inf Regt continued to occupy and improve their positions. They also conducted patrolling.

The 3rd Bn CP moved to Nord Caserne. Division artillery fired routine supporting missions during the period. Defensive fires were planned and adjusted. Eight hundred eighty-three (883) rounds were expended.

The 749th Tank Bn less Co A reported one platoon of Co B fired five hundred (500) rounds in a factory area in support of the 274th Inf. A Co plus one AG of Hqs Co, attached to the 101 Cav Gp were in St Avold. B Co plus one platoon from D Co, attached to the 274th , were located in Forbach. C Co plus one platoon from D Co, attached to the 276th, were also located in Forbach. D Co, attached to the 275th Inf Regt, was in reserve in Spicheren.

A Co remained attached to the 101 Cav Gp and saw no activity. B Co. moved its CP from Kerbach at 1030 hours traveling approximately five miles southeast to a new assembly area in Forbach, arriving at 1100. The 3rd Plt fired six hundred (600) rounds at targets in Simon Mines and a factory area north of Forbach. Several towers and one pillbox were demolished. All suspected Ops such as towers, chimneys, etc., were destroyed. An assault gun fired eighty (80) rounds of 105mm at the same targets. Enemy casualties and damage were not clearly defined. Co C remained attached to the 276th Regt and saw no activity. At approximately 2200 hours, oral word was received from the 70th Inf Div for movements of all units of the 749th Tank Bn to move to an area designed in the area of Rauwiller. Plans for routes and time of departure were coordinated with said division. The following information was extracted from OI from XV Corps:

"749th Tank Bn reverts to control of the XV Corps and move to the assembly area in the vicinity of Sarraltroff in Corps Reserves. Movement will be coordinated with CG XV Corps (G-4 Traffic Control). Radio silence will be maintained until further notice from this Hqs."

Weather was overcast, cold, and rain with visibility poor. Combat efficiency was excellent with morale high.

9 Mar. 1945

Location of troops of the 749th Tank Bn had the CP and Hqs Co at Sarraltroff with Co A at Hellering les Fénétrange that had been changed from Rauwiller as first assembly area. Co D was in Hildesheim, Co C in Oberstinzel, having arrived at 1540, traveling approximately 43 miles and the Svc Co was at Goerlingen.

Operations for the period: In accordance with XV Corps Ops, they moved from the XV Corps area and the battalion reverted to XV Corps Control.

The Bn CP and Hqs Co departed from Vittersbourg and closed in at Sarraltroff at 1400. A Co departed from St Avold at 1200 and closed in at Hellering les Fénétrange at 1545. Distance traveled was approximately 40 miles. Co D departed from Forbach at 1000 and closed in at Hildesheim at 1500. Co D departed from Spicheren at 1200 and closed in at Dolving at 1600. Svc Co departed from Honskirch at 1200 and closed in at Goehlingen at 1330. The companies moved in 30-minute intervals. The maintenance section and gas trucks followed the 1st Plt. Seventeen (17) tanks were operational.

Radio silence was maintained throughout the move and remained so until orders were authorized to break silence.

Commendation: "A and C Cos of the 749th Tank Bn: 275th Inf, during the operation commencing 17 Feb 1945, had Co C, minus one platoon, from the morning of the jump-off until 22 Feb 1945, when they were relieved by Co A, this company supported the regiment in a superior manner. The prior planning, recon, and execution of all assigned missions, and the high professional skill displayed was eminently gratifying to the undersigned. The liaison officer, Capt Swenson, was particularly helpful by his diligent, energetic aggressive performance of duty. Upon attachment of Co A, a continuous high standard was maintained. The efforts in the face of unfavorable terrain, was responsible for the restoration of the regiment's line despite heavy enemy pressure." Signed by John H. McAleer, LtCol, 275th Inf, Commanding. First endorsement "Forwarded with pleasure. It is in a large measure due to the fine work of all supporting units that the teamwork which brings success can be attained." Signed by A. J. Barnett, MajGen, USA, Commanding, 70th Inf Div.

Weather was cold and cloudy. Visibility was fair. Combat efficient was excellent and morale was high.

10 Mar. 1945

The 749th Tank Bn situation showed no changes in the location of troops from the previous period. The battalion remained in Corps Res. The companies continued billeting of troops, cleaning of equipment and weapons, lectures in orientation, and review of recent battle experiences.

The weather was clear and cold with good visibility. Combat efficiency was excellent with high morale of the troops.

11 Mar. 1945

The 749th Tank Bn again showed no change in location of troops. The companies began installation of the 300 series radio sets in the tanks. They also began installation on all the tanks of track extensions for additional traction. The extensions are termed "Ducks".

As of 3 Mar two enlisted men of Co A that had been reported as MIA were T/5 Faust, and Pfc E. E. Cox, were now known to be KIA in the vicinity of Forbach. Sgt. McFadden, B Co, was lightly in action in the vicinity of Forbach. Evacuation is not noted.

The weather was cool and cloudy. Visibility was good. Combat efficiency was excellent and troops' morale high.

12 Mar. 1945

There was still no change in location of the troops of the 749th Tank Bn. The battalion submitted master training schedule to XV Corps G-3. The companies continued to install the 300 series radio sets in tanks and installing track extensions. The companies also started training programs to include cleaning and painting vehicles, care and cleaning of weapons, gas masks training, and first echelon maintenance and orientation.

The weather was cold, cloudy and hazy with fair visibility. Combat efficiency was excellent; morale high.

13 Mar. 1945

The troops of the 749th Tank Bn was still in the same location.

Effective immediately the 749th was attached to the 71st Inf Div. A F.O. provided the following information: "7th Army attacks on D-Day from the present position to destroy the enemy in the zone and seize the west bank of the "Rhine"   . They crossed the Rhine between Mannheim and Mainz to establish a bridgehead in preparation for subsequent advance to the northeast. VI Corps attacked on D-Day and destroyed the enemy in the zone, seized and secured Bitche-Hagenau and Maginot positions in the zone and continued attacks on the general axis of Hagenau-Pirmasens penetrated the Siegfried Line[2] and captured high ground east and northeast of Pirmasens. They assisted in the advance of XV Corps and captured Landau and Neustadt. XXI Corps attacked on D-Day, captured Saarbrucken, Neunkirchheim and St Wendel. They advanced to the Rhine in the zone. XII TAC supported the 7th Army. XV Corps attacked on D-Day at the H hour to make a main effort on the axis including Rimling, Zweibrücken, penetrated the Siegfried Line in the Zone, captured Zweibrücken, Homburg, and Kaiser Slautern, captured Bitche and Camp de Bitche, and secured Bitche and Hagenau roads in the zone. They continued to attack to seize the west bank of the Rhine in the zone. On Army's orders they crossed the Rhine in the corps zone north of Mannheim and secured a bridgehead for further operations toward the northeast. On Army's orders the 1st Inf Div passed to VI Corps in the vicinity of Pirmasens.

"The 44th Inf Div (reinforced) was attached to the 776th TD Bn and continued defensive mission until passed through by the 3rd and 45th Inf Divs on D-Day at H hour. They would support the attack of the 3rd and 45th Inf Divs to limit the range of all available weapons. After being passed through the division with the above attachments, less division artillery, would assemble on Corps' order on D-Day plus 1 in the area of Wittring, Hambach, Saaralbe and be prepared for movement to Army Res to the area indicated by the Army.

The 71st Inf Div (reinforced) and attached to the 749th Tank Bn, effective at once, would continue present defensive mission and support the attack of the 100th Inf Div on D-Day H hour to limit range of all available weapons as desired by the CG of the 100th Inf Div. On Corps' orders after D-Day would relieve elements of the 100th Inf Div in the area to be designated in the vicinity of Bitche.

The 100th Inf Div (reinforced), attached to the 781st Tank Bn and attacked on D-Day at H hour between the point at the division's boundary, passing through the left elements of the 71st Inf Div. They captured Bitche and Camp de Bitche and the high ground in the division's zone to the north and south. Thereafter, on Corps' orders they advanced to the north with all or part of the division protecting the right (east) flank of the Corps. The 3rd Inf Div (reinforced) was attached to the 756th Tank Bn. They attacked on D-Day at H hour passing through elements of the 44th Inf Div making

2   It is believed that the Third Plt of Co B, 703rd TD was the first TD unit to penetrate the Siegfried Line.

the main effort initially in the direction of Schwexen, Ober-Auerbach and breached the Siegfried Line east of Rimschweiler. They captured that portion of Zweibrücken, captured the high ground in the area of Wiesbach in the direction of Kindsbach and captured Kaiser Slautern. They were prepared to assist in the exploitation with at least one RCT motorized.

The 45th Inf Div (reinforced) and attached to the 191st Tank Bn attacked on D-Day at H hour and passed through the elements of the 44th Inf Div, making the main effort initially in the direction of Obergailbach, Seywiller, Wattwille, Hombourg. They breached the Siegfried Line east of the Blies River, captured that portion of Zweibrücken within the zone. They captured Hombourg and the high ground in the area of Reiskirchheim, Hombourg, and Reishoffen. They continued the attack in the direction of Weilerbach and assisted the 3rd Inf Div in the capture of Kaiser Slautern by seizing the high ground in the vicinity of Morlautern. They protected the Corps' left (western) flank and were prepared to assist in the exploitation with at least one RCT motorized.

The 106th Cav Grp were prepared to move on Corps' order on 3 hours notice to cover the Corps' right (eastern) flank from the vicinity of Walsch-Bronn until relieved by the 100th Inf Div, with recon to the east and northeast. After a breach of Siegfried Line was made, cover the Corps' left (western) flank initially from the vicinity of Kusel and St Wendel, and recon to the north and northwest.

6th Armored Div was to be prepared on Corps' orders after D-Day for prompt displacement from its present assembly to the area of Wittring, Sarre-Union, and Butten. They were to maintain after H-hour suitable leaders and commanders with necessary transportation and communication facilities at OPs of the 3rd and 45th Inf Divs. They were to maintain active recon and up-to-the-minute plans for rapid movement to exploit a breakthrough. They were to be prepared on 6-hours' notice to pass through either or both attacking Divs. On Corps' orders, they were to by-pass Kaiser Slautern and secure exits to the Rhine at Bad Dürkheim, Grünstadt, and Derision. They were prepared to continue rapid advance to the Rhine.

Secure any Rhine bridges found intact. Commanders will take all possible measures to attain tactical surprise. Spelling of place names in all orders and reports will conform to spelling on map of France and Germany. Attacking Divs will not relieve front line elements of the 44th Inf Div in position but will pass through these elements at H hour. All combat vehicles operating north of the line of demarcation after D-Day H hour would display cerise or orange panels. All units were prepared to mark targets with smoke on call from the air. All units were prepared to mark targets with smoke and/or panels on call from the air. The attack would be conducted with the utmost vigor and aggressiveness, irrespective of the presence or absence of supporting armor or air. Tanks and air are available but weather may prevent or greatly limit their use. The success of the infantry operation must not depend upon their employment. There is no evidence that the enemy has the means to offer strong coordinated resistance to our advance. It appears that he intends to delay our advance by defending localities such as villages, woods, important CR's, etc., in order to gain time for his elements to effect an orderly withdrawal. Where possible, leading bus will by-pass such resistance, leaving those areas to be reduced by units in the rear. Frontal attacks should be avoided, but every effort should be made to strike the flanks and RR of enemy resistance. In the event a leading battalion becomes involved in enemy action, it must be by-passed by battalions in RR and the advance resumed without delay. Liaison would be established with the 71st Inf Div CP at Ratzwiller."

A Co made recon for firing range for tank cannons. They practiced-fired tank guns at the vicinity of Postroff. D Co. received two new light tanks (M24s) in exchange for old tanks. Companies of the battalion carried out their respective training schedules which included first echelon maintenance, inspection of arms, installation of 300 series radio sets and track extensions, orientation, driver and gunner training. Companies painted vehicles and conducted 1,000-mile maintenance check.

Two enlisted men, Sgt Price and Cpl Race, reported as MIA in the vicinity of Klienbliederstroff as of 3 Mar, now known to be KIA.

Weather was clear and cool. Visibility was good to excellent. Combat efficiency was excellent; morale was high.

14 Mar. 1945

The enemy's front lines were 1,000 yards northeast of Lambrecht and 500 yards northeast of Lambrecht, 1,500 yards north of Lemberg and 500 yards north of Lemberg as well as 200 yards southeast of Lemberg, Goetzenbruck and Sarreinsberg. Enemy units in contact were the 2nd Bn of the 255th Inf, 2nd Bn of the 233rd Inf, and the 1st Bn of the 937th Inf.

The sector was quiet with scattered mortar, light artillery, and MG fire intermittently during the day along the front lines.

The 5th Inf had the 1st and 2nd Bns consolidated and they improved defensive positions. The 3rd Bn reconnoitered routes for counterattacks towards Lemberg and worked in rear of the defensive positions. Approximately 80 rounds of enemy artillery and mortar fire on the 1st and 2nd Bns were received during the period. St Louis received 3 rounds of enemy artillery fire at 1015.

The 14th Inf initiated recon and occupied hasty positions on the corps' right (eastern) boundary. Organization and occupation of positions continued.

The 66th Inf continued to defend in its present position improving ground organization. Scattered enemy artillery and mortar fire fell on the forward position.

The location of troops of the 749th Tank Bn revealed no changes.

Operations for the period showed the battalion received orders from the 71st Inf Div to move to the 71st Div's zone in the vicinity of Diemeringen starting early in the next period. At 1600 all companies were alerted for movement to the 71st Div's area and to be prepared for combat missions. The route to be followed was Sarraltroff, Goerlingen, Rauwiller, Hirschland, Weyer, Drulingen, Durstel, Eschweiler, and Diemeringen.

Co C test fired was done on tank guns in the vicinity of Postroff. For a possible combat mission, all companies continued cleaning of weapons and equipment.

Weather was clear and cool. Visibility was excellent. Combat efficiency was excellent and morale high.

15 Mar. 1945

Enemy front lines were located 1200 yards north of Lemberg, in the woods 500 yards northeast of Lemberg, the southwestern edge of Lemberg, Goetzenbruck and Sarreinsberg. Units in contact were elements of the 1st and 2nd Bns of the 225th Regt, and the 2nd Bn of the 223rd Regt. The sector remained quiet. Some mortar, artillery, and smoke were used scattered along most of the line. Troops heard noises thought to be three enemy tanks in the vicinity of Alt Schmeltz at 2015. These were withdrawn before the info was confirmed.

Sporadic mortar fire fell in Goetzenbruck. Reliable sources indicated that extensive plans were being laid for leaving numerous stay-behind agents, equipped with communication, in Western Germany. The Abwehr has established checkpoints at the Rhine River crossings to screen potential agents from among refugees moving east.

The 9th Army reported possible 5 enemy female agents. Missions were to report military concentrations and insignias.

Successful line crossings had been made across the Lauterbach and Rosselle Rivers and in the St Avold area.

The 5th Inf continues to defend along the present front lines. All units were consolidated and improved their positions.

The 3rd Bn in Regimental Res reconnoitered routes for counterattacks and improved the regimental reserve line position. They patrolled vigorously during the period. Scattered artillery and mortar fire fell on the front line positions. Contact was maintained with the 42nd Inf Div on the right.

The 14th Inf organized and improved defensive positions protecting the Corps' right (eastern) boundary. They initiated recon of front line units with view to relieving elements of the 5th Inf.

66th Inf continued its defensive mission. They assisted the 100th Inf Div attack. The 2nd Bn relieved elements of the 100th Inf Div between limiting the point and new limiting point. The 2nd Bn closed on and occupied position at 1830. They patrolled vigorously during hours of darkness to protect the regiment's rear.

The troops of the 749th Tank Bn showed their locations to be as follows: Bn Hqs and Hqs Co were in Diemeringen. Co A, attached to the 5th Inf Regt was also in Diemeringen after having left Hellering les Fénétrange at 1200. Co B, attached to the 14th Inf Regt after having departed Hildesheim at 1000, was there as well as was Co C, attached to the 66th Inf Regt after having left Oberstinzel at 0800. D Co was in reserve in Dolving and the Svc Co was in Goerlingen.

Operations for the period: The companies started infiltrating to the 71st Inf Div's zone at 0800, all traveling approximately 25 miles to the new locations and on call, was prepared to move from there. There was friendly air activity throughout the period. A Co departed from Hellering at 1200 hours arriving at Diemeringen at 1330. B Co departed Hilbesheim at 1000 hours arriving at Diemeringen at 1130 with platoons leaving Hilbesheim at 30 minute intervals. Company CO departed from Oberstinzel at 0800 hours arriving in Diemeringen at 1430. Friendly air activity was extensive throughout the period.

Weather was warm and clear with excellent visibility. Combat efficiency was excellent and morale high.

16 Mar. 1945

Enemy front lines were located 1,000 yards east of Sarreinsberg, 800 yards east of Goetzenbruck and 1,200 yards northeast of the same town; 1,000 and 1,200 yards east and northeast respectively of Lemberg; Fort Domaniale in the vicinity of Wolfsbrunn; 1,000 yards south of Schwangerbach, and 1,500 yards south of Bitche.

No enemy units were given. The sector was quiet except for intensive light artillery and scattered mortar fire along the central and southern part of the line during the period. A few enemy were seen in the vicinity of Lemberg. Vehicles were observed in the vicinity of Waldeck with about 35 enemy tanks that were bombed by our planes. Many were destroyed. At 1700 division artillery fired on 7 trucks or tanks in the vicinity 3,000 yards north of Mouterhouse. Three to five tanks were also observed 1,500 yards west of Bousseville.

The 5th Inf continued improvement of their defensive positions as well as defensive missions. They executed vigorous officer-led platoon strength patrols encountering MG fire and mine fields. During the period 0001 to 0315 hours, the front line position of the 1st Bn were under heavy artillery fire receiving an estimated 200 to 300 rounds on A Co's position south of Lemberg. Daylight patrols met little enemy opposition.

The 14th Inf continued during most of the period a defensive mission improving positions protecting Corps' right flank. Beginning at 1400, the unit began execution of XV Corps' order to move by motor to the vicinity of Bitche to relieve elements of the 100th Div. At the close of the period, relief was in progress that was completed at 2340.

The 66th Inf continued its defensive mission. The 1st and 2nd Bns, by aggressive patrolling, moved northeast establishing a strong OPL east of Lemberg and Bitche Roads. Engineers and regimental platoons cleared the road of mines by 1800. The improvement was for vehicle traffic. The CP was displaced from Montbronn to Enchenberg at 0900. The 564th FA Bn fired on 7 enemy tanks and rendered them inactive.

The 749th Tank Bn's CP and Hqs Co were located in Diemeringen. A Co, plus one assault gun from the French Hqs Co were attached to the 5th Inf Regt, also in the same town. Co B plus one assault gun from the French Hqs. Co were attached to the 14th Inf Regt located in Reyersviller. Co C plus one assault gun from the French Hqs Co was attached to the 66th Inf Regt and located in Diemeringen as was D Co (light tanks) in the same town in reserve. The Svc Co was in Goerlingen.

Operations for the period: At 1500 Co D moved from Diemeringen to rendezvous with the infantry at the southern edge of le Nassenwald. The tanks traveled via Montbronn to Reyersviller. They met the infantry southwest of Montbronn where the infantry was motorized and then proceeded with the tanks to Reyersviller. There the infantry left the trucks. The 3rd Plt was attached to the 1st Bn; the 2nd Plt attached to the 2nd Bn. The 3rd Bn moved to Siersthal and closed at 2130. Tanks and infantry took up defensive positions along the north-south road running south from Bitche to the road junction in the vicinity of Reyersviller. The tanks closed into the area at approximately 1700.

Co COs and their platoon leaders contacted regimental companies of the 71st Inf Div and reported results to this Hqs. One assault gun (105mm) was attached to each medium company from the Assault Gun Plt of Hqs Co.

D Co moved at 1500 from Dolving and arrived at Diemeringen at 1700 in the area previously occupied by B Co. Capt Ancel L. McNeely, Co CO of A Co was evacuated for battle fatigue. 1st Lt Conway assumed command.

C Co remained in Diemeringen. Two tanks left behind in the previous period rejoined the company. First echelon work was carried on and also company maintenance work was begun changing radio frequencies.

Five enlisted men, Sgt Bishop, Col Mahoney, T/5 Webber, Pfc Smith, Pfc Loia had been previously listed as MIA and now reported as KIA.

Weather was cool and clear with excellent visibility. Combat efficiency was high as was the morale of the troops.

17 Mar. 1945

The enemy front lines were not definite but they scattered at points along the line. They were 1,000 yards east of Sarreinsberg and in the woods 2,000 yards east of Goetzenbruck in the vicinity of the intersection of the road west of Alt Schmeltz. They were in the woods 2,000 yards east of Lemberg on the line running north and south 2,000 and 3,000 yards south of Bitche, and on the road leading out of Bitche to the south. New enemy identifications were as follows: 4th, 5th and 6th Batteries of the 410 Volks Artillery Corps, with a strength of 100 men each. Weapons noted were 4 - 105mm guns each and were last reported moving from the vicinity of Bitche. The sector continued quiet.

Patrols encountered a few passive enemy with several positions found abandoned. Three rounds of artillery and an estimated 15 rounds of mortar fire fell during the period. Enemy patrols were seen in the vicinity 1,000 yards southeast of Reyersviller at 0720. Scattered sniper fire was reported in the northern part of the sector during the night. There was small arms fire at 1635. A smoke screen was reported in Fort Domaniale approximately 400 yards east of Enchenberg.

The 5th Inf, attached to Co A of the 749th Tank Bn, continued defensive missions.

They established an OPL north of Lemberg-Mouterhouse Road on the corps' boundary. Contact was established with the 42nd Inf Div on that road outside of Mouterhouse.

An AT mine platoon swept the Lemberg-Sarreinsberg Road from Lemberg east to Corps' right boundary. The 3rd Bn was alerted by division to be prepared to move on one hour's notice by foot or motors. They had encountered no enemy opposition except mined areas. Vigorous patrolling was pushed to the north and east with any opposition.

14th Inf, attached to Co B, 749th Tank Bn, occupied and improved defensive positions in the vicinity of Bitche and Camp de Bitche. Relief of elements of the 100th Inf Div was completed during the period without incident or enemy opposition. Regimental CP was displaced from Siersthal to Bitche. There was vigorously patrolling to the east and southeast without opposition.

66th Inf, attached to Co C of the 749th Tank Bn, continued a defensive mission. A strong OPL was established on the dominating terrain east of Lemberg and Bitche Road-Bitche Road. Daylight combat patrols swept the area east to the regimental boundary. Contact was established with the 5th Inf without opposition.

A Co from the 749th Tank Bn plus one assault gun moved two platoons from the vicinity of Reyersviller to Bitche. The remaining platoon stayed in defensive positions in Reyersviller. No casualties or losses were sustained.

Results of Operations: On Corps' order relieved elements of the 100th Inf Div in the vicinity of Bitche and Camp de Bitche was completed. Patrols pushed vigorously forward into the division's zone meeting light opposition gaining control of and opened roads in the division's zone forward of the front lines for traffic. Div's CP opened at Montbronn at 1130.

The 749th Tank Bn's CP and Hqs Co were located in Diemeringen as previously. A and B Cos remained with the same infantry units as during the previous period. C Co plus one assault gun from the French Hqs Co was attached to the 66th Inf Regt. In Enchenberg. D Co remained in reserve in Diemeringen and the Svc Co remained in the same town as previously - Goerlingen.

There was no change with Co A, remaining in bivouac. One tank was used for recognition training for the infantry. The company also conducted familiarization firing on the tank guns for 20 reinforcements.

Co B moved from the vicinity of Reyersviller to Camp de Bitche and set up defensive positions relieving elements of the 100th Div. No contact was made with the enemy. The 2nd Plt. moved to Bitche at 1100 while the 1st Plt moved from Siersthal at 1400 to Camp de Bitche.

The Co CP and Maintenance moved from Diemeringen at approximately 1030, closing in Bitche at 1200, having traveled 12 miles to the northeast.

Co C moved from Diemeringen to the vicinity of Enchenberg at 1415 and completed the changeover of radio frequencies. The call signs within the battalion were changed as follows: Hqs and Svc Cos - RUPPERT; A Co – RED TOP; Co B - BURGER; C Co - SCHMIDT; D Co - BOCK; and Assault Gun Plt - PABST.

The weather was cool, cloudy and hazy with fair visibility. Combat efficiency was excellent with high morale of the troops.

18 Mar. 1945

The enemy front lines were still indefinite as they continued to withdraw toward the Siegfried Line. No enemy units were in contact with our troops. It was apparent that all units formerly in contact had withdrawn to the Siegfried Line.

The 5th Inf, attached to Co A of the 749th Tank Bn continued its mission along the general line of Ropplerviller and Walschbronn and maintained contact with the 42nd Inf Div on the right and the 100th Inf Div on the left. They patrolled day and night with no contact with enemy forces.

14th Inf, attached to Co B, 749th Tank Bn, continued defensive mission with improved positions and maintained contact with the 117th Cavalry Recon Group.

The 66th Inf, attached to Co C, 749th Tank Bn, continued its defensive mission and conducted platoon-firing problems, trained in attack of a fortified position. They also maintained the OPL protecting the Lemberg and Bitche Road-Bitche Road.

The 749th Tank Bn moved from Montbronn to Bitche. The troops saw no action during this period.

Results of Operations: The division continued a defensive mission, holding Bitche, Campe de Bitche, and protecting the corps' right flank. They patrolled vigorously during the night and day maintaining contact with the 117th Cav Sqd and the 42nd Inf Div on the right as well as the 100th Inf Div on the left. Combat teams 5 and 14 ceased on division's orders.

The weather was cool, cloudy with haze. Visibility was fair. Combat efficiency was excellent with morale of the troops high.

19 Mar. 1945

The location of troops of the 749th Tank Bn were as follows: The Bn CP was in Bitche; Hqs Co in Montbronn; A Co was 1,000 yards southwest of Liederschiedt; B Co had two platoons at Camp de Bitche and one platoon at Haspelschiedt. D Co was in St Louis; the Svc and Maintenance Cos were in Montbronn.

Operations for the period: Bn Hqs moved from Montbronn at 1300 en route to Bitche opening a new battalion; they traveled approximately 15 miles.

A Co remained in its defensive position in the Bitche Road. Assault guns, 1st and 2nd Plts were at Liederschiedt with the 3rd Plt at Roppeviller.

B Co had one platoon move to Haspelschiedt at approximately 0800, took up defensive positions but saw no action. The remaining two platoons remained in Camp de Bitche and also saw no action.

C Co remained in Enchenberg and saw no action.

D Co remained in Div Res at St Louis. They fired familiarization firing using the two M24 light tanks with 75mm guns, and conducted driving instructions. There were no casualties or action throughout the battalion for the period.

The Svc Co left bivouac in the vicinity of Goerlingen at 0900 and moved to Montbronn, arriving at 1100, going approximately 22 miles.

The weather was cool and clear with excellent visibility. Combat efficiency was excellent and the morale high.

20 Mar. 1945

The enemy front lines were at the Siegfried Line. The following units were believed to be in the Siegfried Line in front of the 71st Inf Div (XV Corps): Mar. Bn 1-Volks Werfer Regt (210mm mortars); elements of the 16th VGD; elements of the 36th VGD; Volkssturm units. Contact was made near the road junction near étang (pond) de Hasselfurt and Walshausen. The enemy continued harassing artillery and mortar fire from its Siegfried Line positions. Small arms and MG fire came from Walshausen.

The 5th Inf, attached to Co A, 749th Tank Bn reported during the early part of the period the defensive mission was continued along the line of Roppeviller-Walschbronn with patrolling aggressively to the east and northeast. Patrols maintained contact with the 117th Cav Sqd and were relieved by the 14th Inf Regt beginning at 2130. The 5th Inf moved to the assembly area. The CP was displaced to Walschbronn.

The 14th Inf, attached to Co B, 749th Tank Bn, reported during the early part of the period they continued defensive mission, holding Bitche and Camp de Bitche areas and the line running northward to Roppeviller. They also patrolled east to Corps and Corps boundary, contacting elements of the 117th Cav Sqd by pre-arrangement. On division's orders, relief of the 5th Inf was carried out along the line of Roppeviller to Walschbronn.

The 66th Inf, attached to Co C, 749th Tank Bn, continued their defensive mission until 1200. Rear training area until 1200 consisted of tactical work with tanks in village fighting and assault of a fortified position with the execution at 1300 of tactical work for motors and 1345 for foot elements. Motor elements closed the rear area at 1430. Foot elements were still en route at 1800.

The 749th Tank Bn situation had the Bn CP, Hqs Co, and Bn Maintenance at Bitche. A Co, attached to the 5th Inf Regt had its CP in the vicinity of 1,200 yards south of Liederschiedt along with one platoon approximately 1,000 yards west of Liederschiedt and one platoon at Reppeviller.

At 0800 one platoon of tanks moved from Reppeviller with a company of infantry to Eppenbrunn in a sector formerly secured by elements of the 117th Cav. The town was supposedly cleared but tanks assisted the infantry in taking nine POWs. The platoon of tanks returned to Reppeviller at 1200. The 5th Inf Regt returned to Div Res.

B Co, attached to the 14th Inf Regt, was in Camp de Bitche. All platoons assembled at a new area in Camp de Bitche. Co Hqs moved from Bitche at 1100 to Camp de Bitche. There was no contact with the enemy but remained on alert with the 14th Inf Regt to relieve the 5th Inf. All company tanks were camouflage-painted by the 88th Engineers. The 1st Plt moved from Camp de Bitche at 1715 to the vicinity of Liedersheim. A platoon in mobile reserve was with the 3rd Bn, 14th Inf, closed at 1900. The 2nd Plt moved to Reppviller at 1800, also in mobile reserve. The 2nd Bn, 114th Inf Regt, closed in at 2100. The 3rd Plt went in a defensive position at Haspelschiedt.

C Co, attached to the 66th Inf Regt, was in Olsberg closing in at approximately 2030. One tank left Enchenberg due to mechanical failure. The 1st, 2nd, and 3rd Plts reported to their respective infantry battalions.

D Co was in Div Res in Camp de Bitche and conducted tank training with the infantry. They moved from St. Louis to Camp de Bitche closing in at 1700, traveling approximately 10 miles.

Service Co was in Montbronn.

The weather was clear and cool. Visibility was excellent, combat efficiency excellent, and the morale of the troops also excellent.

21 Mar. 1945

The enemy front lines were still located at the Siegfried Line. The following units are believed to be facing the 71st Inf Div - elements of the 16th VGD; elements of the 36th Volksgrenadier; and Volksturm Units. Reports from POWs indicate that the Volksturm troops are manning the Siegfried Line to cover the withdrawal of regular troops. Artillery fire was reported in Ruppertsweiller. The enemy continued intensive mortar and artillery fire from the Siegfried Line positions. Contact was made with the enemy in the vicinity of Walshausen. An enemy company manned pillboxes reported to be in the vicinity of Vinningen. Elements of the 3rd Inf Div was attacking across the 71st Inf Div's front in the direction of Walshausen and Windsberg.

The 14th Inf relieved the 5th Inf, attached to A Co, 749th Tank Bn. The regiment moved to the assembly area in Div Res.

The 14th Inf: Co B, attached to the 749th Tank Bn, relieved the 5th Inf along the lines of Ropplerviller-Walschbronn that was completed at 0615. The 2nd Bn moved forward on the right regimental sector beginning at 0800 and established a new MLR extending from Eppenbrunn-Walschbronn.

The 66th Inf, with Co C of the 749th Tank Bn attached, assumed a defensive mission. The 1st and 3rd Bns relieved the 1st and 3rd Bns of the 397th Inf. The 2nd Bn, less Co G, relieved the 2nd Bn of the 399th Inf. Co G went to Regimental Res.

Results of Operations: There was continued defensive mission at the Dietrichingen-Walschbronn line and Eppenbrunn. Relief of the elements of the 100th Div on the right and the 3rd Inf Div on the left was completed.

The following info was extracted from a FO of Hqs, 71st Inf Div:

The enemy has withdrawn to the Siegfried Line defending with Volkssturm troops. Regular troops had withdrawn to the Rhine River. Initial resistance in strength was to be expected.

"The Div was attached to XXI Corps.

XXI Corps would attack the following day with the Divs abreast with the 71st Inf Div on the right and the 100th Inf Div on the left. Advance would be in its zone of action to the Rhine River and be prepared to assist the VI Corps on the south.

The 71st Inf Div, reinforced by the 749th Tank Bn, the 530th AAA AW Bn, the 635th TD Bn, and the 93rd FA Bn upon joining.

The Div would attack at 0800 22 Mar, 1945, seizing Pirmasens and continue in its zone of action to the Rhine River.

The 66th Inf, attached to the 749th Tank Bn, Co C and the 635th TD Bn, both of which would advance in the extreme northern part of the Div's zone of action, seizing and capturing Pirmasens.

CT 5, less the 607th FA Bn, motorized, was attached to the 749th Tank Bn, Co A.

Co B of the 635th Tank Bn would initially be in Div reserve. They would be prepared to proceed to the vicinity of Münchweiler as the first objective and further to the east along the main axis of advance on Div's order.

The 14th Inf, attached to Co B of the 749th Tank Bn, and Co C of the 635th TD Bn would continue its present defensive mission and protect Div's right flank. They would be prepared to assemble on Div's order as Div reserve and initiate vigorous patrolling on Div's right flank.

The 749th Tank Bn minus the companies listed above, would be in Div reserve."

The situation of the troops of the 749th Tank Bn had the Bn CP, Hqs Co, and Bn Maintenance still in Bitche. Co A, attached to the 5th Inf Regt, had no change in its location and remained in reserve. Co B, attached to the 14th Inf Regt, it's CP and one platoon at Roppeviller, one platoon in Kerbach, and one platoon at Haspelscheidt. Co C, attached to the 66th Inf Regt, was in Olsberg. D Co was in division reserve and Svc Co were both in Camp de Bitche.

The platoons of Co B moved to Roppeviller, Kerbach, and Haspelscheidt without incident. The CP moved to Roppeviller. Co D was alerted at 0900 for a possible combat mission with CT 5 (5th Inf Regt) and its CP was at Walschbronn. The Svc Co moved from Montbronn to Camp de Bitche closing in at approximately 1600. Hqs Co and Svc Co vehicles were camouflage painted by the 84th Engineer Co.

At 1700 the 749th Tank Bn was attached to XII Corps from XV Corps per OIs, Hqs XV Corps.

The weather was foggy and hazy early in the period with clearing in the afternoon. Visibility was fair to good. Combat efficiency was excellent with morale of the troops high.

22 Mar. 1945

No definite line exists in the enemy's front lines. Enemy units in contact were the Volkssturm units, miscellaneous units of 16 VGD and other small, disorganized groups of units making their way to the Rhine. The enemy withdrew from positions in the Siegfried Line and was retreating to the Rhine in areas where we contact the line. POWs deserted their units during the retreat when they realized the uselessness of further resistance. They preferred American captivity to taking a chance on being killed five minutes before the end.

The uncertainty whether the road across the Rhine was still open contributed to their decision to desert.

The 5th Inf Regt, attached to the 749th Tank Bn, was in Div Res. They conducted road recon in the zones of the 66th and 14th Infs.

14th Inf Regt, attached to Co C, 749th Tank Bn, completed relief of the 5th Inf during the early part of the period and held the defensive positions until 1200. Then they advanced to the north and northeast with the 2nd and 3rd Bns abreast, capturing the towns of Liedersheimstedt, Thulben, Uniwinger, Obersinten, and Widerzinten. The advance was made against light and scattered enemy resistance over mined and obstacle-covered terrain. The roads were impassable to vehicles except 1/4-ton trucks and penetrated the Siegfried Line.

The 66th Inf, attached to the 749th Tank Bn, Co C, and continued defensive missions until 0800 at which time the line held by the 3rd Inf Div was crossed with the mission of seizing Pirmasens. Foot elements closed into Pirmasens and closed into the town by 1215 without opposition. They immediately began reorganization to secure the town.

The division launched the attack at 0800 seizing and occupying Pirmasens with the 66th Inf and pushing northeast into Nieder Sinten with the 14th Inf penetrating portions of the Siegfried Line against light enemy resistance. The south flank was the most vulnerable to enemy attack.

CT 5 (motorized) was attached to A Co of the 749th Tank Bn and would move at 0600 on 23 Mar by motor on the routes indicated, would detruck at designated points and proceed by marching to a concentration area. They would outpost on the western bank of the Rhine River in the division's zone of action.

CT 66 (motorized) and attached to Co C of the 749th Tank Bn would move by motor on the routes indicated and continue as CT 5 had done. Movement of said CT was initiated upon return of the trucks attached to CT 5.

The 749th Tank Bn minus the above companies would move with the division to the forward echelon. Co D would provide advance guard for motor columns, both to the detrucking points and return. The CTs would provide their own flank protection after the detrucking point was reached. Particular attention was paid to the right (southern) flank. If forced to detruck prior to reaching the detrucking point, attached vehicles would return to the initial point without delay.

The 749th Tank Bn CP, Hqs Co, and Bn Maintenance remained in Bitche. Co A, attached to the 5th Inf Regt, was last reported in the vicinity of Walschbronn. Co B, attached to the 14th Inf Regt, was still in the same location. Co C, attached to the 66th

Inf Regt, was located in Pirmasens.

B Co was in Div Res. The 1st Plt moved at 1200 from the assembly area in support of the Res Co to Vinning, closing at 1600. The 2nd Plt moved at 0800 in support of the Res Co with the 2nd Bn to Trublen, Germany, closing at 1300. There was no change in the 3rd Plt.

C Co supported the infantry in their advance to Pirmasens. The company left Olsberg at 0530 moving to and arriving at rendezvous point at 0730 where briefing was completed for an attack at 0800. The 3rd Plt moved out without the infantry, followed at 200 yards by the 1st Plt carrying 30 riflemen on tanks with the remainder of the 66th Inf Regt following at 4 to 8 hundred yards. The lead tanks reached Pirmasens at 1000. The tanks captured 10 POWs and arrived at the objective by 1030. The city was officially cleared at 1202.

Div Res, D Co, moved from Camp de Bitche to join CT 5 at Walschbronn arriving at 1200. Mission was not defined. At 0001 hours the 749th Tank Bn was relieved from the present attachments to XV Corps and were attached to the XXI Corps for other operations. Co D, also attached to the 5th Inf Regt, was in Div Res and reported to be in the vicinity of Walschbronn.

Operations for the period: Co A moved to Walschbronn at 0800 joining CT 5 with the mission to assist the advance of the 66th Inf Regt and A Co of the 749th Tank Bn if needed. An active recon of the sector made by the Co CO, A Co, the line officer and the 2nd Plt leader captured three POWs. A Co was prepared to leave Walschbronn at 1200 with the motorized infantry in their advance to their first objective of Münchweiler.

The weather was foggy and hazy early in the period with clearing in the afternoon. Combat efficiency was excellent and morale of the troops high.

23 Mar. 1945
The general situation of the 71st Inf Div revealed no enemy front lines were present. Enemy units in contact were stragglers and small groups fighting the rear guard actions. There was not much enemy activity as this division continued its advance to the Rhine. Blown bridges, craters, and roadblocks delayed the advance. Firefight was located in the vicinity southeast of Münchweiler.

The location of the 749th Tank Bn troops was as follows: A Co, attached to the 5th Inf Regt, was in Altdorf. B Co, attached to the 14th Inf Regt, was in Pirmasens.

C Co, attached to the 66th Inf Regt, was in Landau. D Co, attached to the 5th Inf Regt, continued in Div Res, was in Pirmasens. Bn Hqs, Hqs Co, and Svc Co were located in Sarnstall. They, along with medics, left Bitche at 1415 en route to Pirmasens and crossed the German frontier in the vicinity of Walschbronn, arriving at Pirmasens at 1615. On arrival orders were changed and were ordered to follow the division column, destination Gommersheim. They reached Sarnstall at approximately 1930 and bivouacked here for the remaining of the night, using surrounding fields for bivouac. From Bitche to Sarnstall it was approximately 58 miles.

A, B, C, and D Cos supported their respective regiments to which they were attached, assisted in mopping up pockets of resistance. Co C moved from Pirmasens and arrived at Landau at 1700. A Co was ordered to move to the vicinity of Speyer at 0600 and arrived at Altdorf at approximately 1930, traveling approximately 60 miles. B Co CP moved from Reppeviller at 0900 and closed at 1000, traveling approximately 7 miles. The company assembled at Liedersheimstedt. D Co left Walschbronn at 0645 for Altdorf. En route the 2nd Plt encountered enemy small arms fire and artillery. It returned fire. A rifle grenade hit one of our tanks. Our troops by-passed the enemy. Tanks reconnoitered for the 5th Inf Regt and arrived in Altdorf at 1930, approximately 60 miles.

T/4 Kurz and Pfc Wood were slightly wounded but not evacuated.

Weather was cool and clear with visibility good to excellent. Combat efficiency was excellent; morale high.

24 Mar. 1945

The situation of the 71st Inf Div showed the enemy front lines had local scattered resistance. There was no definite front line. Enemy units in contact were elements of the 104th Panzer Grenadier Div with only one positive contact during the period. One company of the Panzer Jaeger Div had been reinforced and was reported to be in position along the Rhine River bank in the vicinity southeast of Mechtersheim. They resisted our advance to the Rhine fighting delaying action in the vicinity 1,000 yards south of Lingenfeld from behind a minefield. A bridge at Gommersheim was blown at 0915. 88mm time fire was received at 1845. Intermittent fire, believed to be 105mm came from the vicinity of Lingenfeld during the morning. Sniper fire was received from the same vicinity. One enemy tank was reported 1,000 yards south of the same town.

The 5th Inf Regt, attached to Co A, 749th Tank Bn, was give the order to move at once that had a change in its mission. They were to move at once to Weingarten and attack without delay along the axis of Weingarten, Westheim, and Gommersheim to seize bridges along the Rhine at Gommersheim. This attack was launched at 0500 in conjunction with the CCR of the 12th Armored Div. They were to move on Gommersheim from the direction of Speyer but were to cease if the enemy blew bridges prior to the execution of the mission.

At about 1030 reports were received that both bridges at Gommersheim had been blown. This report was verified and at 1104 the attack was dropped. The 5th Inf Regt was ordered to remain in position until further orders. At 1800 the advance was resumed towards Gommersheim with the limited mission of securing the town. This advance was halted upon receipt of info that the 12th Armored Div had already secured the town.

The 14th Inf Regt, attached to Co B, 749th Tank Bn, with CT 14 moved via motor from Pirmasens to the assembly area in the vicinity of Gros Fischlingen. On division's order it started moving to the east at 1700 to the Rhine River to establish an OPL. By 2200 the 2nd Bn on the right and the 3rd Bn on the left, were in position. The remaining elements moved east as the period ended.

The 66th Inf Regt, attached to Co C, 749th Tank Bn, moved by motor from Pirmasens to the assembly area in the vicinity of Landau. On division's orders they moved east to Freimersheim and launched an attack south and east on the right of the 5th Inf Regt to seize bridges at Gommersheim. It was launched at 1015 and carried to a position against scattered emery resistance but stopped at 1250 on division orders. The regiment organized defensive positions for the night.

The 749th Tank Bn, with 3 medium companies, supported the operations of infantry units to which they were attached; they furnished armored spearheads in conjunction with infantry attacks.

Results of Operations: The division-completed movements from Bitche-Pirmasens area by CTs to a position near the western bank of the Rhine. In conjunction with elements of the 10th and 12 Armored Divs cleared numerous small towns and villages in the division's zone, capturing large numbers of POWs. The mission of establishing an OP along the western bank of the Rhine extended along the Rhine, extending north of Speyer.

Location of the troops of the 749th Tank Bn showed the Bn CP, Hqs Co, and Bn Maintenance was at Gros-Fischlingen. A Co was in Lingenfeld, B Co in Höchstadt, C Co in Kirrwiller, D Co in Lingenfeld, and Svc Co in Edelsheim.

The Bn CP, Hqs Co and Bn Maintenance as well as the Medics left Sarnstall at 0800 and arrived in the vicinity of Edelsheim at approximately 1100 traveling approximately

28 miles. They closed in the new area in the vicinity of Gros-Fischlingen at 1645.

A, B, C, and D Cos supported the advance of the respective regiments to which they were attached mopping up scattered pockets of resistance. The 2nd and 3rd Plts of D Co left Altdorf at 0645 and arrived at Schwegenheim where they joined the 5th Regt of the 71st Inf Div. Tanks and infantry pushed forward to Lingenfeld and remained there. The 3rd Plt made an advance to Westheim at 0930.

One platoon of Co A and D Co jumped off from Westheim to attack southeast at approximately 1130 to destroy MG nests in the vicinity of the woods. The infantry was pinned down by airbursts and as tanks came to within 50 yards of the woods, 3-88mm AT guns opened fire completely destroying one M24 light tank of D Co at 1200.

Two enlisted men slightly wounded, Sgt Gough with a dislocated shoulder and Lt Hayden, bloody nose from concussion. Whether or not evacuation occurred is not given. One enlisted man, Wilkens, no rank given, was MIA.

Also encountered was sniper fire. Pfc Petillo distinguished himself by going to the aid of wounded infantry on foot under heavy small arms, sniper and automatic weapons fire. He was recommended for the Silver Star. The 2nd Plt of A Co, attached to the 2nd Bn, the 3rd Plt attached to the 3rd Bn, were held in reserve.

The company was ordered to move from Altdorf at 0700 to an assembly area in the vicinity of Schwegenheim, arriving there at 0800. They attacked southeast from this position at 0900, securing the town of Lingenfeld. A blown bridge held up further advance to the south.

Co B left the assembly area at Liedersheimstedt at 2200 and moved to the Vinningen and arrived there at 2230. One hundred thirty-three (133) infantry men of the 14th Regt loaded on tanks to move to a new assembly area. The company moved toward the initial point at Pirmasens at 2230, cross the point at 0430, and moved to Landau, closing in at 1000, approximately 25 miles. The company then moved off into billets at Aber Niemer-Höchstadt, closing at 1200. The infantry dropped off. The 14th Regt was placed in reserve at 1700.

The 1st and 2nd Plts, attached to the 1st Bn, moved to a defensive position at Speyer, closing at 1900. The CP moved forward on the western bank of the Rhine.

Co C, at 0230, left Landau for Kirrwiller. The 1st Plt was attached to the 3rd Bn, the 2nd to the 2nd Bn, and the 3rd Plt was attached to the 1st Bn and assisted the infantry in capturing Nor Hochstädt, Zeiskam, Oberlustedt, and the woods southeast of these towns.

The Svc Co left bivouac at Sarnstall at 0900 and proceeded to Edelsheim, arriving at 1700, approximately 16 miles.

The weather was cool to warm later in the period. Visibility was fair but hazy over 1,000 yards. Combat efficiency was excellent and morale high.

25 Mar. 1945

42nd Inf Div's situation reported there were no enemy front lines and no enemy units in contact. No enemy activity was reported as our troops continued to round up stragglers, POWs and to screen civilians. Our troops continued to demolish captured enemy pillboxes in the first part of the period.

All POWs were processed through the division's collection point were stragglers who had been hiding in the woods. Most of them had been out of food for several days. From civilians we heard that they were totally cut off from the Rhine. One group decided last night to get a good night's sleep and to proceed the following morning to the next village in order to surrender to either the civilian authorities or to troops. Measures were taken to maintain discipline.

Since about 1 Mar all unit commanders of the Wehrmach and other German Army units, from regimental companies and commanders of separate battalions and up, were authorized by official decree to execute any member of their command for the slightest infraction of discipline without court martial procedure.

In the 347th Inf Div; for example, the CO of the Artillery Regt, a full colonel, in disagreement with the division about the form the retreat was going to take, was ordered to report at once to the Div CP about 18 Mar and was executed within two hours of his arrival there. In his place a major from an SS unit was appointed and everybody in the Artillery Regt felt in danger of being shot on the spot for the slightest mistake or indication of inefficiency.

Attitude of German officers were: The greatest majority of all German officers captured in the last few days were not so much concerned about the disaster of the German collapse in this pocket as they were impressed with their personal misfortune of being captured. The fate of Germany to them depended solely on the continuation of their own efforts as an officer of the German Army. At no time did the hopelessness of the general military situation for Germany lead them to the conclusion that Germany had already lost the war, nor would they let conclusions of this nature at any time interfere with their personal efficiency in carrying out whatever mission was assigned to them. "We will fight to the last in the defense of the 'Fatherland' against the onslaught of Russian Bolshevism."

The basic motive which is compelling these German officers to think: "We must fight to the last regardless of the damage done to Germany as a result of this prolonged war," is apparently the idea that victory of Russia means Bolshevism for Germany, and thus the end of Germany. It was amazing to see to what extent Nazi propaganda here had succeeded in totally eliminating any other form of reasoning as to the necessity for a fight to the last from the minds of these officers.

The attitude towards the part of the United States playing in this war is "We cannot understand why the Americans came to the aid of Bolshevism. If the Americans had not created a second front in Europe, we could have defeated Russia." Any consideration of a fight for liberation from dictatorship to overrun European countries or similar reasoning was not understandable to their mind.

According to an older German officer, anti-Nazi, and fully conscious of the necessity of eliminating Nazism from German government, military leadership in the German Army is clearly divided into two camps of men of the older and the younger generation. A majority of the younger officers in the German Army are brought up totally under influence of Nazi ideology and know of no other form of reasoning." To question the solution to this problem of re-education, he had no solution to offer. "One cannot condemn all these young men as criminals. They firmly believe to be in the right in carrying out the Fuhrer's orders and are willing to fight unselfishly to the end." With the Nazi firmly in control of public opinion and the Army disagreeing, officers of the older generation are unable to influence the course of events.

Division operations for the period: All infantry regiments completed the mopping up of rear areas and present assembly areas. Work on destruction of the Siegfried fortifications was halted at 1400 by corps order when VI Corps notified that this work would be taken over by the French. All regiments were moved from defensive positions to assembly areas with outposts established to protect the division assembly areas.

Results of Operations: Mopping of rear areas and division assembly areas were completed. There was improved protection against aerial bombardment. First echelon maintenance of vehicles and equipment was conducted. The troops were prepared for future operations.

The 749th Tank Bn was relieved from the 71st Inf Div at 1200. The 71st Inf Div was now attached to the VI Corps after being relieved from the XXI Corps. The Bn CP, Hqs Co, and Bn Maintenance were in Gros-Fischlingen. A Co was in

Geinsheim, B Co in Dutweiler, C Co in Kirrwiller, D Co in Geinsheim, and the Svc Co in Edelsheim. The battalion was ordered to move from Lingenfeld at 1330 and closed into Dutweiler at 1500 in the Corps Res Area.

There was no action during the period for A Co. B Co, attached to the 14th Inf Regt, moved from Höchstadt at 1400 and closed in at Dutweiler at 1530 without any action during the period. C Co, attached to the 66th Inf Regt, was relieved from attachment to the 66th at 1200. Platoons assembled and moved to join the remainder of the company in Kirrwiller. Maintenance and repair work commenced on vehicles. The battalion took 9 POWS in the vicinity of Bn CP, two in uniform who were SS troopers and seven in civilian dress.

At 0930 D Co received a mission to recon the route into Gommersheim. The mission was accomplished at 1030 without resistance. The company returned to the assembly area at Lingenfeld.

The weather was warm and clear with good visibility. Combat efficiency was excellent and morale was high.

26 Mar. 1945

The 42nd Inf Div situation revealed there were no enemy front lines and no enemy activity in the division's zone during the period as our troops continued rounding up enemy troops still in hiding in our zone. One armed enemy soldier attempted to infiltrate the CP at 0515, was shot and killed by a guard.

POWs stragglers who have lost any contact with their units three or more days ago. A number of these stragglers were still hiding in the woods with sufficient rations to last them a few more days. This particularly was true for the Fortress troops who had ample quantities of "iron rations" stored in their bunkers.

Definite orders were issued to retreating units to destroy all weapons if capture was imminent. Upon the question whether or not some units had orders to bury their weapons, the questioned officers looked up in surprise and laughed. The reason for not burying their weapons were: (1) If buried and not destroyed weapons would ultimately fall into our hands; (2) There was no time to do such a job properly; and (3) If not buried properly, rust would destroy weapons in a short time.

The 749th Tank Bn situation showed no change of troop locations. The battalion remained in Corps Res and remained in position. Maintenance was performed on equipment. Vehicles were dispersed and camouflaged to the furthest extent possible. Ten POWs were taken wearing civilian clothes. At 0900 OIs were received which attached the 749th Tank Bn to the 42nd Inf Div. A second instruction stated the "units would not expend explosives in destroying the Siegfried Line fortifications that recently passed through or captured, except as necessary to mop up isolated resistance."

The weather was cool and hazy with scattered clouds and rain. Visibility was fair to poor. Combat efficiency was excellent and the morale of the troops was high.

27 Mar. 1945

The 42nd Inf general situation showed there was no enemy front lines nor was any enemy units in contact. No activity was reported during the period. Our troops continued the job of locating and capturing occasional POW stragglers still hiding in the division's zone. All POWs have lost contact with their units almost a week ago. They had some rations with them. As soon as they would run out of food they would generally proceed to the next village and surrender if they had not been rounded up before. POW comments on past operations were that "the last defense of the West Wall had to be carried out with only about one-third of the number of personnel originally contemplated and considered necessary minimum strength to effectively operate the fortifications. With the insufficient number of men and weapons to operate and occupy the defensive, fortifications became a liability rather than an asset in the defense of the sector."

A POW officer stated that the secret American plan for breaking the West Wall prepared before the invasion of the continent began, had already fallen into German hands in the form of a document as early as Aug or Sept 1944. It was translated and issued in pamphlet form to all commanders of WestWall units by November 1944, with specific instructions as the type of countermeasures needed to make the contemplated American tactics for the conquest of the West Wall ineffective.

The American plan was based on an analysis of the weak points of the West Wall fortifications. The main conclusion was that "pillboxes defended chiefly from the inside are extremely vulnerable to infiltration tactics of small assault groups armed chiefly with TNT, who under the cover of smoke or darkness could tackle pillboxes individually and blow them up or otherwise put them out of action."

To make infiltration of this sort impossible, the German High Command immediately shifted the emphasis of the contemplated defense of the West Wall on "defense of pillboxes from the outside." For that purpose, hundreds of labor battalions of foreign laborers were put to work in installing a system of trenches and infantry firing positions for the outside defense of the pillbox system. Also, at least one-half of the crew of each pillbox had to be on guard duty outside the pillbox at any time ready to defend the fortification in the open. In view of the insufficient number of personnel, later on, neither pillboxes nor the outside trench system could be manned or defended.

The system for directing artillery fire accurately to each spot of the defended ground within the field of vision of the pillbox crew was further perfected to the point where signs were installed every 50 to 100 yards. They were numbered from "A to Z" marking barrage fire zones for the supporting artillery. If an infiltrating enemy patrol was sighted in the vicinity of such a sign clearly, it would accurately describe the location of the enemy patrol at barrage fire zone "A", in pillbox sector 343, etc. This way, even the dumbest Volkssturm recruit could accurately give the firing orders to the supporting battery.

In order to camouflage pillbox positions against frontal view, entire sectors of the woods were replanted by the Fortress troops up to one week before the attack in this sector.

Many comments were made from POW officers and enlisted men to the effect that dissenting generals and higher commanders had secretly aided the American advance by issuing orders that clearly did not make sense. Particularly, orders prohibiting artillery fire on recognized American targets was deliberately not opened under the pretense "we must save ammo." Later on entire stores of artillery ammo were either abandoned or moved around so that they were never available at the right time when needed.

THE NATIONAL REDOUBT:

Accumulated ground information and a limited amount of photographic evidence now makes it possible to give a more definite estimate of the progress of plans for the "Last Ditch Stand" of the Nazi Party. Theoretically, the last stronghold of Germany consists of the Alpine block covering the western part of Austria and extending as far north as the lakes below Munich and south to the Italian lakes. Within this natural fortress area are inner zones of defense centered on Berchtesgaden and possibly also on some alternative GHQ further south in the neighborhood of the Italian frontier. Here, defended both by nature and by the most efficient secret weapons yet invented, the powers that have hitherto guided Germany will survive to organize her resurrection. Here armaments will be manufactured in bomb-proof factories, food and equipment will be stored in vast underground caverns and specially selected corps of young men will be trained in guerilla warfare, so that a whole underground army can be fitted and directed to liberate Germany from the occupying forces.

In fact, the main trend of German defense policy does seem directly primarily to the safeguarding of the Alpine zone. Although both in the east and the west Allied attacks are thrusting toward the heart of northern Germany, defenses continue to be constructed in depth in the south. They extend through the Black Forest to Lake Constance, and from the Hungarian frontier to the west of Graz, while in Italy, Kesselring continues to hold his ground desperately as the defense lines in the foothills of the Italian Alps are built up in his rear. This area is, by the very nature of the terrain, practically impenetrable. The few passes into it could be blocked by minimum of normal defense measures and even without any additional construction, underground shelter for both men and material is plentiful.

Air cover shows at least 20 sites of recent underground activity, as well as numerous natural caves, mainly in the regions of Edlesheim, Kuestein, Berchtesgaden, and Göllin, where ground sources have reported underground accommodation for stores and personnel. The existence of several reported underground factories has also been confirmed. In addition, several new barracks and hutted camps have been seen on air photographs, particularly around Innsbruck, Landeck, and the Berghof. It thus appears that ground reports of extensive preparations for the accommodation of the German Marquis to be are not unfounded. As regards the actual amount of troops, stores and weapons already within the Redoubt area, only ground info is available. The evidence indicates that considerable numbers of SS and specially chosen units are being systematically withdrawn to Austria. A definite allocation of each day's production of food, equipment, and armaments is sent there; and that engineer units are engaged on some type of defense activity at the most vital strategic points.

The Swiss frontier including the Brenner Pass, the Inntal, the Puster and Gail Tal seems reasonably certain that some of the most important ministries and personalities of the Nazi regime are already established in the Redoubt area. The party organization is reported to be in the Vorarlberg region. The Ministry for Propaganda and the Diplomatic Corps were reported to be in the Garrisch-Partebjurcgeb area, and the Reich's Chancellery at Berchtesgaden. Goering, Himmler, Hitler and other notables are said to be in the process of withdrawing to their respective personal mountain strongholds.

The location of the troops of the 749th Tank Bn had no change. The battalion remained in position. The companies continued maintenance work on equipment. Bn Staff and Co COs contacted by division staff and regimental commanders of the 42nd Inf discussed future plans and methods of employment of tanks with the infantry.

The weather was cloudy with thick overcast and rain continued off and on throughout the period. Visibility was poor. Combat efficiency was high as was the morale.

28 Mar. 1945

There was no change in the location of the troops of the 749th Tank Bn. The companies continued maintenance work on equipment. An oral message was received from the Bn Line Officer that the 749th was detached from the 42nd Inf and was now on 24-hour alert for movement outside of the Army sector. All companies were alerted for a possible move.

At 1900 an advance party left the CP for XX Corps Hqs in Weinerhof (Third Army) but complete info was not available as to status of the battalion in regard to attachments. Movement orders giving route to the assembly area in the vicinity of Kriegsfeld was issued to all companies at 2200: "Bn would move from its present position to the vicinity of Kriegsfeld under "Bn Control". Initial point was the road junction west of Kirrwiller. Another initial point was Diedesfeld - Neustadt - Lambrecht - Neidenfields - Weidenthal - Frankenstein - Fischbach - Enkenbach - Münchweiler - Winnweiler - Hochstein - Schweiswolten - Insweiler - Rockenhausen - Ratzenbach - Kielkirchhen - Gerbach - Kriegsfeld.

The order of the march was Hqs and Hqs Co with the Medical Detachment, C Co, B Co, A Co, D Co, Bn Maintenance, Svc Co. Speed would be 15 miles per hour with maximum speed for individual vehicles 20 miles per hour. Interval between vehicles would be 50 to 60 yards. Interval between the marching units would be 5 minutes. Radio silence was to be maintained. The first vehicle in each serial would display a green flag and marked with chalk "1st Vehicle." The last vehicle in each serial would display an orange flag and would be marked with chalk 'Last Vehicle.' All tops on 1/2-tracks and 1/4-ton trucks would be down unless it was raining. All marching units had maintenance halt of 15 minutes every 1-1/2 hours after the head of the column crossed the IP. All crews would keep to the right of vehicles during the halt. All tank crews would ride inside of tanks."

The weather was hazy, cloudy, and cool. Visibility was fair to poor. Combat efficiency was excellent with morale high.

29 Mar. 1945

There was no change in the location of the 749th Tank Bn troops. The companies remained alert for possible movement and the "Movement Orders" were received. "The 749th would move without delay to Kriegsfeld with the following instructions to apply: advance detachment report would immediately be sent to Hqs XX Corps, at Weinerhof. Coordinate route clearance with Traffic Control. Radio silence would be maintained during the move. Morning reports and allied records of the unit would be serviced. Effective upon departure the 7th Army area unit is relieved from its present attachment to XXI Corps, 7th Army and passes to control of the 12th Army Group. Report time and date of departure and estimated time of arrival to destination would be reported to Hqs. The 749th Tank Bn would be attached to the 65th Inf Div effective 1800. Head of the column would reach Kriegsfeld at 2200, this date."

Weather was hazy, cloudy, and cool. Visibility was only fair. Combat efficiency was excellent with morale high.

30 Mar. 1945

The entire 749th Tank Bn would be in bivouac in a field west of Höchheim. The battalion would now revert to XX Corps under the control of 3rd Army. The battalion left the vicinity of Gros-Flischling at 0800 and crossed the IP at Neustadt at 0830. The battalion arrived at Kriegsfeld at approximately 1400, approximately 55 miles. The battalion was then ordered to proceed from Kriegsfeld to cross the Rhine River doing so at Mainz, crossing at 2215. The battalion then proceeded on a road march to the bivouac area in a field west of Höchheim on Frankfurt Road, closing in at 2400.

After crossing the Rhine, the head of the battalion column was fired on by a passing vehicle going in the opposite direction by what was believed to be a subMG. No casualties were sustained. The battalion crossed the Rhine on what is believed to be the longest bridge constructed by Army Engineers over the Rhine - 154 pontoons. The battalion traveled approximately 91 miles during the period. Vehicles that would not fit a treadway bridge across the Rhine were ferried across north of Mainz.

The weather was cool with scattered clouds and visibility was good. Combat efficiency was good and morale high.

31 Mar. 1945

The 749th Tank Bn showed the line companies en route on a 30-mile road march from Ruppersburg that was where Hqs and Svc Cos were located and remained for the night while the remaining line companies continued to march with the infantry on the back deck of tanks.

The battalion left the bivouac area in the vicinity west of Höchheim at 0730 over the "autobahn" highway to Ossenheim, arriving at 1130. They left this area at 1245 and arrived at Ruppersburg at 1500 where contact was made with elements of the 65th Inf Div. The entire battalion was attached to the 260th Inf Regt. At 1320 an infantry of battalion size mounted on the back of 10 medium tanks for the 30-mile road march.

Weather and visibility: It was cool and cloudy with good visibility. Combat efficiency was excellent while the morale of the troops remained high.

1 APRIL TO
30 APRIL 1945

1 Apr. 1945

According to the 65th Inf Div XX Corps, our front lines had no contact with the enemy. The division's CP was at Hatterbach, Germany. The 259th Inf attached one light tank with two platoons from the 749th Tank Bn and moved into the assembly area. Preparations were made for an attack. The 260th Inf less one battalion was attached to one medium tank, one light tank with two platoons from the 749th Tank Bn. They also moved into the assembly area and made preparations for the attack. The 3rd Bn was in Div Res and the 261st Inf moved into the assembly area making preparations for an attack and attached to the 6th Armored Div.

Result of Operations showed the division moved into the assembly areas and would attack through the 3rd Cav Grp across the Fulda River. An undetermined number of POWs were taken.

Orders received stated that XX Corps would continue attacking to seize Erfurt and Weiler. The 6th Armored Div would continue the attack to the east. The 80th Inf Div was on the left (north) flank and attack to seize Kassel. The 90th Inf Div (XII Corps) would be on the right (south) flank and continue their advance to the northeast.

The 65th Inf Div less one RCT would pass through the 3rd Cav Grp and attack aggressively and continuously to seize the corps' objectives - Erfurt and Weiler.

The 259th Inf would be attached to A Co and two platoons of light tanks from the 749th Tank Bn and would attack aggressively, cross the Fulda River and seize the initial objective. They would be prepared to continue their advance to the east on division's orders utilizing transportation of attached and supporting units to the maximum. They would also protect the division's right (south) flank, maintain contact with the elements of the XII Corps on the right and the 260th Inf on the left.

The 260th Inf, less one battalion, was attached to B Co and one platoon of light tanks from the 749th Tank Bn. They would attack aggressively, cross the Fulda River and seize the initial objection; they would be prepared to continue their advance to the east on division's orders utilizing transportation of attached and supporting units to the maximum and would protect the division on the left (north) flank. They would maintain contact with the 60th Inf Div on the left (north) flank and the 259th Inf on the right (south) flank.

The 749th Tank Bn was in Div Res in the present location. AT weapons would have high priority in crossing the river. After the initial objective had been seized the advance to the corps' objective, on division's orders, would be continuous until all objectives were seized.

Formation: The regiments would be abreast with CT 259 on the right. CT 260, attached to D Co and one platoon of light tanks from the 749th Tank Bn, would move rapidly on motors of attached and supporting organizations, would protect the left flank of the division and follow the route indicated to seize the division's objective. The battalions would be in columns, maintain contact with the cavalry group, the tank destroyer company that was initially attached to the 3rd Cav Grp.

CT 259 would move rapidly on motors of attached and supporting organizations. They were to protect the right flank of the division and follow routes indicated to seize the division's objective. The tank destroyer company would revert to CT control when it passes through the 3rd Cav Grp.

Orders were that we were to bypass enemy pockets that cannot be reduced by the advance guard. A distance of 60 yards will be maintained between vehicles.

The location of the troops of the 749th Tank Bn were: Hqs, Hqs Co and the Svc Co were in Kirchheim with A Co in Hersfeld, B Co in Erstrode, C Co and the forward battalion CP were in Hainrode.

This is the 273rd day in combat; the consecutive number of days on the line ended 13 Jan 1945 (194 days).

Hqs Co and the Svc Co left bivouac at Ruppersburg at 0930 en route to Kirchheim, arriving at 1545. A Co plus two platoons of D Co were attached to the 259th Inf Regt and left Ulrichstein at 0600 and arrived in the assembly area in the vicinity of Hainrode at 1230. They then proceeded to Hersfeld. Upon arrival at Hersfeld late in the period, they made preparations for an attack in compliance with OIs.

B Co, plus one platoon of D Co was attached to the 260th Inf Regt. Then the company moved from Ulrichstein at 0600 and traveled approximately 38 miles northeast to the infantry dismount point in the vicinity of Hainrode, closing in at 1200. At 1300 the company moved into billets at Erstrode, traveling approximately another two miles northeast, closing in at 1400. One platoon of Co D with this battalion was attached for a combat mission.

Co C, under battalion control, was in Div Res and remained in Hainrode. At 0600 the company left Ulrichstein and moved in position with a battalion column that traveled in a northeasterly direction to Hainrode.

Co D, with two platoons attached to A Co and one platoon was attached to E Co. The company CP left Ruppersburg at 0930 for a new bivouac area and arrived at Hersfeld at 1730 traveling a distance of approximately 50 miles.

The Svc Co left the bivouac area at 0830 and proceeded to a new bivouac area at

Kirchheim arriving at approximately 1600 having traveled approximately 48 miles.

The 749th Tank Bn signed by MajGen F. W. Milburn and endorsed by MajGen received the following commendation. A. J. Barnett, CG of the 70th Inf Div. "It is my desire to commend the 70th Inf Div on the capture of Forbach, Stiring-Wendel and Saarbrucken and on the crossing of the Saar River. The successful completion of this mission is one in which the 70th Inf Div may take justifiable pride. The courage of your men is evident in their victory in the face of the enemy's stubborn resistance and employment of natural obstacles. It is in a large measure due to the fine work of all supporting units that the teamwork which brought success was officially recognized by the CG, XXI Corps."

2 Apr. 1945

The general situation of the 65th Inf Div that the enemy front lines were in the zone of the division's advance and was generally along the north and south lines east of the Wehre River. There were many remnants of different enemy units in contact. No heavy organized resistance was encountered. There was a roadblock on the bridge at Braasch. Tanks were reported in the town by the 3rd Cav Grp capable of an attack further east. Fresh tank trucks were reported in Sontro at 1700 by the 65th Recon Troops. Another civilian saw trenches being dug on the north side of Sontro. The enemy destroyed the bridge in the vicinity of Braasch. Small arms fire from scattered localities and pockets of resistance was received by our forward elements but was generally light.

One vehicle was hit by enemy fire and one enemy aircraft, identity unknown, flew from west to east over the Div CP at 0825. No attempted attack was made. Six FW 190s and two ME 109s strafed one of our convoys but no damage was done. All eight planes were reported destroyed.

The following message from the CG, XX Corps, stated, "It has been reported that persons in civilian clothes are mining roads, bridges, and attempting to sabotage US military installations in occupied areas. Such persons when caught in the act will be shot. You will see that all units of your command are informed and comply. This will be read to all troops by an officer immediately upon receipt."

A civilian POW states that 70 tanks arrived via rail from the vicinity of Erfurt and unloaded at Bebra on 29 Mar. They proceeded under their own power to Hersfeld where some of them apparently took part in defense of that town. He surmised that the balance of the tanks entered the autobahn in the vicinity of Hersfeld and headed northeast in the direction of Eisenach. Enemy troops were moving out of Melsungen northeast towards Quentel early this morning. Heavy motorized tanks and tracked vehicles (no tanks) were heard moving northeast from Melsungen.

Operations for the period had the 259th Inf Regt attached to A Co and two platoons of light tanks from Co B from the 749th Tank Bn. They attacked at 0600 in elements of battalions with the 3rd Bn leading. They crossed the Fulda River and captured the towns of Braubach, Braasch, Rotenburg and continued their advance to the northeast making rapid progress against scattered enemy resistance. The town of Bebra was cleared by elements moving in the rear of the assault battalion. The bridge was captured intact at Braasch that was being used for all division traffic except tanks. At the close of the period the 2nd and 3rd Bns were in the vicinity of Contra and continued their attack to the east.

The 260th Inf Regt was attached to Co B and one light tank from platoon from Co D of the 749th Tank Bn, crossed the Fulda River and captured the towns of Heimbach, Bergersmausen and Alta. A bridge at Konnefeld was captured intact. At the close of the period the advancing units had passed through the line. The 3rd Bn was in Div Res in the vicinity of Wichte.

The 261st Inf Regt was attached to the 6th Armored Div. There were continuous recon routes of the advance and flanks. Artillery was in close support of the infantry units was accomplished with rapid displacements and aided by transporting infantry troops. At the close of the period all division artillery had crossed the Fulda River.

The 65th Recon Troops crossed the Fulda River and passed through elements of the 259th Inf Regt to screen the advance at the close of the period. Elements passing Sontra made rapid progress.

Location of troops of the 749th Tank Bn was as follows: The Bn Hqs and Hqs Co were in Hainrode. After having left Kirchheim at 1230 having traveled 15 miles; they closed in at 1330. At 2000 orders were received from the 65th Div to move Hqs and Svc Co across the Fulda River on a wheel vehicle bridge by noon the next period and into the assembly area.

Co A plus four tanks of B Co were attached to the 259th Inf Regt and two assault guns were located in Hersfeld. They moved from Hersfeld to Braasch. They advanced up to the Fulda River and assisted the infantry in capturing the bridge intact. The bridge would not take the tanks so the tanks moved south to Hersfeld to be in position to cross the river at this point.

B Co, plus one platoon of D Co was attached to the 260th Inf Regt and moved at 0800 from Ersche to advance to the Fulda River carrying the 3rd Bn Inf on the back decks.

The traveled approximately six miles northeast to the advance assembly area in the vicinity of the Braubach Bridge to carry the tanks across which was not completed at 2400. Six POWs were captured and turned over to the MPs at Baubach.

C Co was in Div Res in Oberellenback. They left at 1215 from their position at Hainrode and moved through Esrode, Starkelshausen to Oberellenback. They arrived at 1300 and were prepared to cross the river. Oil shortage prevented further movement of the company.

D Co had one tank of the 3rd Plt was abandoned in Hersfeld, Germany due to maintenance trouble.

The clocks were moved ahead one hour at 0200 hours to DOUBLE BRITISH SUMMER TIME. Two ME 109s strafed in the vicinity of the Bn CP but sustained no damage. Planes were fired on but no hits were observed.

The weather was windy, cool, raining with poor visibility. The combat efficiency was excellent and morale high.

3 Apr. 1945

The enemy front lines were fluid and many enemy units in contact had different remnants as previously. Enemy tanks were reported in Bad Sooden the night of 2 and 3 Apr. Fifteen to 18 tanks, plus unidentified infantry units were moving from Ronada to Grossburschla. No enemy ground resistance was encountered during the period. Several enemy aircraft were active over the division's zone. Three ME 109s were reported over the 259th Inf Regt area at 1550. No hostile acts were reported.

From 1700 to 2000 several enemy aircraft were active over the Div CP at Bernburg without damage. Sporadic enemy resistance between Brandenburg and Eschwege was conducted. The predominant note among all ranks of POWs continued to be a sense of confusion and disorder. Most of them wander about, heading east.

The 356th Inf Div left Italy at the end of Jan; they were a German division. There were two regiments of this division, the 870 and 871st, having gone first to Hungary while the 869th was sent to Schwarzenborn to be reformed there. Some recruits arrived, plus some rifles. When our troops broke through, an Alarm Co was formed to defend Resfeld. The balance of the embryo regiment was committed piecemeal along our path of advance. This battalion with approximately 150 men had manned the 88mm AA guns in the Rotenburg area. After their guns were knocked out, they fell back in scattered groups, and were committed in local defense.

In accordance with the division's orders of the 276th VGD, this unit plus all other units in the corps' zone were absorbed by the 276th Div Staff, and then were located in Kellbach. The division is now a part of the 89th Corps. The 2nd Co of the GHQ NCO School was located in Eisenach. The 600 men attending this school were organized into four companies and committed as infantry. It was armed with six MGs, 15 Panzerfausts, and a few MPs.

The 259th Inf Regt was attached to Co A and two platoons of D Co of the 749th Tank Bn. They continued their advance to the east occupying the towns of Lauterbach, Detra, Rittmannshausen, Ifta, Scheroda, and Kreuzberg. They crossed the Fulda River and occupied the high ground to the east thereof. Good progress was made against scattered enemy resistance.

The 260th Inf Regt was attached to B Co and one platoon of D Co of the 749th Tank Bn. They continued their advance to the east occupying the town of Ronada and other populated localities. Rapid progress was made against very slight enemy resistance. At the end of the period regrouping forces awaiting the passage of the 6th Armored Div on roads before continuing the advance in the zone.

The 261st Inf Regt was attached to the 6th Armored Div. Air operations continued recon routes of the advance and their flanks. Artillery was in close support of infantry units by rapid displacements and continued to transport infantry troops.

The 65th Recon troops continued to screen movement of the division and reconnoitered routes in the zone of advance. One platoon searched the woods for the enemy. Some of our troops made it across the Werra River. The division was now in position to continue its attack to the east. Three hundred thirteen (313) prisoners were cleared through the Prisoner of War camp.

The following info was taken from Hqs, 65th Div: "Any person found cutting telephone wires or tampering with any communication installations will be regarded as committing a hostile act against US forces and would be summarily shot. The body would be left on the spot as warning to others with like intentions."

The Bn CP of the 749th Tank Bn as well as Hqs Co and the Svc Co moved at 0900 from Hainrode and traveled 23 miles to Rocensuss. The new CP opened at 1100. The route taken was Hainrode, Erstrode, and then Erstrode to Braäsch crossing the wheeled vehicle bridge, then to Rotenburg, Bebra, Conneburg, Rittman and Shausen and then Rocensuss.

A Co plus two platoons of D Co were attached to the 259th Inf Regt and were en route to Kreuzberg. The company had been ordered to move from Braäsch via Hersfeld and Sontra. The conpany was taken from general support and assigned to the 1ˢᵗ, 2ⁿᵈ, 3ʳᵈ Plts of the 1ˢᵗ, 2ⁿᵈ, and 3ʳᵈ Bns, respectively. The tanks moved out at 1300 en route to Ronada with infantry on the back decks with the objective to take Kreuzberg. Their route was Sontra, Weissenborn, Drauthausen, Brettau, Grandenborn, and Ronada. Upon reaching Ronada the order was received to continue the advance at 1800. Columns moved east to Kreuzberg via Lauterbach and Ifta. The company, less light tanks, had crossed the Fulda River early in the period at Hersfeld and advanced to Sontra, arriving at 0800. Light tanks had crossed during the previous period and proceeded to Sontra. The medium tanks could not cross the bridge at Braäsch because of tonnage and had to detour and cross.

B Co moved from the assembly area at Braäsch at 0630 to cross the Fulda River. They crossed the bridge at Hersfeld because the bridge would not carry medium tanks. After crossing the river, the company moved to a new assembly area in the vicinity of Elthansee, closing at 1400 but orders were changed and tanks with infantry on back decks advanced to Kreuzberg. Routes taken were through Sontra, Wichrannshausen, Metra, Rittmannsausen, Ifta, and Kreuzberg. The 3ʳᵈ Plt and a light tank platoon moved at 1800 to join the 1ˢᵗ Bn as advance guard. There was no contact with the enemy.

Co Hqs and trains crossed the river at Braasch at 0700 moving to Sontra at 1530, closing at 1700.

At 1215 C Co left Oberellenback on a road march to Weissenborn closing in at 1630. Two tanks and one assault gun had mechanical trouble. C Co was then in Div Res in Weissenborn.

The CP of D Co left Hersfeld at 0730 for a new bivouac area and arrived in Rocensuss at 1400 having traveled a distance of approximately 55 miles.

Svc Co and Bn Maintenance left the bivouac area at Kircheim at 0830 and proceeded to their new bivouac area in Rocensuss arriving at 1600 with a distance traveled of approximately 40 miles.

Two enemy planes fired upon the vicinity of the Bn CP at 1330 and again at 1830; no hits were observed but the planes were chased.

The weather was of scattered showers and cloudy with fair visibility. Combat efficiency was excellent and the morale, as well, was excellent.

4 Apr. 1945

The following OIs were issued from Hqs, 65ᵗʰ Inf Div. "VIII Corps will become operational within the next 48 hrs in the zone between XII and XX Corps. The

65th Inf Div passes to the command of CG of the CG, VIII Corps when VIII Corps assumes responsibilities for its zone of action. Roads and routes are shown to be effective. Drivers will maintain the distance of 60 yds between vehicles. The doubling of columns on the road is prohibited. The 259th Inf Regt will continue on the mission as directed by the CO, 65th Inf Div. The 265th Engineer Bn will continue close support of the advance."

The 749th Tank Bn showed the Bn CP, Hqs Co and Svc Co in Rocensuss. Co A plus two platoons of D Co would be attached to the 259th at Bischofrode. The company was ordered to move at 0700 from Kreuzberg but platoons would remain attached to their respective battalions. The 1st Plt seized and secured Mihla by 1800. The 2nd Plt seized the towns of Langula and Kellerforst by 2100. The 3rd Plt moved as reserve arrived in Langula at 1930.

B Co plus the 1st Plt from D Co would be attached to the 260th Inf in the vicinity of Falkenberg. They would support the infantry to the vicinity of Falkenberg, Treffurt and Schweppenhausen. The 1st and 2nd Plts moved into position as advance guard for the 3rd Bn at 0900. The 3rd Plt moved from Kreuzberg to a rendezvous point at Weissenborn at 1500. Route of march and marching orders were changed several times during the day while the column waited on the road. At 1830 the company was ordered to assemble in the vicinity of Gros Burschla. The company closed in at 2400.

C Co was in Div Res in Weissenborn and had no action during the period.

Weather was thickly overcast with breaking clouds, intermittent rains, and very cool. Visibility was good. Combat efficiency was excellent as was the morale.

5 Apr. 1945

The 65th Inf Div general situation revealed the operations for the period was that the 259th Inf Regt was attached to A Co and two platoons of D Co from the 749th Tank Bn. They continued to advance to the east capturing the towns of Mihla, Nazza, and Kellerforst as well as other populated localities. Good progress was made against scattered enemy resistance. A bridge was captured at Nazza capable of carrying 2-1/2 ton trucks.

The 260th Inf Regt was attached to B Co plus one platoon from D Co light tanks from the 749th Tank Bn. Initially, they were held up by the movement of the 6th Armored Div. They continued the advance to the east following closely behind them. They occupied the towns of Treffurt, Diedorf, and Gros Burschla.

The 261st Inf Regt was held from attachment to the 6th Armored Div for 1200. The assembled troops were located as follows: The 1st Bn was in the vicinity of Grossengottern, 2nd Bn in the vicinity of Manfred, and the 3rd Bn in the vicinity of Nieden. The remainder of the regiment was in the vicinity of Eschwege and given the mission of protecting the divisions left flank and guarding a warehouse at Eschwege and enemy Class V supply dump in the vicinity of Meyerode. The 2nd Bn liberated 400 British Officer prisoners at Lingenfeld at 1700. Artillery, in close support of infantry units by rapid displacement, continued to transport infantry troops. The cavalry continued to screen movement of the division and reconnoitered routes in the zone of advance.

The division continued its advance in the new zone occupying many towns and populated communities. The only obstacle to the advance was the 6th Armored Div. Preparations were completed to occupy a line running from Mülhausen to Lancensalza and regroup forces before continuing the advance on corps' orders. An accurate account of POWs was not available but 129 had been cleared through Prisoner of War Camp.

The location of the troops of the 749th Tank Bn showed that Bn CP, Hqs Co, and the Svc Co were in Hockensuss. A Co plus two platoons from D Co were attached to the 259th Inf Regt. The 1st Plt was at Heroldishausen, the 2nd Plt at Lancensalza, and the 3rd Plt at Weberstedt. Co B plus one platoon of D Co was attached to the 260th Inf Regt was in Mülhausen. C Co was in Div Res at Weissenborn.

Operations for the period - the 1st Plt of Co A was ordered to move to Langula. The advance continued and the towns of Grossengottern and Schonstedt were seized. Orders were received to continue and seize Heroldishausen; the mission was accomplished. The 2nd Plt was ordered to leave Kannerforst at 1100 and seized Flarchheim, Mülverstedt, Weberstedt, Zimmern, Ufhort, and Lancensalza. Resistance was light with only small arms fire. Two enemy OPs and MG nests were destroyed. The 3rd Plt moved from Langula to Weberstedt arriving at 1500. The town was outposted. All platoons remained attached to respective organizations.

The 2nd Plt from B Co moved from Gros Burschla to Treffurt to form an advance guard for the 3rd Bn, 260th Inf Regt. The CT moved out at 1000 with the objective of Mülhausen and the high ground east of Formar that were taken at 1700. Resistance was very light. The 3rd Plt plus light tanks formed an advance guard of the 1st Bn, 260th Inf Regt. and moved out from Falkenberg at 1000. The objectives were Mülhausen and the high ground west of Bollstedt. The objectives were taken at 1600 against light resistance.

After the infantry consolidated positions, the platoon moved to the company assembly area of Mülhausen in regimental reserve and remained in Formar. The 1st Plt, in support of the 2nd Bn was in regimental reserve and moved from Grossburschla at 0900 to Mülhausen, arriving at 1400.

Co Hqs moved from Gros Burschla at 1200 to Mülhausen, closing at 1800. Nine POWs were captured.

Co C had no activity during the period and remained in position in Div Res and was alerted for movement to the 76th Div's zone in the vicinity of Hess-Lichtenau, arriving at 2000. Work progressed on vehicles, radio maintenance and repair.

Bn Co and S-3 contacted the 707th Tank Bn at Schwartzmannshausen for details of relief for this battalion. The following message was received at 1600: "Move elements of your command as released to the assembly area in the vicinity of Hess-Lichtenau and report to Div for further instructions."

The weather was scattered showers, cloudy and cool with fair visibility. Company efficiency and morale of the troops were both excellent.

6 Apr. 1945

The 65th Inf Div's general situation showed the operations for the period to be the 259th Inf Regt attached to Co A and two platoons of D Co from the 749th Tank Bn. They continued their advance to the east and captured the towns of Mülverstedt, Flarchheim, Uphoven, and Lancensalza as well as other populated places. Resistance at Lancensalza was fairly heavy but over 300 POWs were captured. Mopping up continued throughout the period. The regiment occupied positions on the line at Mülhausen-Lancensalza in the zone as ordered.

The 260th Inf Regt was attached to B Co and one platoon from D Co of the 749th Tank Bn. They also continued their advance to the east occupying the towns of Pfafferode, Oberdoria, and Mülhausen. The advance was held up due to the use of roads by the 6th Armored Div. The regiment fulfilled its mission and occupied a portion of restraining the line at Mülhausen-Lancensalza in the zone.

The 261st Inf Regt was attached to Co D and one platoon from Co C from the 707th Tank Bn. The regiment continued to assembly troops in preparation to become Div Res. The 1st Bn finally assembled in the vicinity of Schontheim, the 2nd Bn in the vicinity of Wanfried, and the 3rd Bn in the vicinity of Eigenweiler. They continued to protect the left flank of the division. Aggressive patrolling was in progress with stiff resistance in the vicinity of Geismar. They established roadblocks on roads leading into the division's zone along the left boundary. Air observation points continued reconnaissance of routes of the advance and flanks. Artillery was in close support of the infantry units by rapid displacement and continued to transport infantry troops.

Relief was in progress by the 707th Tank Bn for the 749th Tank Bn. The cavalry continued to screen movement of the division and reconnoitered routes in the zone's advance. They assisted in the capture of Lancensalza protecting the right flank of the division.

The general situation of the 76th Inf Div showed there were no enemy front lines. An enemy of unknown strength occupied critical areas north of and then east of the Werra River. Elements of D IV and D XVII Bns, elements of the 166th Inf Div, elements of KG Kuebler, and 10 or more miscellaneous enemy units were in contact. Mines and other material were on the road 1,600 yards west of Bad Sooden and roadblocks were in the town. An estimated two companies were entrenched in the high ground north of Truttenhausen and one plane reported the infantry entrenching in the streets of Altendorf. A civilian stated that as of 5 Apr the road was mined at the entrance to Asbach in the vicinity of the woods. Approximately 500 Wehrmach trucks, three tanks and two armored cars were in Asbach. Five troop carrier trucks were seen along the road 200 meters from Asbach.

From Altendorf to the west there were two bridges across the river with one blown; there was a crater approximately 10 meters, but was unable to be used for foot troops. In the hills around Düdenrode approximately 30 men were there with Panzerfausts. A laborer stated he did not know if there was infantry in Grebendorf, Schweb, or Frieda as of this date.

Despite stubborn organized resistance, the enemy was forced to withdraw from Helsa and Grossalmerode. A strong counterattack by infantry of unknown strength in Bad Sooden forced friendly elements to withdraw during the night but the town was re-entered and fighting continued at the end of the period. A counterattack by an estimated platoon, the infantry repulsed without loss of ground. Three rounds of 105 mm (estimated) were received on the western edge of Helsa at 1120. Small arms and mortar fire was received from Grossalmerode during the entire period.

There was sniper fire on friendly wire team in the vicinity of Huterode at 1030. Twenty enemy were seen in the vicinity of Frankenhausen at 1100. A small group of infantry attempted an ambush near Weissenbach and 7 tanks entered the woods at 0845. Five tanks from Grossalmerode at 1000 and one tank was seen at 1015.

Our operations for the period: The 417th Inf moved by motor. One platoon of Co

C moved to Lauterbach to furnish protection to the Div CP. The 2ⁿᵈ Bn continued to attack to the east in the zone and captured Helsa. One tank was knocked out with bazooka fire. The 3ʳᵈ Bn launched an attack in the east. By the end of the period it had advanced against heavy enemy resistance. Two counterattacks were repulsed. The AT Co placed nine 57mm guns in position to protect the division's left flank against an attack.

CT 304 moved east by motor and through elements of the XX Corps. It had reached a position in the vicinity of Schonstedt.

The 385ᵗʰ Inf Regt had Co C of the 749ᵗʰ Tank Bn attached. The 1ˢᵗ Bn, minus B Co attacked Grossalmerode at 0700 and captured it at 1610. A reinforced A Co was holding the town. The battalion moved to the assembly area in the vicinity of Oberdunzebach. B Co crossed Werra River going through the 304ᵗʰ Inf and assisted the advance of the 2ⁿᵈ Bn. The 2ⁿᵈ Bn attacked and captured Bad Sooden but a counterattack forced a temporary withdrawal from the town to high ground to the rear. By 1615 the town was retaken with E Co now holding the town. The battalion assembled in the vicinity of Wiederhone. The 3ʳᵈ Bn continued to attack in the zone and captured Truttenhausen with K Co holding the town. They received a counterattack at 1640 that was beaten off. Twenty-five (25) POWs were taken and 11 enemy killed. The battalion then assembled in the vicinity of Eschwege.

The 901ˢᵗ FA Bn destroyed one enemy tank. The 364ᵗʰ FA Bn fired on an enemy counterattack and other targets of opportunity. The 749ᵗʰ Tank Bn had C Co attached to the 385ᵗʰ Inf Regt.

Bn CP, Hqs Co, and Svc Co of the 749ᵗʰ Tank Bn was located in Rocen. Co A plus two platoons from D Co was attached to the 259ᵗʰ Inf Regt and located in Sontra. B Co plus one platoon of D Co was attached to the 260ᵗʰ Inf Regt and located in Mülhausen while C Co was in Hess-Lichtenau.

Co A plus two platoons from D Co and their attachments were relieved from the 65ᵗʰ Div at 1200. They were ordered to withdraw from the 65ᵗʰ Div's zone and assemble in the vicinity of Sontra. First the assembly occurred in Mülverstedt at 1700 and then road marched to Sontra, closing at approximately 2100. The 1ˢᵗ Plt was ordered at 1100 to seize Allengotten. The move was completed at 1445.

B Co, plus one platoon from D Co would remain in assembly in Mülhausen and had no contact with the enemy. They were ordered to withdraw from the 65ᵗʰ Div's zone and assemble in the vicinity of Reyerode in the early hours of the next period.

C Co, attached to the 385ᵗʰ Inf Regt, 76ᵗʰ Inf Div, joined at 1615. The company's joined their respective battalions at 2100. The company then moved to the vicinity of Weissenborn at 0900 to the assembly area in Hess-Lichtenau, the 76th's Div zone, closing in at approximately 1615 having traveled approximately 30 miles. Platoons were attached to the 1st, 2nd, and 3rd Bns of the 385th Inf Regt as follows: The 1st Plt with the 1st Bn, the 2nd Plt with the 2nd Bn, and the 3rd Plt with the 3rd Bn. The Co CP remained in Hess-Lichtenau. Two tanks were out of action due to maintenance trouble.

The following message was received at Bn Hqs at 1500 from the CG, 65th Inf Div: "The 749th Tank Bn is relieved from attachment to the 65th Inf Div and will comply with instruction from the CG, XX Corps with clear movement through the 65th Div G-4 Traffic Control."

Bn staff contacted the 76th Div staff at their CP at Lauterbach to coordinate plans for battalion movement upon relief to the 65th Div by the 707th Tank Bn. As per verbal agreement between the CG of the 65th and the 76th Inf Divs, the 749th Tank Bn less Co C is to remain with the 65th Inf Div for operations until present mission is completed. Further orders for movement for the balance of the battalion to the 76th zone would be issued. D Co's 3rd Plt was relieved from attachment to Co A, this battalion, and joined D Co in Rocren.

The weather was cloudy with heavy overcast, rain and cold. Visibility was fair. Combat efficiency and morale were both excellent.

7 Apr. 1945

The 76th Inf Div's general situation showed there were no cohesive enemy front lines. Friendly advancing elements were operating in the vicinity of Lancensalza and Mülhausen. The enemy units in contact were elements of the 166th Div, elements of GHQ Engineer Brigade, elements of the 593rd Inf Regt, D-IV Bn, D XVII-Bn, 5th Co. from the 3465th Fortress Inf Bn, 2nd Battery from the 541st Reich Labor Service Bn (RAD), the 15th Armored Inf Replacement Bn, the 309th Artillery Signal Replacement Bn, the 6th Battery of the 393rd Anti-Aircraft RAD Bn, and 17 other miscellaneous units.

In the division's zone, the enemy continued to offer stubborn resistance. During the early part of the period two unsuccessful counterattacks were launched in the vicinity of Truttenhausen. During the remainder of the period, resistance varied from moderate to light. The 65th US Inf Div reported strong counterattacks in the vicinity of Katharinanenberg and Struth with tanks and infantry. Struth was reported cleared by the end of the period. The 65th US Inf Div also reported Eigenrieden heavily shelled by guns of undetermined caliber at 0900. One plane strafed the northern edge of Lancensalza at 0920. Four planes flew over at 1105. One ME 109 flew over Lauterbach about 1300. Counterattacks by enemy supported by heavy MG and mortar fire in the vicinity of Truttenhausen was repulsed at 1900; a second counterattack at 1950 was repulsed by friendly artillery at 2015.

Three enemy soldiers were observed in Rebach at 1000. The bridge at the northern end of Eschwege was under small arms fire at 1215. A jeep was ambushed in Schwedda at 1230. The road between Schwedda and Frieda was under fire at 1400. An estimated 100 enemy entered Altendorf at approximately 1400. The bridge at Wanfried was out as was the bridge at Frieda and both were booby-trapped. As of this date the bridge at Grossburschla was intact. Civilians stated bridges at Witzenhausen and Lindewerra were intact but unusable for tanks. The bridges at Kleinvach and Witzenhausen were intact as well but tanks could not use them; this was as of 6 Apr. Three enemy soldiers were dressed in US uniforms and armed with M1's entered a house in Truttenhausen and killed one sergeant; that enemy was still at large.

Air Recon reported elements on the roads north and west of Kefferhausen and in the vicinity of Struth consisting of horse drawn vehicles, tanks, infantry, and bicycles at 1340. The 691st TD Bn on a destroyed train found maintenance and operational file with blueprints, photographs, and construction details of a V-2 rocket.

The 417th Inf had the 1st Bn in regimental reserve. The battalion, minus one platoon from C Co, moved by shuttling to the vicinity of Truttenhausen. One platoon of C Co furnished protection to the division CP. The 2nd Bn continued the attack to the east in the division's zone, captured Ferhenbach and Hundelshaufen against light resistance. At the close of the period they had advanced to their next position. The 3rd Bn continued the attack to the east in the zone, captured Rosbach, Lohrenbach, and Wintershausen against slight resistance.

CT 304 will be attached with Co A from the 749th Tank Bn on 8 Apr. The 1st and 2nd Bns continued their advance to the east against light resistance and reached the line where B Co awaited further orders. The 3rd Bn moved to Mülhausen to maintain law and order. They were attached to the 6th Armored Div on the corps' orders.

The 385th Inf was attached to Co C of the 749th Tank Bn. The 1st Bn continued the attack, cleared Jested, crossed the river at Grebendorf and pushed forward toward Volkerode. The 2nd Bn attacked to the east and cleared the woods. The 3rd Bn continued its attack, cleared Grebendorf and advanced along the river to Altendorf to secure a bridgehead. At the close of the period, they were on the high ground overlooking Altendorf.

As per a top-secret directive, "message through channels from the Supreme Headquarters Allied Expeditionary Force (SHAEF), enemy supply dumps overrun during our rapid advance may include unmarked gas shells or gas bombs. Greatest care must be taken in making use of captured munitions to insure that gas is not employed against the enemy. The unfortunate consequences that might result from accidental or unwitting initiation of gas warfare by our army will be impressed upon all personnel who handle or employ German ammunition against the enemy."

Locations of the 749th Tank Bn troops were as follows: Bn Res, Hqs Co, and D Co were in Rocren. A Co was still in Sontra, B Co in Reyerode and C Co, attached to the 385th Regt, 76th Div and the Co CP was at Eschwege. The 1st Plt was at Grebendorf, the 2nd Plt at Wiederdurzebach, and the 3rd Plt at Jested.

Operations for the period: A Co arrived at Sontra at 0200 hours after leaving Lancensalza the previous evening. They performed first echelon maintenance on tanks, cleaned weapons, and prepared for movement to the 76th Inf Div's zone. B Co moved from Mülhausen at 0630 and traveled approximately 30 miles southwest to a new assembly area in Reyerode, arriving at 0930. The company was released from the 65th Inf Div's control.

The CP of Co C moved to Eschwege at 0700 hours. The 1st Plt was with the 1st Bn of the 385th Regt moved northwest towards Schwedda but the tanks were held up due to a blown bridge. The platoon moved to Jestad and crossed on a pontoon bridge, then moved east to Grebendorf. The 2nd Plt supported the advance of the 2nd Bn, 385th Regt, to Frieda. The platoon lost two tanks due to breakdown. The entire platoon joined the 2nd Bn group in Niederdurzebach. The 3rd Plt, in support of the 3rd Bn, 385th Regt, moved southwest to Frieda and fired on the town to reduce enemy resistance of small arms fire that was halting advance of our infantry and construction of a bridge over the Werra River. Seventy (70) POWs and six MG were captured. After the bridge was completed the tanks started across at 1800 but the bridge broke down and the remainder of the platoon was delayed in crossing until 2000. The platoon then moved into Jestädt with the 3rd Bn. D Co's 2nd Plt was relieved from attachment to B Co, this battalion, and joined D Co at Rocren.

Weather had scattered clouds; it was also cold. Visibility was good. Combat efficiency and troops' morale was excellent.

8 Apr. 1945

The 76th Inf's general situation revealed there was no cohesive line to the enemy's front lines, but it runs generally along the west bank of the Werra River, then south on the western bank of the Frieda River. Enemy front units in contact were the 2nd Co of the 688th GHQ Engineer Brigade, elements of the 39th Fusilier Regt, D-IV Bn, D-XVII Bn, elements of the 26th Fusilier Bn, a signal platoon of the 2nd Bn Regt "Donau", the 4th Co. KG 26th VGD with the CP located at Grebendorf, the Hqs of the 661st Regt and miscellaneous straggler units. Scattered enemy groups offered light resistance as friendly troops cleared 22 towns: Wintershausen, Ellenhausen, Ahrenberg, Altendorf, Kleinwach, Albungen, Furstensteim, Jestädt, Motszenrode, Hitzelrode, Volkerode, Kella, Neuerode, Grebendorf, Oberrieden, Völkershausen, Frieda, Schwedda, Topfe-niedehone, Nierderzebach, and Oberdunzebach.

An estimated 105mm fell in Grebendorf at 2000. Artillery fire of undetermined caliber fell on the bridges in the vicinity of Jestad and Grebendorf at about 1930. Two ME 109s flew over Oberdorla at 1900. Two planes dropped two bombs on the west end of Lancensalza at 2430. One plane strafed west of Spangenberg at 0120 hours and two planes over Lancensalza at 1126.

There was small arms and MG fire from north of Grebendorf at 1700. One hundred (100) enemy was observed moving east from Altendorf with MGs and mortar at 1715. An MG fired on friendly patrol at 1830.

The 385th Inf Regt with the attached C Co of the 749th Tank Bn had the 1st Bn advance to high ground southwest of Kella, attacked and captured Kella, Metzenrode, and Detzerode. The 2nd Bn advanced to high ground, occupied Topfe, Pffaffschwende, and Sickerode against light enemy opposition. The 3rd Bn advanced in the zone, captured and cleared Altendorf.

CT 304 with Co A from the 749th Tank Bn was attached. The 1st Bn maintained defensive positions along a temporary phase line with B Co; the 2nd Bn extended its position to protect the left flank and occupied Bothenheillngen, Kleinwelsbach, Kirchdeilingen, Sundilensen, and Klettstedt. The 3rd Bn was detached from the 6th Armored Div and reverted to Regimental control in the vicinity of Dingelstadt. Cannon Co assumed the mission of guarding approximately 700 wounded POWs in Lancensalza.

Co B from the 749th Tank Bn, was attached to the 417th Inf Regt, and was relieved in the zone by the 3rd Cav Grp. The 1st Bn moved by motor to the vicinity of Eigenrieden, flushed the woods and established defensive positions for the night. The 2nd Bn moved from the vicinity of Heyerode at Regt Res. The 3rd Bn moved by motor to the vicinity of Lingenfeld and established a defensive position area.

All battalions of the FA fired on targets of opportunity and displaced as necessary to closely support operations of the division. The 736ᵗʰ FA Bn fired a preparation on Altendorf with good effect. The 19ᵗʰ TAC flew two armed recon missions on the division's flank at the request of the division. Results were unreported.

The following information was taken from a FO: "Army Plt report of a sortie flown 1600 7 Apr was shown at the large woods northeast of Mülhausen. Sixty (60) or more tanks were in the woods, 30 or more vehicles, 53 SP guns and numerous small pieces. Camouflaged tanks were reported to be well dispersed. XX Corps continued their advance to the east in the zone on the left of the XX Corps. The 65ᵗʰ Inf Div would move south via routes commencing north to the assembly area of the VIII Corps. The 6ᵗʰ Armored Div would continue present missions. The 3ʳᵈ Cav Grp would relieve elements of the 76ᵗʰ Inf Div along the Werra River from the vicinity of Unterrieden, exclusive, to the vicinity of Bad Sooden, inclusive, commencing early this date. Elements (TF LA Grew) of the 6ᵗʰ Armored Div would move north from the vicinity of Dingelstadt with the mission to clear enemy in the zone to the west as far as the eastern bank of the river."

"The 76ᵗʰ Inf Div was attached to the 749ᵗʰ Tank Bn and would continue their present missions and relieve elements of the 6ᵗʰ Inf Div and prepare to resume their advance to the east on corps' orders. The CT 304, attached to A Co of the 749ᵗʰ Tank Bn. The Bn, would continue to clear the area enclosed by a line on the west, the temporary boundary between the 76ᵗʰ and 80ᵗʰ Inf Divs on the south. A temporary line on the east and between the First and Third Armies on the north and from a point of contact with elements of the 80ᵗʰ Div on the south to establish a screen generally the line of advance elements. They were also west along the First and Third Armies' boundary to the point of contact with elements of the 6ᵗʰ Armored Div. They would be prepared to continue to advance to the south as far as the 80ᵗʰ and 76ᵗʰ Inf Div's boundaries and as far east as the line south, on order. They would maintain line with elements of the 6ᵗʰ Armored Div in the area and contact and line with elements on the first-third Army boundaries and maintain line with elements of the 80ᵗʰ Div on the right. They would resume when the 3ʳᵈ Bn passed through by the 417ᵗʰ Inf."

The 385ᵗʰ Inf Div was attached to the 749ᵗʰ Tank Bn. The 1ˢᵗ Bn advanced to the high ground southwest of Kella, attacked and captured Kella, Metzenrode, and Detzerode. The 2ⁿᵈ Bn advanced to high ground and occupied Topfe, Pffaffschwende, and Sickerode against light enemy opposition. The 3ʳᵈ Bn continued its advance in the zone, captured and cleared Altendorf.

The 304ᵗʰ CT was attached to A Co of the 749ᵗʰ Tank Bn. They maintained defensive positions along a temporary phase line while the 2ⁿᵈ Bn extended its position to protect the left flank and occupied Bothenheillngen, Kleinwelsbach, Kirchdeilingen, Sundilensen, and Klettstedt. The 3ʳᵈ Bn was detached from the 6ᵗʰ Armored Div and reverted to regimental control in the vicinity of Dingelstadt.

The Cannon Co assumed the mission guarding approximately 700 wounded POWs in Lancensalza.

The 417ᵗʰ Inf was attached to B Co of the 749ᵗʰ Tank Bn. They were relieved in the zone by the 3ʳᵈ Cav Grp. The 1ˢᵗ Bn moved by motor to the vicinity of Eigenrieden and flushed the woods and established a defensive position for the night. The 2ⁿᵈ Bn moved to the vicinity of Heyerode at Regimental Res. The 3ʳᵈ Bn moved by motor to the vicinity of Lingenfeld and established a defensive position in the area. All battalion FA fired on targets of opportunity and displaced as necessary to closely support operations of the division.

The 736ᵗʰ TAC flew two armed recon missions in preparation on Altendorf with good effect. The 19ᵗʰ TAC flew two armed recon missions on the division's flank at their request. Results were unreported.

Results of operations: The division continued to clear enemy from woods and towns against moderate resistance. The 304ᵗʰ CT continued to hold positions along the temporary phase line and the following information was taken from FO #9, 76ᵗʰ Div: "1. Army report of sortie flown shows at large woods northeast of Mülhausen. 60 or more tanks were in the woods, 30 or more vehicles, 53 SP guns and numerous small pieces. Tanks were reported to be well dispersed and camouflaged. 2. XX Corps continues to advance to the east in order from right to left of the 80ᵗʰ Inf Div, 76ᵗʰ Inf Div. The 69ᵗʰ Inf Div advanced to the east in the zone. The 65ᵗʰ Inf Div moved south via routes shown commencing from 1-3 Apr to the assembly area some of the VIII Corps. The 6ᵗʰ Armored Div continued to present missions. The 3ʳᵈ Cav Grp relieved elements of the 76ᵗʰ Inf Div along the Werra River from the vicinity of Unterrieden, exclusive, to the vicinity of Bad Sooden, inclusive, commencing early 8 Apr. TF LA Crew, elements of the 6ᵗʰ Armored Div, moved north from the vicinity of Dingelstadt with the mission to clear enemy in the zone to the west as far as the eastern bank of the Werra River."

"The 76ᵗʰ Inf Div, attached to the 749ᵗʰ Tank Bn, continued its missions and relieved elements of the 65ᵗʰ Inf Div and prepared to resume its advance to the east on corps' orders. The CT 304, attached to Co A of the 749ᵗʰ Tank Bn continued to clear the area enclosed by a temporary line on the west between the boundary of the 76ᵗʰ and

80th Inf Divs on the south. There was also a temporary line on the east and the boundary between the 1st and 3rd Armies on the north. They established a screen along the line of advance elements of the 6th Armored Div. They would resume contact with the 3rd Bn when it passed through the 417th Inf."

"The 385th Inf, attached to the 749th Tank Bn's Co C, would continue to advance to the north to clear it with enemy troops. It would relieve elements of the 65th Inf Div and establish beachheads east to the bank of the Werra River at Altendorf, and upon clearing enemy forces from the area, limit responsibility on the north. They would establish a screen along the boundary from the eastern bank of the Werra River in the vicinity of Ahrenberg east to the vicinity of Effelder until uncovered by friendly troops on the north. They would establish and maintain contact and lines with elements of the 3rd Cav Grp and maintain a line with the 417th Inf until further orders. They were prepared, when assigned missions were completed, to move east on short notice of orders."

"The 417th Inf would hold on the western bank of the Werra River until relieved by elements of the 3rd Cav Grp. They would move by shuttling without delay via previously reconnoitered routes to previously reconnoiter detrucking area south of the line of Wanfried-Diedorf and advance west approximately 7 kms extending from the left boundary to contact with elements of the 6th Armored Div on the right, clear enemy troops from the area and also relieve elements of the 65th Inf Div and the 3rd Bn of the 304th Inf. Upon clearing enemy troops from the area, they would establish a screen along the boundary between the 1st and 3rd Armies with the 385th Inf in the vicinity of Effelder east to a point of contact with elements of the 6th Armored Div until they reached friendly troops on the north. They would maintain contact with elements of the 69th Div on the left until relieved by the 3rd Cav Grp. Upon entering the new zone, establish and maintain contact and line with the 385th Inf on the left and with elements of the 6th Armored Div."

The 3rd Cav Grp released the 76th Recon Troops, minus one platoon, to the 385th Inf effective upon relief of the 417th Inf. The 749th Tank Bn with Co A attached to the 304th Inf and Co C attached to the 385th Inf would assemble in the vicinity of Eschwege and await orders. The Div CP opened at Eschwege and closed at Lauterbach this date with the hour to be announced.

The location of the 749th Tank Bn troops had Bn Hqs Co, Svc Co, and D Co in Eschwege. A Co, attached to the 304th Regt, was at Lancensalza. B Co, attached to the 417th Inf, was in Treffurt. C Co, attached to the 385th Inf Regt, was in Eschwege.

Bn Hqs, Svc Co and D Co left Rockensuss at approximately 1000. They went 15 miles arriving at Eschwege at 1130. Co A, with one assault gun attached from Hqs Co was ordered to move from Sontra at 0930 to Lancensalza, arriving there at approximately 1500. Distance traveled was about 48 miles. This company was attached to the 304th Inf Regt, 76th Div, for a combat mission. D Co received orders at 0800 to move to Treffurt by 1200 to join the 417th Inf Regt. They moved from the assembly area of Reyerode at 1100, traveled approximately 20 miles northeast, arriving at the new assembly area of Treffurt. It closed at 1300. They were relieved from the 65th Inf Div and attached to the 417th Inf Regt, 76th Inf Div. C Co's 1st Plt was assigned to the 1st Bn of the 385th Regt moved from Treffurt north through Neuerode and Volkerode. Ten POWs were taken during the period but there was no other contact with enemy troops. The platoon returned to Grebendorf at 1700. The 2nd Plt moved from Niederdurzebach to Pffaffschwende with the 2nd Bn, 385th Inf Regt. The 3rd Plt remained in Jestad.

The weather consisted of scattered clouds, windy, and cool with visibility fair that was limited by haze. The combat efficiency was excellent as was the morale.

9 Apr. 1945

The enemy front lines were not cohesive. Elements of the 26th Fusilage Bn, KG Schaefer, the 14th Air Protection Bn, 4th Co. of the 44th Armored Bn, the 10th Co of the 15th PGR, elements of the 688th GHQ Engineers Brigade, elements of the Regiment Kirschfeld, elements of the 15th PGR and several other miscellaneous units were the enemy units with whom we had.

Enemy air was active with strafing and bombing of our forward elements. Ground resistance was negligible as mopping up operations continued. Six (6) FW 190's flew west at 1610, unknown how many bombs were dropped but we had no damage.

A jet-propelled plane strafed Lancensalza at 1909 and at 1915 two planes attacked our aircraft. Unknown number of planes dropped flares at 2300.

Sniper activity was reported at Lancensalza on 8 Apr. A grenade was thrown at our guard at 0100 hours. One tank was reported in the vicinity of Bursestedt and was firing southwest. In Bad Tennstedt five motor transports were scattered in the town section where twenty (20) flat cars were loaded with transport and armor. The transport was destroyed and the armor damaged as of 1020. We located Germans in American uniforms. They were prisoners from SS Jagdeinsatz who stated the unit was composed of men trained for espionage and sabotage missions behind our lines using captured US uniforms and equipment. One group was commanded by Lt Stein and composed of men of French nationality. The other was commanded by Lt Kallenberg and made up of men from Langemarck Div (the 27th SS Div) and Dutch SS personnel.

The French group has 41 men with 16 having received parachute training but Allied bombing the training grounds interrupted it. The other group has about 50 men from Langemarck Div and 50 Dutch SS. The Dutchmen have completed training but men from the Langemarck Div were still undergoing such training at last account.

SS Jadgeinsatz has United States helmets, sweaters, field jackets, and trousers, combat shoes and some British battle jackets. The men are armed with Thompson subMGs, carbines, or M-1 rifles. Five of our jeeps were known to be available for use. Lt Stein is 25 years old, 5'5", slim build, black hair, blue eyes, small face, fine features, and high voice. He speaks very good English and French. Lt Kallenberg is 22 years old, 5'9", athletic, black wavy hair, dark eyes, narrow face, and scar on his left hand. On 26 Mar both groups were reported to be behind our lines, either now or in the immediate future with missions of espionage or sabotage.

Our operations for the period had the 385th Inf attached to Co C of the 749th Tank Bn. The 1st Bn less B Co, motorized, closed in at Ballstadt while B Co remained in Volkerode. The battalion advanced to the eastern zone and occupied Kleinfahner and Gierstadtrt. At the close of the period they advanced to a new position. The 2nd Bn minus one company, motorized, closed in at Burgtona. They also advanced to the east occupying Gross fanner and Döllstäd. The 3rd Bn assembled in the vicinity of Elleben.

The 417th Inf was attached to B Co of the 749th Tank Bn, motorized. The 1st Bn flushed enemy from the area, and moved to a new assembly area in the vicinity of Lancensalza as regimental reserve. The 3rd Bn cleared enemy from the area and maintained contact with the 3rd Cav Grp. They were to be prepared to move on short notice. One platoon protected the 364th FA in the vicinity of Buttstadt, CT 304, who was attached to A Co of the 749th Tank Bn. They continued to hold positions along a temporary phase line and cleared enemy from the woods in the vicinity of Kellerforst. They were also prepared to advance to the east.

Results of Operations: The division continued to mop up wooded areas and towns in the division's zone. CT 304 continued to hold positions along its temporary. The following info was taken from a secret message, Hqs, 76th Div, dated 9 Apr:

"The 3rd Cav Grp plus a platoon would move east early via the vicinity of Wickerode and thence north to protect the left flank of the corps.

The 76th Inf Div would continue its present mission and prepare to resume their advance to the east in the assigned zone.

The 385th Inf plus a platoon would screen along the line of advance elements until they uncovered friendly troops on the north. Then they would move by motor and shuttling would commence to the detrucking areas in the vicinity of Ballstadt, Aschlura, and upon detrucking, establish a screen without delay from the point of contact. The contact was to be with the elements of the 80th Div on the south generally along its temporary line in the zone to a point of contact with the 304th Inf on the east. They were to establish and maintain contact with the 304th Inf on the left and with elements of the 80th Div on the right. The 76th Recon Troops minus a platoon were to continue the 417th Inf and be prepared to resume advance to the east on order.

The 417th inf plus a platoon would continue its advance to the north to clear enemy in the 417th's assigned zone and the Westerode area. Upon completion of their assigned missions, screen generally along the First and Third Army Bns in the zone from the point of contact with the 6th Armored Div on the right. A point of contact with the 3rd Cav at Effelder would then be carried out, and then be prepared to move by motor and/or shuttling to the east on short notice of order. They would assume contact with the 76th Recon Troops, less 1 platoon, from 385th Inf and Co B of the 749th Tank Bn at Treffurt at once.

CT 304 would continue present missions and clear enemy from the woods in the vicinity of Kellerforst area. They would establish a line with the 385th Inf after the latter closed in the forward area. They would be prepared to resume contact with the 3rd Bn and advance to the east on order.

TF LaGrew would continue its present missions prepared to revert to the control of the CG, 6th Armored Div on order.

The 76th Div Artillery, plus a platoon, had no change in organizing for combat and continued present missions with prepared displacement to the east without delay to reconnoiter position area from which artillery would be able to assigned in verbal orders."

The 749th Tank Bn (medium tanks) were prepared to organize for combat, effective at once; and Co B was attached to the 417th Inf. The battalion minus one platoon was prepared to move to the vicinity of Mülverstedt on order. As per operation directed #16, Hqs, 76th Div, the following info was taken:

"XXth Corps was to attack to the east with the 80th Inf Div on the right and the 76th Inf Div on the left. They would continue the advance to their temporary phase line. The 6th Armored Div with Recon elements would protect the left flank (north) and the 3rd Cav Grp would be assisted by TF LaGrew as they continued to clear the enemy in the area northeast of Altendorf of the ZK XX Corps.

The 76th Inf Div plus platoons attacked to the east and was prepared to resume advance to the east on corps' orders. The LD was present on the front line.

The 385th Inf was attached to Co C from the 749th Tank Bn and would attack to the east making their main effort on the right. They would continue their advance to the division's zone and would pass elements of the 6th Armored Div through the zone and were to advance to the east on short notice on orders. They would protect the right (south) flank of the division. They were to maintain contact with the line of the 304th Inf on the left and in line with elements of the 80th Div on the right.

The 304th Inf Div was attached to Co A of the 749th Tank Bn plus platoons. They would attack to the east and make a main effort on the left, continuing their advance in the zone as well as to pass elements of the 6th Armored Div through the division's zone. They also would resume their advance to the east on short notice on orders. They were to protect the left flank (north) with the division and maintain line with elements of the 6th Armored Div on the left and with the 385th Inf on the right.

The 417th Inf was attached to Co B of the 749th Tank Bn. They were to screen to the north on a line generally along the First-Third Army Bn with contact of elements of the 6th Armored Div on the right to a point of contact with elements of the 3rd Cav Grp. They were not to exceed one platoon of A Co, motorized, and to protect left of the rear flank of the division and secure the road to Mülhausen-Diedorf-Wanfried. They were to be prepared to pass through either assault regiment on short notice and repel the enemy's counterattack from the north or northeast."

Location of the troops of the 749th Tank Bn revealed the Bn Hqs, Hqs Co, and Svc Co as well as A Co was in Lancensalza; B Co was in Katharinanenberg; C Co was in Eschwege with one platoon in Pfaff-Schwedda, one platoon in Kella; and one platoon in Wiederdurzebach. D Co was in Mülverstedt.

Operations for the period had the Bn Hqs, Hqs Co, and the Svc Co moved from Eschwege at 1500 and closed into its present position at approximately 1730, traveling about 34 miles.

A Co, attached to the 304th Inf Regt, three platoons with three tanks of the 1st Plt had been ordered to Flarcheim, leaving at 1230 and arrived at 1300.

B Co, attached to the 417th Inf Regt, moved from Treffurt traveling approximately 8 miles north to its present assembly area, closing at 1445. No contact was made with the enemy.

C Co of the 1ˢᵗ Bn with the 304ᵗʰ Inf Regt arrived at 1500. The tanks were divided into three TFs and advanced with the infantry policing the wooded area west of Langula. Five POWs were taken. After the mission was completed, all tanks returned to Lancensalza, arriving at 2215.

C Co, attached to the 385ᵗʰ Inf Regt, had all platoons relieved from battalion control and assembled in Bringendorf. The company moved as a marching unit from Grebendorf to Eschwege. The platoons were attached to battalion control upon arrival as follows: The 1ˢᵗ Plt was attached to the 1ˢᵗ Bn at Schönberger, the 2ⁿᵈ Plt to 2ⁿᵈ Bn at Burgtona, and 3ʳᵈ Plt to the 3ʳᵈ Bn at Elleben.

D Co moved from Eschwege at 1600 for a new bivouac area. They arrived at Mülverstedt at 1930 with a distance traveled of about 30 miles. One platoon was attached to the 304ᵗʰ Inf Regt and one to the 385ᵗʰ Inf Regt effective tomorrow's date.

The Svc Co left the bivouac area at Eschwege at 1500 and proceeded to a new bivouac area in Lancensalza, arriving at 1800 with a distance traveled of about 30 miles.

Weather and visibility was cold, hazy, and scattered clouds with visibility poor to fair. Combat efficiency was excellent as was morale.

10 Apr. 1945

The 76ᵗʰ Inf Div revealed the enemy front lines were not cohesive. They generally were east of a line near Gebessee-Elleben-Tiefthal areas. POWs taken continued to be from hastily formed miscellaneous units. Civilians stated an infantry of unknown strength were dug in at Andisleben, Walschleben, and Elleben. They also stated Erfurt was defended by 800 men from the 71ˢᵗ Training Regt. The Inf March Bn Klaff and KG Faller were two regiments with 1,000 men each.

Air Recon reported pieces of undetermined caliber weapons were scattered in the area of Wittenbach-Hausen. An escaped French POW stated between 6 and 7 Apr approximately 5 to 6,000 troops had an unknown number of half-tracks at Bleicherode. Three to four thousand enemy with tractors were hauling 150mm artillery at Obergebra. Three to four thousand enemy troops were at the airfield at Halberstadt with 70 or 80 enemy fighters. Enemy resistance was extremely heavy in the vicinity of Dachwig and Wittenbach with light to moderate resistance in the remainder of the division's zone.

Air activity increased as enemy advance attempted to disrupt communications and supply traffic in the rear areas and harassed friendly forward elements. One plane strafed at 1030. Five planes strafed the vicinity of Bad Tennstedt at 1030. Approximately five planes dropped unknown number of bombs at 1215. One ME 109 flew over Halbruck at 1315. Two FW 190s strafed and two ME 109s strafed at about 1325.

Bridges were blown facing the east, northeast, and north at Genesee, the east bridge at Elleben was out, the railroad bridge west and east of Kuhnhausen were also out. The bridge at Klineber caved in at 1030 and the footbridge south of Kuhnhausen caved in at 1030.

Four enemy troops in a jeep in the vicinity of Klettstedt at 1640; three were killed, one escaped in a five-man patrol in the vicinity of Döllstädt about 0100 hours.

Small arm fire was received from the vicinity of Herbsleben and from west of Bad Tennstedt at 0800. A jeep and armored car were fired on by automatic weapons fire from a building at 1930.

One platoon of infantry was seen in the vicinity of Bruchsted at 0840. We received MG and AA fire at 1910. An unknown number of enemy infantry was dug in 200 yards northwest of Witterda at 1000 and small arms fire from the woods south of town at 1030. Sixty enemy infantry were seen in the vicinity of Bad Tennstedt at approximately 1930. One tank moved west from Schwerstedt at 1105.

The following info was taken from OD #3, Hqs, and CT 385:

"This CT will attack with CT 417 on the left and CT on the right. It would advance in its zone to the east, two Bns abreast. The 3rd Bn would be on the left, the 1st Bn on the right. The 3rd Bn would pass through the 2nd Bn by shuttling. The 3rd and 1st Bn would cross the line at 0700. 2nd Bn would initially go into Regimental Res in the vicinity of its' present position and be prepared to follow the 3rd Bn by bounds on order. The 2nd Bn will shuttle with its' own vehicles."

Attachments to the 1st Bn would remain the same. All attachments of the 2nd Bn, except for one platoon of medium tanks would revert to the control of the 3rd Bn upon passing through the 2nd Bn area in addition to one platoon of medium tanks attached to the 3rd Bn upon receipt of this order. Co B Engineers would report to the CO of the 1st and 3rd Bns by 0600 hours all night.

Transportation: Initially six AT 2-1/2 ton trucks to the 3rd Bn until shuttle is completed. Upon completion, the 3rd Bn Shuttle Co, the 3rd Bn would send three 2-1/2 ton trucks to Co's 1st Bn. Each attacking battalion, in addition to the three AT trucks would have available its kitchen trucks in order to facilitate moving of reserve companies.

Service Co was in Walschleben.

Axis Signal Communication. Note: The CG had noted that in almost every instance, towns had been taken by frontal attacks, thus allowing many enemy to escape from the rear and flanks. Taking towns from flank and rear as well as from the front shall prevent this."

The following info was taken from Message #11, Secret, 76th Div:

"The 76th Inf Div plus a platoon with the 385th Inf on the right and the 417th Inf on the left and resume advance to the east in the zone early the following day, reaching the line by dark.

The 385th Inf plus attachments would resume their advance early. Tomorrow with missions directed to reach the line on the right by dark.

The 417th Inf plus attachments would advance early with the mission with the 304th Inf and reach the line by dark.

The 304th Inf plus attachments would close in the assembly area at Bad Tennstedt-Arleen, Gruargula-Herbsleben-BadTennestedt in Div Res and be prepared to repel any enemy counterattack from the north or northeast and to advance to the forward assembly area to the east.

The 749th Tank Bn: Co A was attached to the 304th Inf; Co B was attached to the 417th Inf; Co C was attached to the 385th Inf; Co D with one platoon attached with B and C Cos."

Our operations for the period had the 385th Inf with Co C attached from the 749th Tank Bn; 1st Bn would attack to the east on the zone and clear Witterda, Friedrichs, Bleyleben and Huhnhausen against moderate resistance. The 2nd Bn would attack to the east and clear Lachwig against heavy enemy resistance. They would continue to attack and capture Andisleben and Walschleben. The 3rd Bn was in Regimental Res in Lachwig.

The 417th Inf with Co B from the 749th Tank Bn attached, would have the 1st Bn less one company of reinforcements moved by motor and close in the vicinity of Allengotten and pass Regimental Res. One company was screened to the west along the 1st and 3rd Armie Bn west of Mülhausen. The 2nd Bn would move by motor to the vicinity of Hassleben. Relief of the 1st Bn in the zone was in process at the close of the period. The 3rd Bn would move by motor to the vicinity of Hergenfeld to the vicinity of Allengotten. Relief of the 2nd Bn with the 304th Inf was in process at the close of the period.

The 304th Inf with Co A from the 749th Tank Bn - the 1st Bn would attack to the east and clear Hershleden, Genesee. The 2nd Bn would attack to the east and clear Bad Tennstedt against moderate opposition and capture Ballhausen, Schwerstedt, Hassfurt, Verra and

Werninghausen. The 3rd Bn was in Regimental Res in the vicinity of Ballhausen.

The regiment was prepared to move to assembly area after relief by the 417th Inf. Battery A, 778th AAA AW Bn were engaged with a total of four ME 109s, 3 FW 190s and claimed two enemy planes. D Battery engaged 28 ME 109s, claimed 3 planes.

Results of Operations: The division attacked to the east with the 385th Inf on the right and the 304th on the left. At the close of the period they had advanced to positions to accomplish their missions. The 417th Inf was in process of relieving the 304th Inf in the zone with the division prepared to renew the attack early on 11 Apr.

The location of the troops of the 749th Tank Bn had the Bn Hqs and Hqs Co in Grafentonna. Co A, attached to the 304th Inf Regt, was in Gebesee. Co B was attached to the 417th Inf Regt in Altengottern. Co C, attached to the 385th Inf Regt, was in Grossfanner. D Co with one platoon was in Div Res in Lancensalza. One platoon was attached to A Co and one to C Co. Svc Co was also in Lancensalza.

Operations for the period: Bn Hqs and the Bn CP was in the vicinity of Lancensalza and was bombed and strafed by five ME 109s with the probable target being enemy planes still intact on the airfield. No enemy planes were seen to have been shot down. Later in the period in the vicinity of Grafentonna, the Bn CP, two enemy planes appeared high over the area. Ack-ack knocked down one of them. The pilot parachuted down and was taken prisoner. The other plane was driven off.

At 1600, Bn Hqs and Hqs Co moved from Lancensalza to Grafentonna, arriving at 1650, traveling about 5-1/2 miles.

Co A, plus one D Co Plt, attached to the 304th Inf Regt, supported the advance of the infantry up to the line. The company left Lancensalza at 0503 to reach the assembly point. The 304th Regt attacked at 0700 supported by the 1st and 2nd Plts, plus one light tank platoon and two assault guns on the left. The 3rd Plt was on the right flank. The objective was taken by 1400 and reassembled at Gebesee. The company knocked out 10 enemy MG nests, two bazooka teams, two tanks (Mark IVs) and took approximately 500 POWs. The column was strafed twice but suffered no casualties.

Orders were received at 2300 for withdrawal to Bad Telstedt. One enlisted man, Pfc Aber, was slightly WIA and evacuated when a hatch fell on his forehead while firing. One medium tank fell through a bridge causing no casualties but was considered a combat loss. B Co, attached to the 417th Inf Regt, moved from Kathaninenberg at 1100, moving approximately 20 miles northeast to Altengottern, closing in at 1430. Tanks were refueled and at 1930, the 2nd and 3rd Plts moved out. The 2nd Plt was attached to the 3rd Bn and the 3rd Plt attached to the 2nd Bn.

The Co CP and the 1st Plt were in reserve moved from Altengottern at 2130, traveling approximately 22 miles to the east to a new assembly area at Schwerstedt, closing in at 2400. C Co, plus one platoon from Co D, was attached to the 385th Inf Regt. The 1st Plt moved to Kleinfahner and moved from here in support of the infantry's advance along the route to Witterda, Friedrichs, Tiefthal, and Lexeben but were halted here by a blown bridge. They assisted in capturing 50 POWs, destroyed seven MGs, one bazooka, and crew. The 2nd Plt moved from Burgtona to Bollstedt, and then attacked Dachwig where small arms fire fatally wounded a platoon leader, Lt Leovelton Malloy, by sniper fire.

At Walschleben one tank fell through a bridge at 2100 in trying to cross it; no casualties resulted. The two remaining tanks crossed a stream at 2330 and continued to attack, assisting the infantry in the night attack. The 3rd Plt with the 3rd Bn moved to Dachwig without incident and remained in reserve. Co CO, Lt McProuty, was slightly wounded but not evacuated.

Hqs Section and Co CP moved from Aschera to Grossfanner. D Co's 3rd Plt left Mülverstedt at 0730 and joined C Co for a combat mission. The 2nd Plt left Mülverstedt at 0730 and joined C Co, also for a combat mission. D Co's CP plus 1st Plt left Mülverstedt at 1100 for a new bivouac area in Lancensalza, arriving at 1145, traveling approximately three miles.

Weather and visibility - it was cool in the forenoon with a heavy haze that cleared later in the period; it was warm in the afternoon. Visibility was zero in the early hours but later became fair in the afternoon. Combat efficiency was excellent as was the morale of the troops.

11 Apr. 1945

There was no cohesive line of the enemy but they were generally east of the line at Grossneuhausen-Vogelsberg-Kleinbrenbach-Drautheim-Newlark-Grossrudestedt-Kleinrudestedt-Eckstedt-Schwerbrun. Enemy units in contact were miscellaneous replacement units from Eisenach, Erfurt, and Weimar as well as training u\areas of which the 59th AA Replacement Bn, 3rd Co, 2nd Panzer Replacement Bn and the regiment Obitz of Feller Div. None of these units is believed to have the strength in excess of 500 men with the average strength approximately 150 men. They have little or no heavy weapon support. Total enemy strength in the division's zone is estimated at 3,000 men and 40 tanks. Enemy resistance was generally moderate to light except in the vicinities of Mittelhausen and Stotternhein where heavy small arms, mortar, and direct weapons fire was encountered. Their advance continued to be active in the zone.

One of our planes was shot down by friendly AA fire in the vicinity of Döllstädt at 1930. Three unidentified planes flew over at 2330, with four planes flying west at 0840. Two planes strafed Walschleben at 0905, four ME 109s flew south at 0910 with one being shot down. At 0910 two FW 190s flew north and two flew to the east. Another four FW 190s strafed at 1300. Two bridges north and one south of Gebesee were out. Heavy small arms fire from the vicinity of Sommerda, Scholossvippach and Grossrudestadt, and small arms and automatic weapons fire from Nora and Stotternhein at 1100. Tanks were heard leaving Reithnordhausen going east was reported at 0400 hours.

At 0950 our artillery fired on an undetermined number of tanks. Tank activity was reported in the vicinity of Stotternhein at 1135. Two tanks were destroyed, three damaged, and one set afire by friendly advance at 1430.

A KNIFE IN OUR BACK: American officers were freed after five days as German POWs testify to facts that are of great concern to our security. They report German women and children on bicycles crossed our lines at will and kept enemy commanders informed on movement of our troops. Civilians manned GPs in tall buildings and key terrain features and spread the alarm quickly when our troops were seen. The civilians spit on captured Americans and taunted them with mocking jeers when they were led through enemy held towns. When enemy troops moved through a town, civilians gave them food and hot drinks and advised them of the location of the Americans. The civilians we are now encountering are as much a part of Germany as enemy troops we engage in battle. Realizing they have no love for ideals, which we cherish, we may expect to be treated scornfully whenever they may be in position to choose their own line of action.

When death and destruction become evident, German civilians rapidly display white flags of meekness. Remember these flags are serving as a means of sparing German lives and property. It is true they are lessening the cost of victory - but they also allow German individuals who have no understanding of humane treatment to carry out activities that are nothing less than despicable collaborations. All of these indications prove any outward sign of friendliness by civilians toward our soldiers have no foundation in sincerity but must have an ulterior motive.

The bridge at Bad Kösen was prepared for demolition, guards posted on the morning of 7 Apr. About 1,000 SS personnel were seen at Hardisleben on 8 Apr and some wore Totenkopf[1] armbands. Several POWs stated some officers and SS personnel were trying to escape in civilian clothes.

The following info was taken from FO, Hqs, 76th Inf Div:

"XX Corps continues to attack to the east in the zone with the 4th and 6th Armored Divs leading to disorganize enemy resistance and with the 80th and 76th Divs following to clear enemy pockets bypassed by friendly armor.

The 9th Armored Div followed by the 69th Inf Div advanced to the east on the left (north) flank of XX Corps.

The 3rd Cav Co plus other Plts protected the right (south) and left (north) flanks of the XX Corps.

XIX TAC supported the XX Corps.

The 416th FA Group reinforced firing of the 76th Inf Div Artillery.

The 1139th Engineer Co Group supported the 76th Inf Div. They continued to attack to the east until passed through by the 6th Armored Div and then followed an armored group to clear the zone of enemy. They would protect the left (north) flank of the corps and maintain contact with elements of the 9th Armored Div as well as the 69th Inf Div on the left.

CT 385 with attached Co C from the 749th Tank Bn would continue to attack to the east and be prepared to pass through elements of the 6th Armored Div in the zone early on this date. They would follow the armored attack closely to clear any enemy bypassed.

TF, composed of one infantry motorized, one tank Plt, one TD Plt and one Cannon Plt would maintain close contact with elements of the 6th Armored Div. The TF would have close contact with elements of the 6th Armored Div, also in the zone. They would engage strong points or formations of enemy only in self-defense, advancing rapidly in the zone. When forced to halt for extended periods of time, they were to await resumption of the Armored advance or to fight or by shuttle limit, trucks would return immediately for the infantry or parent regiment on foot. They would also protect on the right (south) flank of the Div and maintain contact with the 417th Inf Regt on the left and maintain line contact with elements of the 80th Div on the right.

CT of the 417th, attached with Co B of the 749th Tank Bn, would also continue to attack to the east and be prepared to pass elements of the 6th Armored Div through the zone early this date and follow the attack closely to clear enemy earlier bypassed.

The 304th Inf Regt with Co A of the 749th Tank Bn attached, were in Div reserve in

---

1   The Totenkopf was infantry units, one of which could be motorized or cavalry regiments.

their present position but be prepared to follow closely the left assault and to repel enemy counterattacks from the north and northeast. They were to be prepared to use organic motors with the 1st Inf Bn on short notice on order and release the motorized Bn.

The R Co would be released to protect supply installations on call."

Our operations for the period: CT 417 with Co B from the 749th Tank Bn plus the 1st Bn was motorized and designated for TF Tette. Co B's 1st Plt would assemble and move out behind elements of the 6th Armored Div and reached the phase line by the end of the period. The 2nd Bn continued to attack to the east that was occupied in Hassleben, Kranischberg, Schloscippach, Spratan, Vogelsberg, Kleinenhausen and Grosbreitesberg against moderate resistance. The 3rd Bn continued their attack to the east and occupied the following towns against moderate resistance: Wundersleben, Trengenhausen, Schallenburg, Sommerda, Nohrbarn, Oblershausen, Schloscippach, Kleinenhausen, Grossneuhausen, Ellersleben, Obersleben, Guthmannshausen, and Mannstedt. By the end of the period they had advanced to Bullstädt.

The 304th Inf Regt with Co A from the 749th Tank Bn - the 1st Bn continued its attack to the east and captured Stotternhein against heavy resistance as well as capturing Schwerborn, Unestedt, Hatttedt, and Ottmaunushsn. The 2nd Bn continued its attack to the east and captured Schwausee, Kleinrudsdt, Eckstedt, Diesdorf, Markvippach, Vippachedelshein, Bollstedt, Ollendorf, and Bullstädt.

The 3rd Bn (motorized) followed closely the elements of the 6th Armored Div and captured Rohrbach, Leutenthal, Sachsennausen, and Neumarkt.

On division's request two P-47s from XIX TAC intercepted a flight of enemy planes over the division's zone. Results were unreported. Three flights of P-47s attacked enemy tanks. They claimed two destroyed, two possibles, one damaged and also one-armed vehicle destroyed.

The situation of the 749th Tank Bn had their Bn Hqs and Hqs Co in Grafentonna. A Co was attached to the 304th Inf Regt and was in Bad Tennstedt. B Co was attached to the 417th plus one platoon of Co D was located in Vogelsberg. C Co, attached to the 385th Inf Regt plus one platoon of D Co, was in Walschleben. D Co was in Div Res in Lancensalza.

Operations for the period had Co A with 304th had finished their move from Gebesee to Bad Tennstedt at 0300 hours. They remained in Div Res with no activity during the period. B Co was attached to the 417th and one platoon of light tanks from Co D was attached to the company for a combat mission. The 2nd Plt jumped off at 0630 hrs in support of the 3rd Bn and advanced 10 kms against light opposition until they passed through by the 6th Armored Div at Sommerda. The platoon then continued east with the 3rd Bn to the new assembly area of Hennstedt. The 3rd Plt was unable to move because of a blown bridge. Bridge was completed and platoon finally moved out at 1100 joining the 2nd Bn and marched east to assembly area of Grossbrembach. The 1st Plt plus a platoon of light tanks formed an advance guard of Regimental TF mission to maintain contact with the 6th Armored Div. The TF moved out at 1700.

The Co CP and trains moved to a new assembly area in Grossbrembach at 1830 traveling approximately 20 miles southeast closing in at 2030. Fifty-two (52) POWs were captured during the period.

Co C was attached to the 385th Inf and supported the infantry in their advance. The 3rd Plt plus a platoon of light tanks moved as advance guard for the 3rd Bn in their movement to Bullstädt. The 2nd Plt moved with the 2nd Bn to Vippadredefhausen. The 1st Plt moved with the 1st Bn to Ottstedt from that point they carried the infantry to Kalsia, then returned to Altendorf. Hqs section and Co CP moved from Grossfahner to Eckstadt. No tanks were lost during the period.

Weather and visibility - it was clear, warm with excellent visibility. Combat efficiency was excellent as was the troops' morale.

12 Apr. 1945

The 76th Inf Div reported there were no enemy front lines. They were generally east of the Saar River with no change in enemy units. There was a brief but ineffective resistance offered by miscellaneous remnants as friendly elements advanced approximately 18 miles and overrunning more than 65 towns. They continued to advance and harassment continued of the forward elements and railroad areas in the south. An MP reported seven SS men harbored by civilians in Wallstedt. There was a Russian prison camp in Nirmsdorf.

The following info was taken from FO #1:

"The 76th Inf Div plus other Plts continued their present missions.

CT 385 plus Plts continued its present missions and were to maintain a line with the 304th Inf to the front.

CT 417 with Plts would continue its present missions and maintain a line with the 304th Inf to the front. The Reserve Bn would follow to the left and assault along the left flank in the Div's zone.

CT 304 with Co A from the 749th Tank Bn would move by motor without delay to the east via reconnoitered routes in the Div's zone and pass through elements of the 76th Div. They would continue to advance to overtake and thereafter follow closely with the assault elements of the 6th Armored Div and be prepared to facilitate rapid advance of armor by removing obstacles and reducing enemy strong points that the Armor would be unable to surmount or bypass. They would maintain contact with elements of the 6th Armored Div. The 749th Tank Bn would continue its present missions.

Road priority was in this order: The 6th Armored Div, CT 304, CT 385, and CT 417 with its respective attachments and after passage of CT 304 through forward elements of the 76th Div. Combat echelons of the 304th Inf would thereafter lead and other elements would come abreast of or pass through the forward elements of the 304th Inf on order of the Div only."

1.   As per FO#32, CT 304:

"The 6th Armored Div had established 3 bridgeheads across the Saar River. This CT would move by motor in two elements to the east to overtake and thereafter follow closely assault elements of the 6th Armored Div. They would facilitate their movement to the east by removing obstacles and reducing enemy strong points which armor was unable to surmount or bypass.

The 3rd Bn would move on the northern route, contact and support CC-B, 6th Armored Div. Co A from the 749th Tank Bn was attached to the 3rd Bn with the remainder of the CT would move on the southern route. ICR??? Plt would precede both elements on the recon routes and make a prompt report on necessary alternate routes to the 1st Armored 3rd Bn as well as the Regt CP. They would also establish contact with the 6th Armored Div.

Operations for the period: The 417th plus attached Co with the 1st Bn initially motorized, dismounted and continued to attack to the east clearing eight towns in the zone against moderate resistance. The 2nd Bn would continue to attack to the east and clear 19 towns against light resistance. The 3rd Bn was motorized and continued to maintain close contact with elements of the 6th Armored Div in the regimental zone. Co C from the 749th Tank Bn was attached to CT 385. The 1st Bn would advance to the east, capture and clear Apolda against moderate resistance. The 2nd Bn would advance on the left, detruck at Calburg, seize the town, and force a crossing of the Saar River. The 3rd Bn would advance to the east on the right to seize Stodra, Utenach, and Darndorf. CT 304 with Co A from the 749th Tank Bn attached would move by motor to the east and pass through elements of the 76th Div and continue their advance to the east. During the period the Div advanced over 25 miles in the zone, clearing woods and towns; over 700 POWs were processed."

The 749th Tank Bn 's location was as follows: Bn Hqs and Hqs Co were in Nirmsdorf. Co A, attached to the 304th Inf Regt., was in Camburg. Co B, attached to the 417th Inf Regt plus one platoon of D Co had the 1st Plt in Neldschutz, the 2nd Plt in Leislau, and the 3rd Plt in Apolda. Co C, attached to the 385th Inf Regt plus one platoon of D Co was: the 1st Plt was in Apolda, 2nd Plt in Schkölen, and the 3rd Plt in DÖRNBURG. The Svc Co and Co D's CP were in Oberhausen.

Operations for the period: Bn Hqs and Hqs Co moved from Grafentonna traveling about 34 miles, closing into Nirmsdorf at 1900. Co A, attached to the 304th Inf Regt were divided into two TFs. The 1st and 2nd Plts with two assault guns crossed the IP at 1230 and proceeded to Osterfeld with the infantry, arriving at 2030.

The 1st Plt, without the infantry, continued on to Kretzschau arriving at about 2400, with no resistance from the enemy. The 3rd Plt, with infantry, crossed the IP at 1230 and proceeded to Doschwitz, arriving at approximately 2400. The company traveled approximately 70 miles during the period closely following the 6th Armored Div. Co B was attached to the 417th Inf Regt; the 3rd Plt was a part of the 2nd CT; they moved to Osterfeld where it remained for the night. Small arms fire was encountered at Abt-lobnitz. Eighty (80) POWs were taken, three of which were officers. The 1st Plt plus one platoon of Co D (light tanks) became a part of the TF formed by the 1st Bn; they then moved to the vicinity of Eckatsberga where at 1400, the battalion was reverted to CT status. The light tanks were transferred to the 3rd Bn that then became the regimental TF. The 1st Plt then moved to Neldschutz and assembled, remaining in this area for the remainder of the night.

The 2nd Plt, as part of the 3rd Bn CT moved to Eckatsberga where the battalion became a part of the regimental TF joining the 1st Plt. The Co Hqs and train moved to Bad Sulza traveling approximately 20 kms east, and closed in at 2020. B Co, attached to the 385th Inf Regt's 1st Plt moved with the 1st Bn of the 385th from Ollendorf to Apolda. The 2nd Plt moved with the 2nd Bn of the 385th from Vippadredefhausen to Schkölen.

The 3rd Plt moved from Buttelstadt to DÖRNBURG with the 3rd Bn of the 385th. Hqs Plt moved from Eckstadt to Camburg. Co D, minus two platoons, moved from Lancensalza for a new bivouac area at 1030 and arrived at Oberhausen at 1915, having traveled a distance of approximately 50 miles. The Svc Co left the bivouac area at Lancensalza at 1300 and proceeded to its new bivouac area at Oberhausen, arriving there at 1800 after having traveled approximately 43 miles.

Weather was warm, with scattered clouds, and a few scattered showers. Visibility was good to fair. Combat efficiency and morale were excellent.

13 Apr. 1945

The 76th Inf Div reported the enemy front lines were not found but was located generally east of the Weisse Elster River. There was no change in enemy units but resistance was light to moderate as our troops advanced to the Weisse Elster River and Zeitz. Small arms and scattered artillery fire was encountered in Zeitz but decreased as the town was entered. No enemy air activity was reported.

Undetermined number of enemy rounds of unknown caliber fell in the vicinity of Grana at 1100. Eight rounds of unknown caliber fell on Kretzschau at 1240. An infantry of approximate strength of a company with SA and bazookas fired on Kretzschau at 2301 hours followed by heavy sniper fire in the same town at 1430 hours. The bridges over the Weisse Elster River in our zone were intact.

CT 305 had its 1st Bn (motorized) passed through the 2nd Bn in the vicinity of Stalzlinhain. They captured Hesse and continued their advance, also clearing Droyssig, Mansdorf and Salsitz against light opposition. The 2nd Bn continued to attack to the east and cleared Sliglitz, Hainohan, Pratschutz, and Kleinsdorf. The 3rd Bn continued to attack to the east after clearing Larnsburg, crossed the Saar River and cleared Wetzdorf, and Dothen. They continued their attack and occupied eight other towns.

CT 417 had its 1st Bn continuing to attack to the east and cleared 21 towns against little or no resistance. They engaged in the relief of elements of CT 304 in Zeitz at the end of the period. The 2nd Bn also continued to advance to the east and cleared 25 towns against very light opposition and also engaged in relief of CT 304 in Zeitz at the end of the period.

The 3rd Bn plus the motorized regimental reserves moved by the end of the period. An AT company established and maintained order at Sommerda. Over 1,000 POWs were processed during the period. As per operation secret message: "All haystacks and woodpiles would be flushed by MG fire. The line of fire would be carefully observed to prevent accidents to friendly troops."

Location of troops of the 749th Tank Bn showed that Bn Hqs and Hqs Co were in Bonau. Co A, attached to the 304th Inf Regt was in Kretzschau with one platoon in Zeitz. Co B plus one platoon of D Co, attached to the 417th Inf Regt was in Osterfeld. C Co, plus one platoon of Co D, was attached to the 385th Inf Regt and was in Droyssig. Svc Co and the remnant of D Co were in Preissen.

Operations for the period: Bn Hqs and Hqs Co moved from Nerlsdorf at 1000 and arrived at Bonau at 1900, traveling 43 miles. While en route to Bonau, the convoy stopped for a two-hour layover at Aue that was 27 miles from their starting point.

Co A, attached to the 304th Regt had the 2nd and 3rd Plts move from Osterfeld and Doschwitz respectively to Kretzschau, arriving at 0700. The 1st Plt crossed the Weisse Elster River at 0300 hours and proceeded to Zeitz. The 2nd Plt cleared out the town of Kretzschau with the infantry capturing approximately 200 POWs and 12 FA pieces.

B Co, attached to the 417th Inf Regt, had the 1st Plt as part of the 1st Bn CT moved to Gladidtz and prepared to cross the river. The 2nd Plt as part of the 3rd Bn Inf CT moved to the vicinity of Lobitz while the 3rd Plt, as part of the 2nd Bn Inf CT moved to Doschwitz. The CTs halted because of lack of bridges across the Weisse Elster River. There was no contact with the enemy.

The Co Hqs and trains moved from Bad Sulza at approximately 0600 and traveled about 21 kms to a new assembly area of Osterfeld, closing in at 0930. The 1st Plt of Co C, attached to the 1st Bn of the 385th, moved from Apolda across the Saar River and advanced to the east to Salsitz, assisting the infantry in capturing approximately 100 POWs. The 2nd Plt with the 2nd Bn moved from Schkölen across the Weisse River and advanced to Dietersdorf. The 3rd Plt with the 3rd Bn moved from Dörnburg across the Saar River and advanced to the vicinity of Mon. A headquarters platoon and the Co CP moved from Camburg to Droyssig. There were no losses or casualties for the period. Svc Co and the remaining D Co left Oberhausen at 1230 for a new bivouac area and traveled 45 miles, closing in the new area at Preissen at 1800.

Pfc Wilkens of D Co was reported a slightly wounded on 24 Mar was now carried as KIA.

As per a letter from Hqs, 6th Army Group, dated this date with the subject: Unit Assignment Order No. 65: "Effective on 30 Mar the 749th Tank Bn, having been relieved from assignment to the 6th Army Group and assigned to the 12th Army Group, are relieved from assignment to the 7th Army."

Weather was cold, scattered clouds turning to heavy black rain clouds in the afternoon with poor visibility. Combat efficiency was excellent and the morale of the troops was high.

14 Apr. 1945

According to the 76th Inf Div general situation, the enemy's front lines ran east of Dageistedt, Grafentonna, Eckardteleben, Aschera, and Ballstadt. They had no enemy units in contact. A POW stated batteries of unknown caliber weapons were located on the high ground northeast of Rimsdorf between Thrissen and Ronnewitz. English POWs who escaped from the vicinity of St Gangloff reported 30 tanks, 6 motor drawn artillery pieces, many light vehicles, and 100 trucks that went east through St. Gangloff during the night of the 12-13th of Apr. Resistance increased with stubborn house-to-house fighting in Rasberg and Bergesdorf.

Enemy artillery harassed forward elements and bridge sites. Air was active in the division's zone with bombing and strafing of our advance units. Sniper fire continued in Zeitz.

A 40mm AA fired at one of our planes in the vicinity of Krienlitz at 1815. Ten to 15 enemy planes flew over toward the west at 1930. Two ME 109s circled over the zone at the same time with one enemy plane shot down at 1940. At 1945, one of three FW 190s was damaged, as was one of two ME 109s. A pig-a-back JU88 was shot down at 2015.

Two hundred officers of enemy OCS were fighting house-to-house at 1420. Civilians stated two companies of approximately 200 men guarded a synthetic oil plant at Triplets, each with MGs and MPs. Another POW stated 300 allied POWs were at Gleina-Kechensdorf with 1,000 allied POWs at Rasdorf between Munich and Áltenburg, in good condition. They also reported the 1st Armored Regt, 1st Army Replacement Bn of the 16th Armored Div had Zeitz as an assembly point where various companies were to be newly formed. Lots of high-ranking officers left in civilian clothes. The 3rd Battery, from the 543d Calvary Regt (RR), and an AA battalion had orders to move from Dauben to Borna. One hundred of the men from the Battery were to make their way in small groups. The 2nd Battery of the 535th RR AA Bn left Gtoitzsch on 3 Apr and moved to Kuckenau, lost their guns there and approximately 100 men were employed as infantry. Fifty to 60 boys between the age of 15 and 17 from Zeitz area were trained at Grana from 3-10 Apr and committed, equipped with Panzerfausts. POWs were captured yesterday in Grana.

Our operations for the period: CT 385's 1st Bn moved from the vicinity of Salsitz, crossed Schrauwitz Bridge and continued to advance. They cleared Kleinosida, Grosshabersdorf, and Hohndorf. The 2nd Bn continued their advance and cleared Satzzeichen, Katserbersdorf, Schlekweda, Drossdorf, Frankenhain, and Grusskarten.

CT 417 reported the 1ˢᵗ and 2ⁿᵈ Bns continued successful mopping up operations against stubborn resistance in Zeitz. The 3ʳᵈ Bn's motorized regimental reserve moved to the vicinity of Zeitz. The AA company maintained order at Sommerda. One platoon of Co A, 691ˢᵗ TD Bn knocked out two 20mm flak guns and one 88mm gun. CT 304, leading the advance, had the 1ˢᵗ and 2ⁿᵈ Bns relieved for operations in Zeitz by elements of the 417ᵗʰ CT. They reorganized and moved east by motor with the mission of clearing Áltenburg. The 3ʳᵈ Bn motorized crossed the Weisse River; Regimental Reserve continued their advance to the east.

The following info was taken from an Urgent Secret Message #5:

Attention is directed to letter, Hqs, Third US Army; subject:

"Engagement of Aircraft by Ground Force Troops other than (AA artillery (AAA) will fire at aircraft ONLY WHEN the aircraft attacks THEM with bombs or other weapons, and THEN ONLY by specific order of the senior commander present."

All commanders will require strict compliance with the above.

Any officer issuing an order to fire on aircraft not attacking his own installations or troop dispositions or any EM firing on a plane without an order from the senior commander present, will be subject to severe disciplinary action."

The location of the 749ᵗʰ Tank Bn troops was as follows: Bn Hqs and Hqs Co were in Bonau. A Co, attached to the 304ᵗʰ Inf Regt was in Osterfeld. C Co plus one platoon from Co D, attached to the 385ᵗʰ Inf Regt, was in Droyssig. Svc Co and the remainder of D Co, was in Preissen.

Operations for the period: One platoon from Co A, attached to the 304ᵗʰ Inf Regt, was recalled from Zeitz at 1230. The company, with two assault guns moved from Kretzschau to Drossdorf, leaving at 1700 and arriving at 2345 hrs. They had traveled approximately 15 miles to their new destination. B Co, attached to the 417ᵗʰ Inf Regt, had their platoons move from their respective assembly areas to Zeitz. The 1ˢᵗ and 2ⁿᵈ Plts had no contacts with the enemy. The 3ʳᵈ Plt moved into the attack on the south-western edge of town with the mission to clear a few Germans from two buildings that were giving the foot troops trouble. Their mission was accomplished at about 1900 and the platoon stayed in position to help repulse any sort of a counterattack. Forty (40) POWs were taken. Co Hqs and trains moved from Osterfeld at about 1745, traveled about 12 miles east to a new assembly area in Zeitz, closing in at 1900. Co C, attached to the 385ᵗʰ Inf Regt, had the Co CP remain in Droyssig. The 1ˢᵗ Plt moved with the 1ˢᵗ Bn, 385ᵗʰ Inf Regt, 76ᵗʰ Div from Salsitz to Bergesdorf, firing on enemy positions and assisting in the capture of 50 POWs. The 2nd Plt moved with the 2nd Bn from Dietersdorf to Wildenborn. The 3rd Plt moved with the 3rd Bn from the vicinity of Mon to Rippach.

The weather was cool with scattered high clouds. Visibility was good. Combat efficiency was excellent and the morale of the troops, high.

15 Apr. 1945

Regarding the 76th Inf Div, friendly armored elements established a bridgehead over the Zwickauer-Mulde River as the infantry continued clearing remnants and isolated groups of the enemy in their zone. There was no change in enemy units. Of 905 POWs taken, 585 were from 48 miscellaneous units plus 138 deserters, soldiers on furlough, and convalescents. A POW stated one group of artillery was to withdraw to the Zwickauer-Mulde River line when their present positions become untenable. TAC reported 50 trucks going west on the autobahn from Dresden. Civilians and POWs reported 100 tanks in Dorna yesterday. Resistance was light as the last enemy elements cleared from Zeitz. Negligible air activity was reported. An undetermined number of planes dropped three bombs at 2120. MG fire was received at 2400.

A jeep was ambushed northeast of Zeitz during the evening. Four hundred (400) allied POWs were liberated at Burtschutz. Approximately 150 POWs from the United States, and 250 Russian POWs were liberated at Grossröda.

No surrender following an announcement made at the end of a Wehrmach communiqué over a German radio station on 12 Apr as follows: "All German cities along main roads will be defended. A battle commandant will be assigned the mission of defending each of these cities. No public official will initiate negotiations for surrender to the enemy, and anyone who attempts to do so will be sentenced to death."

A terrible tempered tapper: In the early morning hours of 12 Apr, the switchboard operator of the 175th Signal Repair Co received a telephone call. A male voice in good English informed the operation "This is MASTER calling. There has been a German breakthrough. You may have to move out at any moment. If the telephone rings again, don't even bother to answer it; it will be the signal to move." The levelheaded operator refused to get excited and asked who was calling. The reply was: "This is MASTER, God damn it." Many telephone conversations carried over German civilian lines have Gestapo long standing taps.

CT 385's 1st Bn seized Bergesdorf against stiff resistance; they continued the advance and captured Gensnitz, Zettweil and was passed through by the 3rd Bn.

They reorganized in the vicinity of Bonla. The 2nd Bn continued their advance to the east and cleared Lindenburg, Phohla Lostitz, Grossröda, Kreutzen, Teckwitz, and Goderin. At the end of the period they had advanced to a position in the vicinity of Áltenburg. The 3rd Bn (motorized) passed through the 1st Bn. They met with the 385th Infantry in the vicinity of Nesima and continued the advance clearing Zechan, Leesan, and Lödla. They closed in Áltenburg.

Relieved elements of CT 304 engaged in clearing the town. CT 417's 1st Bn completed mopping up operations in Zeitz. They continued an attack to the east and cleared 14 towns against light resistance. The 2nd Bn continued to attack in the east and occupied 24 towns against little or no resistance. They followed the advance elements of the 6th Armored Div. The 3rd Bn maintained order and mopping up in Áltenburg. They took over 700 POWs with more than 1, 000 POWs taken during the period and over 55 towns had been cleared.

The 749th Tank Bn had their Bn Hqs and Hqs Co was in Wintersdorf. A Co, attached to the 30th Inf Regt, was in Buscha. B Co plus one platoon from Co D, attached to the 417th Inf Regt, was in Leda. C Co plus one platoon from Co D, attached to the 385th Inf Regt, was in Zechan and Lessen. The Svc Co and the remainder of Co D were in Pelicdtedof.

Operations for the period-included Bn Hqs and Hqs Co left Donau at 1500, traveled 20 miles to Wintersdorf, arriving at 1900. The 3rd Plt of Co A (attached to the 304th Inf Regt), left Droissdorf at 0700 with the 3rd Bn of the Inf Regt and escorted FA into a position in the vicinity of Áltenburg. They proceeded with the infantry and seized the town at 1300. The 1st and 2nd Plts, with two assault guns and one light tank left at 1415 and road marched to Áltenburg, arriving at 1730.

The 1st Plt left Áltenburg in support of the 1st Bn at about 1900 and road marched to Mittweida. They arrived at 2345 traveling approximately 47 miles, road marched towards Mittweida, arriving at 2400. D Co, attached to the 417th Inf Regt's 1st Plt, as part of CT's 1st Bn of the 260th Inf Regt, moved to Roda. The 2nd Plt, as part of CT of the 3rd Bn, moved to Rohron. The 3rd Plt, as part of CT's 2nd Bn moved to Fockendorf. The platoon leader of the 3rd Bn and platoon leader from the TD Bn captured 183 POWs while on foot for recon in the vicinity of Zeitz.

Co Hqs and trains moved from Zeitz at approximately 1500, traveling approximately 12 miles east to a new assembly area of Leba, closing in at 1930. Co C, attached to the 385th Inf Regt's 1st Plt moved with the 1st Bn of the 385th from Hergesdorf to Nessa. The 2nd Plt moved from Wiedenborn with the 2nd Bn of the 385th to Áltenburg.

The 3rd Plt moved with the 3rd Bn of the 385th from Rippach to the vicinity of Áltenburg. Co Hqs and the CP moved from Droyssig to Zechaulessen.

There were no losses or casualties during the period. Svc Co left the bivouac area of Preissen at 1700 and proceeded to a new bivouac area at Flectdorf, arriving at 1900 with approximately 20 miles having been traveled.

The weather was cool with high overcast. Visibility was good. Combat efficiency was excellent and morale high.

16 Apr. 1945

The 76th Inf Div reported the enemy was generally east of the line at Rackwitz-Sittweida. There was no change in enemy units in contact. Captured documents showed clothing warehouses at a stove and porcelain factory in Altmugehn, and a clothing office at Plauen. On 6 Apr friendly troops met no enemy resistance as an area east of Zwickauer-Mulde River was cleared and a bridgehead was secured. Hundreds of POWs surrendered without firefight. One jeep was captured in Munsa by the enemy and ambushed at 0930. Five hundred (500) French POWs were liberated at Benndorf.

POW statements included in total were 76 officers, 38 of whom were from the School Hqs in Zeitz. Part of the school was formed into Regt Eich with CO being Maj Eich. There were two battalions, each with four companies of 50 men committed to defend Zeitz. The 18th Armored Replacement Bn arrived in Borna on 12 Apr with about 400 men and 50 tanks. The tanks moved from Borna with the CO being Maj Hemprich. Officer POWs of GHQ Relief Agency stated that carloads of chlorine gas was hit during an air attack on the railroads near Zeitz on 10 Apr and that several casualties were killed and wounded. The gas was destined for commercial use.

One POW stated that Div Gross Deutschland with the CO being General Maj Lorenz had been dissolved. Panzer Corps (armored corps) of Gross Deutschland was formed consisting of armored infantry divisions named Brandenburg, Fuehrer Begleit Brig and Fuehrer Inf Brigade. He stated he saw and spoke to a soldier wearing an SS Armband "Eltz 1944" who claimed his unit was a regiment in a newly formed SS Div located at Garnisch-Partenkirchheim in the Bavarian Alps. The division consisted exclusively of German SS personnel and were supposed to remain in that area.

A sabotage booby trap apparently mounted on the spring of a one-quarter ton vehicle cost one soldier both feet and injured another in Neunkirchheim. The explosive was detonated when one of the men stepped into the vehicle. Only little scraps of brown paper and a battered eight-inch piece of aluminum of the bomb and its precise specifications were not known. Examination of the vehicle indicated the explosion was not caused by a mine in the road but a bomb mounted in the spring or slightly higher in the right rear underpinning of the vehicle. The vehicle was stationary when the explosion occurred and the bomb was evidently a pressure type. The booby trap was believed to have been placed between Apr 9 and Apr 15 while the vehicle was parked outside an American occupied building under general surveillance of a guard in the vicinity. The vehicle was driven to another part of town at 0915 and parked outside a unit headquarters for approximately one-half hour and was under constant observation of American soldiers standing nearby. It was driven a few yards to the center of the road with the explosion taking place as other members of the party were climbing in.

The following info was taken from OD #17, Hqs, 76th Inf Div:

"XX Corps would establish and hold a beachhead east of the Zwickauer-Mulde River and be prepared to resume an advance to the east on orders. The 6th and 4th Armored Divs initially would assist the corps in establishing the beachhead and when relieved by the 76th and 80th Divs, elements of the 6th and 4th Armored Divs would assemble in their assigned areas. The 3rd Cav Grp plus a platoon would protect on the right (southern) flank of the corps and be prepared to pass through those elements of the 76th and 80th to reconnoiter to the east.

The 76th Inf Div plus assigned company would continue its present missions and relieve elements of the 76th Armored Div in its assigned sector. It would then hold the line at the beachhead and be prepared to resume advance to the east on order.

The CT 304 plus its assigned company would continue its present missions and relieve elements of the 6t th Armored Div at the Zwickauer-Mulde River beachhead. They were to hold the line until relieved by the elements of CT 417 plus its assigned company in the northern portion and then with elements of relieved, move south running generally east and west between Königstein and Mittweida.

CT 417 plus the assigned company would continue its present missions and then cross the Zwickauer-Mulde River over the bridge in the vicinity of Kochlitz. They would continue marching on the road in Dorfen, Zolinitz, and Wiederau and relieve elements of the 304th CT without delay in the northern portion of the Div's sector; they would hold the line at the bridgehead.

CT 385, plus the assigned company, would continue its present missions and upon arrival of the Zwickauer-Mulde River, move into its assigned assembly area and await orders in Div Res.

All other organizations would continue their present missions.

a. Seize any bridges found intact over the Zschopau River between Schönberg and Merzdorf, both inclusive.

All echelons would be prepared to resume their advance to the east on order of short notice.

New bridges would be effective when the infantry initiated relief of armor in the zone. General uses of the roads were authorized but clear convoys through Div Traffic Control.

Time for the Div CP would open at Wiederau and close at Gorna with the hour to be announced."

Operations for the period: CT 385's 1st Motorized Bn would attack to the east clearing the wooded areas and towns as far as the Zwickauer-Mulde River and on completion of the mission, would close in the assembly area and establish all-around security.

The 2nd Bn would relieve elements of CT 304 in Áltenburg and continue to clear the town of the enemy and maintain order there. The 3rd Bn would continue their advance to the river clearing the towns and wooded areas of the enemy. They would then close into the assembly area and establish perimeter defense.

CT 417's 1st Bn continue to attack to the east, mopping up enemy in the zone, cross the Zwickauer-Mulde River in the vicinity of Nochlitz and relieve elements of this CT in the area of the beachhead. The 2nd Bn moved by motor to the vicinity of Königstein.

Regimental Res had its 3rd Bn attack to the east and cross the river in the vicinity of Rochlitz and relieve elements of CT 304 in that area.

CT 304 had its 1st Bn relieve elements of CCB, 6th Armored Div and assumed defense of the bridgehead in that sector. They were relieved bye elements of the CT 417. Their 1st Bn relieved the 2nd Bn of the 304th Inf on the left of the regimental's zone. Co E and two MG Plts from Co H guarded the bridgeheads at Gonren, Lunzena, and Garitzhain. Over 800 POWs were taken during the period.

The troops from the 749th Tank Bn had Bn Hqs and Hqs Co in Topseifersdorf while the Svc Co was in the same location. Co A, attached to the 304th Inf Regt was in Rollingshain. Co D, attached to the 417th Inf Regt was in Chalhein. Co C plus one platoon of D Co, attached to the 385th Inf Regt, was in Mansdorf. D Co, minus one platoon, was in Div Res in Frankenau.

Operations for the period: Bn Hqs and Hqs Co left Altersdorf at 1315 and traveled approximately 32 miles to Topseifersdorf. Co A's 2nd and 3rd Plts with two assault guns

WHAT DID YOU DO IN THE GREAT WAR GRANDPA

and one light tank arrived in Wiederau at 0430 hours. At 1200 they left Wiederau and marched to Rollingshain, arriving at 1500. The 1st Plt left Mittweida at 1500 and assembled with the company at Rollingshain, arriving at 1630. The 1st Plt was ordered to Altmittweida at 2030 to get into position for repulsing a possible counterattack. The distance traveled from Buscha was approximately 7 miles. B Co, attached to the 417th Inf Regt moved from their respective assembly areas to the company assembly area at Chalhein, closing at 2000.

Co Hqs and trains moved from Lena at 1500, traveled approximately 30 miles east to the same town, closing in at 1700. D Co was in Div Res. All platoons reverted to company control this period and the entire company was in Div Res, and moved from Plichtendorf to Frankenau. The Svc Co left the bivouac area at Plichtendorf at 1300 and proceeded to their new bivouac area at Topseifersdorf arriving at 1700, having traveled about 32 miles.

1st Lt Leighton, CO of Co B was promoted to Capt this date. 1st Lt McProuty, CO of C Co was promoted to Capt this date. Second Lts Bobbett, Co B, and Rosencrantz, also from Co B, were promoted to First Lts this date. 1st Lt Wilhelm, CO of Svc Co was promoted to Capt this date.

The weather was clear and warm. Visibility was excellent. Combat efficiency was excellent as was the troops' morale.

17 Apr. 1945

According to the 76th Inf Div there was no change in the enemy's front lines and no change in enemy units. A liberated Yugoslav POW reported 200 troops with 10 bazookas were in Hernsdorf yesterday. Scattered groups offered slight resistance to our mopping up operations. There was light artillery fire including Nebelwefer fire that harassed our forward elements. Three rounds of undetermined caliber fell on Gainsdorf at 0200 hours. One ME 109 was shot down in the vicinity of Erlau at 2050. At 1030 ten enemy troops were located and had dug in the vicinity of Rimsdorf. Three tanks and 3-1/2 track trucks fired on the bridge in the vicinity of Ringenthal at 1815. Enemy equipment captured in the vicinity of Ottendorf included six ordnance trailers, 12 tank motors, 5 light trucks, 12 rocket launchers, 40 motorcycles, 1 sedan, 15-1/2 tracks, and three possible Mark III tanks. More than 100 aircraft of which 15 were JU88 and 15 ME109s were reported. An enemy operated US B-17s believed to be in operating condition. Several crated engines and aircraft instruments were found in a warehouse.

The enemy's Anti-Aircraft School for Armored Inf at Wechselburg had about 400 men and 50 remained there to fight a delaying action but the balance moved toward Frankenberg yesterday. They had with them 12-20mm AA weapons on quadruple mounts. The CO's name was Winkler. Their school was for heavy weapons of Armored Inf in Grinda had about 300 men, now organized into KG Moser. They have 4 armored cars with 75mm guns, 6-150mm infantry Howitzers, motorized, 12-12cm mortars, and 4 AGs with 150mm guns. The KG Moser moved towards Mittweida on 15 Apr. The 2nd Nebelwerfer Replacement Bn with about 500 men, 6-150mm Nebelwerfers with 6 tubes each. The CO was Maj Fechke. The battalion moved from Burstädt toward Helichen on 15 Apr. The 192nd Inf Replacement Bn was stationed in Dobelin and has 300 men with the mission to defend the super highway in the vicinity of Merzdorf. The 102nd Inf Replacement Bn with between 1,000 to 1,500 men was located in Chemnitz at the end of March.

POWs at Mühlberg, east of the Elbe River between Thurgau and Riesa, had an estimated 20,000-allied POWs, mostly British and American fliers at the end of March. The 1003rd Tartar Supply Co worked on road repair in the vicinity of Zeitz.

Intelligence available from higher headquarters indicates the enemy is making substantial use of telephone lines to transmit info of immediate tactical value by stay-behind agents or overrun groups of troops. These circuits may be underground lines not immediately located by our forces. It was suggested all telephone be disconnected promptly as localities are captured to eliminate this use as far as possible.

The following secret message #9 this date stated:

"The 6th Armored Div would relieve elements of the 76th Inf Div north of the line without delay.

The 76th Inf Div plus attached company would relieve elements of the 80th Inf Div north of the line by 18 Apr and continue to defend the line beachhead east of the Zwickauer-Mulde River and be prepared to resume its advance to the east, southeast, or south on order.

The 417th Inf, with B Co from the 749th Tank Bn attached, would be as relieved by elements of the 6th Armored Div via route designated in verbal orders to detrucking area in the vicinity of Hartmannsdorf. Upon arrival they would initiate relief elements of the 80th Inf Div and defend the assigned sector. Relief would be completed prior to 0800 18 Apr. They would protect the right (southern) flank of the Div, establish and maintain contact with the 304th Inf on the left; they would establish and maintain contact with elements of the 4th Armored Div on the right.

The 304th Inf with A Co from the 749th Tank Bn reverted control to the parent organization and continued to maintain defensive positions in the zone. They carried on aggressive patrolling, continued maintenance of their vehicles and weapons. They were prepared to protect the division's left on the north flank. The artillery was in position to support the division and battalions fired on targets of opportunity on harassing and interdictory missions.

The 901st FA Bn moved out of the division's zone en route to a new area. Other battalions were prepared to move the following day."

The 749th Tank Bn's troops were at these locations: Bn Hqs, Hqs Co, and Svc Co were in Topseifersdorf. Co A, having been assigned to the 304th Inf Regt, was in Rollingshain. Attached to the 417th Inf Regt was B Co was in Chalhein. Monsdorf was the location of Co C, attached to the 385th Inf Regt. Div Res was Co D in Frankenau.

Operations for the period: Bn Hqs and Hqs Co remained in their bivouac area. The 1st Plt of A Co, attached to the 304th, returned from Altmittweida at 1300. The company spent the remainder of the day on maintenance work. B Co, attached to the 417th left the assembly area at Chalhein at 1900, traveling approximately 15 miles to the south to a new assembly area of Hartmannsdorf closing in at 2100. There was no contact with the enemy during this period. Co C, attached to the 385th, had their 1st Plt move from the vicinity of Nesima to Monsdorf to join the remainder of the company. The 2nd Plt remained with the 2nd Bn of the 385th Inf Áltenburg. The 3rd Plt moved from Áltenburg, also to Monsdorf. The 2nd Plt joined the rest of the company there. Maintenance and radio repair work was carried on. D Co's platoon that had been attached to B Co was relieved from attachment and returned to the company at Frankenau.

The weather was clear and warm with good visibility. Combat efficiency was excellent, morale high.

18 Apr. 1945

The 76th Inf Div reported no change in enemy lines but was generally east of Mittweida, Krumbach, Oberdichtenau, western outskirt of Chemnitz and Osprung. A civilian stated troops were to set up a defense line east of the autobahn on the road between Seifersbach and Hainichen that had been dug up but there were an unknown number of troops in the woods as of Apr 16.

Another civilian reported an undefended roadblock south of Dratsdorf but there was a defended roadblock at Glosa. A POW taken by the 80th US Div reported 90 troops committed in hasty defense positions west of Borna with rifles, bazookas and a few MGs. A civilian also reported an unknown number of SS troops in Lichtenau. The enemy remained unaggressive, improved their hasty defensive positions, particularly in the vicinity of Chemnitz. Scattered harassing artillery and Nebelwerfer fire was directed against our forward elements.

Enemy air was active with two strafing and one bombing attacks were reported. Two Nebelwerfer shells fell in the vicinity of Seifersbach at 1725. Four rounds of undetermined caliber fell in the Grensdorf area at 2230. An unknown number of rounds of 150mm and Nebelwerfer shells fell in the vicinity of Mittweida Bridge from 0430 to 1015.

BELT BUCKLE PISTOL: A pistol made to resemble a belt buckle was found in this vicinity. The buckle is black, has silver-colored swastika emblem, spread-eagled on the front. The buckle is about 1"x 2-1/2". The cover drops down and by pushing a button, a 2-barrelled 32 pistol flips out, pointing directly to the front. By pressing two more buttons, the weapon can fire two shots. A person standing directly in front of the buckle would be shot. This weapon is an actuality and has been examined by higher headquarters. It was recommended that persons capturing, or talking to any German with a belt buckle that resembles the above, be careful to make the prisoner hold their hands behind their heads and to stand slightly to one side of the person.

Information on Chemnitz: Informant from town reported one roadblock on Leipziger Street and another at Liebacher Street. Unknown number of troops are said to be in the Grembitschauer Forest, armed with infantry weapons, and liberal amounts of Panzerfausten (tank ammunition). Roadblocks were said to be lightly defended by approximately four men each, armed with rifles and AT grenades. He further stated the town was generally held by Volkssturm (Home Guard) and added the majority of the population was hoping for quick Allied occupation of the city.

Oberbuergermeister (Brigadier General – BrigGen) Schmitt of Marine Reconnaissance Brigade was reported to have his family evacuated and was unwilling to surrender the town. The armory, containing a majority of troops, was said to be located just north off the #1 square according to the town plan. Chemnitz police was ordered to remove white flags from the houses on which they had appeared.

Another POW stated the party headquarters was located on Herren Street. An estimated entire garrison including approximately 300 men was reinforced by the Volksturm in the northwestern sector of the town just south of the autobahn but was lightly held by inexperienced troops.

Other POWs corroborate reports that all main entrances of the town had defended roadblocks, held by approximately a squadron of infantry for each. Rumors that the SS was committed in Chemnitz were apparently based on the following facts reported by the POWs. The 1st SS Engineer Replacement and Training Bn, after being upgraded to a two battalion CT was committed in Thuringia. One battalion was killed or captured in total; the other, after reassembling in Chemnitz, was seen there receiving orders, according to former members of that unit. They were to infiltrate through their own lines and reassemble in Dresden.

POWs reported that Grennitz had at least three armories, all occupied, with one infantry, one artillery and one signal corps armory. The 4th PGR Replacement Bn was also located in the town. The GAF Replacement Bn III, strength of 500-600 men, was stationed in barracks in the vicinity of Chemnitz-Ebersdorf.

Counter-Intelligence verified that large numbers of non-combatant German troops had been told officially to don civilian garb, and lose themselves as effectively as possible among the civilian population. This time, they were females of the GAF and males from ordnance shops of an auto-union factory near the railroad station at Oberalt-Chemnitz. When the question on legality of such procedures arose, all were of the opinion that combatant troops have the right of such action. Women AA gun crews for such purposes were defined as non-combatants.

The following info was taken from OD, Hqs 76th Div: "VIII Corps would hold along a limiting line and pass to Continental First US Army on Third U.S. Army order. The 6th Armored Div and the 89th Inf Div would clear enemy and occupy a limiting line in the assigned zone on the left and right respectively of the 76th Div. Upon relief by the 76th Inf Div, the 4th Armored Div would assemble in its area and await orders. The 1107th Engineers, Co C Group would support the 76th Inf."

"The 76th Inf Div, attached to the 749th Tank Bn, would relieve elements of the 4th Armored Div without delay. They would clear the enemy and hold a limited line in its assigned sector. They would maintain contact with the 6th Armored Div on the left (northern) flank."

"The 385th Inf, attached to Co C of the 749th Tank Bn, would relieve elements of the 4th Armored Div in the sector without delay. They would clear the enemy and occupy forward limits lightly and dispose forces in depth with the assigned sector, establishing OPL generally along said line. They would establish and maintain contact with the 417th Inf on the left and establish and maintain line with elements of the 89th Inf Div on the right. They would protect the right (southern) flank of the division, maintain continuous recon and patrolling to the vicinity patrol line."

"The 417th Inf, with Co D of the 749th Tank Bn attached, would clear the enemy in the zone to the limit line and occupy forward limits lightly, dispose of enemy forces in depth within the assigned sector. They would establish an OPL generally along the line. One battalion would be committed on division's order only, would maintain contact and line with 304th Inf on the left and establish and maintain line with the 385th Inf on the right. They would maintain continuous recon and patrolling to the vicinity of the patrol line."

"The 304th Inf, with Co A attached from the 749th Tank Bn would clear the enemy in the zone. They would occupy forward elements lightly and dispose enemy forces within the assigned sector, establish an OPL generally along the line, maintain a line with elements of the 6th Armored Div on the left and maintain line with the 417th Inf on the right. They would protect the northern flank of the division; maintain continuous recon and patrolling to their vicinity of the patrol line.

Operations for the period: The 417th Inf, attached with 749th Tank Bn's Co B would relieve the 318th Inf of the 80th Div in their zone. They would establish defensive positions, patrol vigorously to the front. The 3rd Bn, Regimental Reserve, with one platoon from Co K, would protect division installations at Burstädt. The 385th Inf, Co C from the 749th Tank Bn attached, would close in a new assembly area and relieve elements of the 4th Armored Div. Co G relieved Co C and assumed the mission protecting the airport in the vicinity of Altenburg. Co F maintained order in Altenburg. The regiment established defensive positions in the sector and patrolled vigorously to the front. The 304th Inf continued to maintain defensive positions in its assigned sector. They patrolled aggressively to the front and in regimental area. Co D maintained guard on the hospital and supply trains in Burstädt. FA Bns were displaced to new areas, registered and fired on targets of opportunity. Division artillery and the 416th FA Group fired HEs with quick and delay, and weapons upon the City of Chemnitz. Air and ground observers reported huge fires and explosions.

Location of the troops of the 749th Tank Bn: Bn Hqs, Hqs Co, and D Co were in Taura. A Co, attached to the 304th Inf Regt was in Rollingshain. B Co, attached to the 417th Inf Regt was in Hartmannsdorf. Co C, attached to the 385th Inf Regt, was in Waldenburg. The Svc Co was in Topseifersdorf.

Bn Hqs and Hqs Co departed from Topseifersdorf at 1045 and moved to Taura, arriving at 1145 with the distance traveled, 10 miles. A Co, attached to the 304th Inf remained in position with no activity throughout the period. B Co, attached to the

417th Inf remained in the assembly area in Hartmannsdorf. Crews performed echelon maintenance on tanks. Co C, attached to the 385th, at 0900, marched from Monsdorf through Burstädt, Chursdorf, Penig, and Schrauwitz to Wallenburg where the CP and Hqs Plt remained. The line platoons continued on to close with their respective infantry battalions: the 1st Plt at Oberlungwitz, the 2nd Plt at Glauchau, and the 3rd Plt at Limbach. D Co left Frankenau for a new bivouac area, arrived in Taura at 1215 with a distance traveled approximately 10 miles. The battalion was then attached to VIII Corps, 1st U.S. Army and relieved from XX Corps, 3rd Army, OD #18, Hqs 76th Inf Div, this date.

The weather was warm with dense fog early in the period with clearing in the afternoon. The visibility was very poor early in the period changing to good later in the period. Combat efficiency was good; morale was high.

19 Apr. 1945

According to the news from the 76th Inf Div there was no noticeable enemy front lines nor were there any changes in enemy units contacted. Civilians stated there were bazooka positions at the crossroads on the road between Leukersdorf and Chemnitz, at roadblocks in Hartnau and on the road into Klaffenbach. As of yesterday, there were 40 to 50 tanks in the Ronewisch-Auerbach area with 6,000 SS troops. Also there were 100 troops and a small group of SS in Schneeberg. Civilians also reported many enemy were moving south to Annaberg or Stollberg on 13 Apr. They also stated the Chemnitz airport was intact as the enemy continued to improve a hasty defensive position.

Harassing artillery and Nebelwerfer fire fell on our forward elements. A 50-to 60 man counterattack in the vicinity of Schonborn was repulsed without our losing any ground. One strafing attack was reported. Three rounds of Nebelwerfer fell on Schonborn at 1930. An undetermined number of Nebelwerfer and artillery of unknown caliber fell in the vicinity of the Schönborn Bridge at 1530. Small arms fire as reported at the eastern end of Dratsdorf at 2400.

A counterattack by 50 to 60 enemy troops from the vicinity of Seifersbach at 0545 hours against Schonborn was repulsed at 0730. Four enemy tanks built into houses were reported as of the evening of 18 Apr.

A US air attack in the vicinity of Monsdorf on 12 Apr destroyed one battery from a group of two batteries of six 150mm guns each; fate of the other six guns were not known.

The following information was taken from Secret Message #3 dated this date:

"Effective immediately, corps on the right (south) boundary (becomes boundary between First and Third U.S. Armies on Army order) is announced as follows:

Lann River from its mouth to Aumenau, Giessen, Oberichstein, Fulda, and Wustensachsen (all to First US Army); thence along the northern boundary of Bavaria to the Czechoslovakian border.

Boundary between the 6th Army Div and the 76th Inf Div was extended west as follows: Old boundary at Poleig, Luckenwalde, Rosenthal, Gosen, Poppendorf, and Wichmar (all included to the 76th Inf Div)."

The 385th Inf, with Co C from the 749th Tank Bn continued to hold defensive positions in the sector with the 1st and 3rd Bns. The 1st Bn was in position on the right flank of the zone, maintained contact with elements of the 355th Inf. The 3rd Bn was in position on the regimental front and carried on vigorous patrolling. No enemy contacts were reported. The 2nd Bn with Co F, minus one platoon, moved to Eisenberg and assumed the mission of maintaining law and order. G Co, plus one R Plt and OPs Plt from F Co, were relieved at Altenburg and moved to Gera. They assumed the mission of maintaining law and order in the city.

The 417th Inf, with Co B from the 749th Tank Bn continued to hold their defensive positions in the sector with the 1st and 2nd Bns with the 1st Bn on the left. Both battalions patrolled vigorously to the front. No enemy contact was reported by the patrols. The 3rd Bn was in regimental reserve and was prepared to repel counterattacks in the regimental zone. One platoon of K Co furnished security for the Div CP.

The 304th Inf continued to maintain a defensive position. They patrolled aggressively to the front and in the regimental zone. They repelled a counterattack from the north at 0530 hours, taking over 100 POWs. The 2nd Plt attacked the enemy with force from the rear inflicting casualties. One of our light medium tanks was knocked out by enemy bazooka that had been fired on a gun tube.

The 355th FA Bn and the 901st FA Bn fired missions on Chemnitz with good results. All battalions registered and fired on targets of opportunity.

Troops from the 749th Tank Bn were located as follows: Bn Hqs, Hqs Co, and D Co were in Taura. A Co, attached to the 304th Inf Regt, had its CP at Rollingshain with one platoon at Schonborn and the two remaining platoons in Rollingshain. B Co, attached to the 417th Inf Regt, was in Hartmannsdorf. Co C, attached to the 315th Inf Regt, was in Glauchau and the Svc Co was in Topseifersdorf.

A Co, 749th Tank Bn, attached to the 304th Inf Regt, was ordered to support the advance of the 1st Bn to secure the high ground northeast of Schonborn and southeast of Ottendorf. The 2nd and 3rd Plts moved from the CP at Rollingshain at 0015 hours to Schonborn, via Mittweida, and Uttendorf respectively to take up defensive positions in the event of a counterattack. Sporadic resistance was encountered in Schonborn. The 1st Plt remained in regimental reserve until 0630 when orders to cross the Zschopau River at Mittweida to repel possible counterattacks when an undetermined size of enemy troops came from the north. The 2nd Plt pulled back to Mittweida and traveled east to penetrate the attacking force from the rear. They accompanied advance elements of the 1st Bn in the attack on high ground west of Seifersbach, where they became engaged in a firefight. The 1st Plt was ordered up to assist the 2nd Plt at 1200. About 1430, the 3rd Plt was ordered to return to the CP location and at 1930, the 1st and 2nd Plts were ordered to back to the CP after the infantry had secured the high ground northeast of Schonborn that was the objective. At 1830 the 3rd Plt moved from the CP location to support the infantry patrol east of Schonborn and returned to Rollingshain at 2130.

At 1300 the 3rd Plt moved to Schonborn to be in a position to repel a possible attack. As the tank platoon proceeded down the road to Schonborn from Mittweida, one medium tank was knocked out from a direct hit. The tank didn't burn but will require evacuation. Three men evacuated – Cpl Carver and O'Brien (no rank given) were slightly wounded. The platoon assisted in taking 200 POWs, killed 50, destroyed three MGs, two bazooka teams, and destroyed six houses that were sniper strongholds.

C Co, attached to the 385th Regt had its 1st Plt move from Oberlungwitz. The 3rd Plt moved from Limbach and the Hqs Plt and Co CP moved from Waldenburg to assemble in an area occupied by the 2nd Plt in Glauchau. One liaison tank from the 3rd Plt returned to Limbach at 1700 to remain with the 3rd Bn of the 385th Inf Regt.

The weather was warm and clear with scattered clouds. Visibility was good. Combat efficiency was excellent and the morale of the troops, high.

20 Apr. 1945

The situation of the 76th Inf Div showed enemy units in contact were the KG Gruse, 1st and 2nd Cos, 10th Recon Replacement Bn, the 2nd Co of the 4th Replacement Bn, the 1st and 2nd Cos of the 3rd Nebelwerfer Replacement Bn, elements of the 413th Armored Inf Replacement Bn and the 3rd Air Force Replacement Bn from the GK Thomas.

Our patrols found Seifersbach and Merzdorf occupied by enemy forces. A French

POW stated the entrances to Chemnitz were covered by troops with Panzerfausts and rifles as well as a roadblock near Bensheim entrance. Civilians stated Chemnitz was heavily guarded along the autobahn on the west and north. They also reported AA gun positions in the Auto Union Motor Works, the Alt Chemnitz. Another civilian reported 88mm battery positions.

Other French POWs reported 20 medium tanks and armored vehicles in Nussen. Two barracks with SS troops and two with infantry were reported in Freiberg 14 Apr. As of the 12th and 13th of Apr, many trucks passed through Chemnitz toward Annaberg, many SS troops in Chemnitz, and Tiger Tanks moved into the city.

A civilian reported 12 artillery pieces, five companies of infantry including some SS in Frankenberg yesterday. Another French POW stated an ammunition dump was in a silver mine in Tüttendorf as of 14 Apr. Hostile troops opposed our troops with small arms, automatic weapon, and Nebelwerfer fire. An enemy group of 30 to 40 men attempted to cut off one of our combat patrols. A few rounds of 128mm fire fell in the vicinity of Schonborn.

Enemy aircraft was negligible with only three aircraft reported. Two ME 109s flew southwest at 1400. One enemy plane flew northwest at 1540. Ten men of an enemy group captured a US soldier (no name given) at 2245.

Our patrols destroyed bazookas attached to bicycles and found bazooka positions in the vicinity of Seifersbach and Merzdorf and received automatic weapon, small arms and Nebelwerfer fire at 2240. There was a firefight with 30 to 40 enemy troops at 1430. At 1530 one of our cars received MG and mortar fire from the woods. A civilian stated two enemy officers were observed from a friendly position from Lichtenau and into Frankenberg yesterday to gather info from a German civilian from Bergstadt, Germany. An informant going to Hainichen traveled through town on 13 Apr and heard from soldiers who had been collected there that the town was to be fortified and defended. Panzerfausts and Panzerschreck (bazooka) were the most common weapons in Hainichen. All stragglers were stopped by the town commandant and used in defense of the town. An informant going to Freiberg traveled through the town and he noticed even more soldiers and Volkssturm men there than at Hainichen. He estimated at least three battalions were charged with defense of the town. There were roadblocks made of concrete on all the roads leading to the city. Behind them small (37mm) AT guns were being set up. Many soldiers with Panzerfausts; seven Panzerschrecks were also seen. Freiberg was to be a "fortress."

An informant going to Chemnitz noticed little activity there compared to other towns mentioned above. Small groups of soldiers with Panzerfausts were noted.

The city was ruined to a very large extent on 13 Apr.

The 1ˢᵗ Bn of the 315ᵗʰ Inf Regt secured the division's right flank and maintained contact with the 355ᵗʰ Inf. The battalion less one platoon maintained order in Gera. The 2ⁿᵈ Bn's F Co maintained order in Eisenberg. The 3ʳᵈ Bn maintained defensive positions along the regimental's front and patrolled vigorously to the front.

The 304ᵗʰ Inf Regt's 1ˢᵗ Bn maintained defensive positions along the regimental front. The 2ⁿᵈ Bn was in Regimental Res. Co B and one platoon of G Co guarded hospitals, warehouses, and supply installations in the vicinity of Burstädt and Markersdorf. The 3ʳᵈ Bn patrolled throughout the regimental area and to the front.

The 417ᵗʰ Inf Regt continued to hold defensive positions with elements of the 1ˢᵗ and 2ⁿᵈ Bns. They also patrolled aggressively to the front. The 3ʳᵈ Bn was in Regimental Res. One platoon of K Co furnished security for the division's CP. Eighty-one (81) POWs surrendered by pre-arrangement to the 2ⁿᵈ and 3ʳᵈ Bns.

Location of troops of the 749ᵗʰ Tank Bn: Bn Hqs, Hqs Co and D Co, minus one platoon, were in Taura. A Co and one platoon of D Co, attached to the 304ᵗʰ Inf Regt had its CP at Rollingshain. Two platoons were in Rollingshain as well, with one platoon at Schonborn. B Co, attached to the 417ᵗʰ Inf Regt was in Hartmannsdorf. C Co, attached to the 385ᵗʰ Inf Regt was in Limbach and the Svc Co was in Topseifersdorf.

Co A, attached to the 304ᵗʰ Inf Regt, had the 1ˢᵗ Plt leave the CP location at 1730. They joined the infantry and supported them in a recon force southeast of Ottendorf in the direction of Trumbach and returned at 1400. The 2ⁿᵈ Plt left at 1500 with the infantry as recon in force to Seifersbach, returning at 1900. Resistance was light in both attacks with no ammunition expended. The 3ʳᵈ Plt remained in support of the 1ˢᵗ Bn with the 304ᵗʰ Inf at Schonborn. The light tank platoon had been attached and they reported in at 1900. B Co, attached to the 417ᵗʰ Inf Regt remained in the assembly area with no activity during the period and had no contact with the enemy.

C Co, attached to the 385ᵗʰ Inf Regt, moved at 1100 from Glauchau to Limbach. The march was carried out without incident. Maintenance and radio work was carried on.

D Co's 3ʳᵈ Plt left Taura at 1830 for the assembly area at Rollingshain to join A Co. for tactical purposes.

They received orders and instructions for the following day.

The weather was warm and clear. Visibility was excellent as was combat efficiency and morale of the troops was high.

21 Apr. 1945

The general situation of the 76th Inf Div was no change in enemy front lines as well as no change in enemy units in contact. Enemy infantry was in the woods west of Sachsenburg. They dug in the streets in Borna along the railroad. A civilian stated there were 1,500 troops with small arms in Kruebathal yesterday. They manned and improved defensive positions resisted our patrolling with small arms, automatic weapons, mortar fire, and artillery fire that was light in nature. Our patrol drew fire from the north of the area and in the vicinity of Rabenstein at 1200. Troops in civilian clothes armed with MGs, rifles, and Panzerfausts were in a house. What was thought to be a US vehicle entered Chemnitz after receiving enemy small arms and rifle fire at 1905. Total enemy POWs taken during the period was 317.

The 1st Bn of the 385th Inf Regt continued maintaining defensive positions on their right flank and maintained contact with the 355th Inf Regt. Otherwise, all positions and duties were as the day before. Law and order were also maintained in Eisenberg, Gera, and Jena. All troops were alerted late in the day for possible contact with advance elements of the Russian Army.

The general situation of the 749th Tank Bn regarding location of troops was the same as the day before.

Activity for the companies and platoons remained the same as the previous day. Bn Hqs received a telephone message concerning plans in connection with the proximity of Russians to our lines. It was received at 1545 and was distributed to all companies.

A platoon of Co D, attached to A Co was relieved at approximately 1800 by another platoon of D Co B Co, attached to the 417th Inf Regt remained in the assembly area with no activity during the period. C Co, attached to the 385th Inf Regt remained in Limbach. The first echelon work in maintenance of the battalion was carried on. The 3rd Plt of Co D crossed the initial point for the vicinity of Seifersbach at approximately 0700. They assisted in two strong separate infantry patrols in force in assaulting the town of two separate missions during the day; they also aided in shooting up the woods and dug in positions of the enemy held north and west of the town. They returned to the company area at 1700 after being relieved of the day's assignment. Bn Hqs received a message at 1545 that was distributed to all companies concerning plans in connection with the proximity of Russians to our lines.

Medical Detachment: Capt Mele was relieved of command and transferred to the 66th Field Hospital. Capt French assumed command.

The weather was warm, heavily overcast with rain. Visibility was fair. Combat efficiency continued to be excellent and troop morale high.

22 Apr. 1945

The 76th Inf Div reported there was no change in the enemy's front lines or enemy units in contact. A civilian stated a large tower in the center of Chemnitz was used as an OP. A French POW also stated that as of this date, Two hundred (200) infantry enemy were located in buildings and foxholes in Seifersbach with transportation of two Volkswagens and bicycles. Another civilian reported that as of this date two MG factories and underground airfield was operating in the vicinity one mile south of Chemnitz. They remained quietly on the defensive with only two rounds of artillery fire reported. A small enemy patrol attempted penetration of our lines. Total POWs for the period was 179. Every German was to be an enemy.

At 0955, nine German soldiers stopped a civilian and questioned him as to the location of our positions. Another civilian was observed pointing to an artillery OP about 1,000 yards away. The Germans proceeded north and at 1020, began firing bazookas and burp guns to that site. Shortly thereafter the nine Germans advanced toward the post but were eliminated by our artillery. The German civilian was observed going into the town of Lichtenau followed closely by 60 rounds of US artillery. Two heavy Nebelwerfer units were reported in Hainichen-Seifersbach vicinity.

Medical Corps uniform as a disguise: A fair source reported on 4 Apr many high party officials and experienced agents were now serving with the Wehrmach as Medical Corps personnel in appropriate uniforms. They hope to be taken prisoner by the Allies and to re-enter Germany after the war under false identities, per our Supreme Hqs.

The 1st Bn of the 385th Inf continued to maintain defensive positions on the infantry's right flank. They maintained contact with elements of the 355th Inf, relieved elements of the 3rd Bn on line. The F Co from the 2nd Bn continued to maintain order in Eisenberg while the 3rd Bn maintained order in Gera. They also maintained defensive positions along the regimental front; they were relieved on the right by elements of the 1st Bn. The 1st Bn of the 304th Inf maintained the defensive position along the right flank of the regimental front as well. The 2nd Bn of the Regimental Res Co., Cos E and two platoons of Co G guarded hospitals, warehouses, and supply trains in the vicinity of Burstädt and Markersdorf.

The troops of the 749th Tank Bn passed from the control of VIII Corps and was assigned to the 1st Army this date. The following info was received from G-3 of the

76th Inf Div:

"Russians are 25 kms east of us.

We will hold our present position including the Mulda River bridgehead.

Russian liaison will be permitted to cross our lines but no large bodies.

The Mulda River bridgehead will be abandoned only on agreement by the CG of the VIII Corps and the Russian Commander.

No artillery fire or tank fire will be permitted beyond support of patrols.

You may use Russian personnel now behind our lines to identify Russian units or for translating.

Div will be notified when any of your troops make contact with Russian troops.

You must be careful not to fire on Russian tanks. They will probably be in the leading elements.

Any Russian officer, Col or above, will be brought to Div Hqs by the most expedient means.

CG, 76th Inf Div, will direct each man in your organization be given the above points immediately."

This information reached this Hqs at 1545 from division at 1015: "During the period of link dash up between forces under SHAEF and the Soviet High Command, the following overall recognition signals will apply:

AEF elements will identify themselves by a series of more than two green lights or green star rockets.

AEF Armored and other vehicles will continue to carry markings specified in SHAEF operational memoranda. Soviets have been informed that yellow and/ or cerise panels may be seen from the air depending upon local orders of the day.

Soviet Armored vehicles will carry a white band painted completely around the turret in the center thereof and a white cross on top of the turret.

Aircraft will carry nationally prescribed markings.

This information will be disseminated to all elements likely to make contact with the Soviet forces."

The following Secret Message #3 was received this Hqs: "The following instructions are reproduced for the info and guidance of all concerned and confirm verbal instructions issued to the line officers at this Hqs.

"No one in the 76th Inf Div is permitted to release to the press info of contact with Soviet forces. Higher Hqs will handle such release.

In the future, an officer will lead any patrols in advance of the present front line.

The patrol will be instructed that in case Soviet forces are met, cordial greetings will be extended and the Soviet officer in charge invited to visit the American commander in the locality.

There is a probability that Soviet forces understand that they may advance to the following line from north to south: Zwick-Mulde River from Lunzenau to a point on Div's boundary southwest of Glauchau to Schlunzig to Zwickau. If this be the case the Soviet commander will be informed that the American forces will be withdrawn to the west of the line as soon as Div Hqs can issue appropriate orders. In this case, Div Hqs will be notified promptly of the Soviet Commander's desire.

In the event of withdrawal of troops behind a new line, there will be no change in Div boundaries."

The location of troops of the 749th Tank Bn was Bn Hqs, Hqs Co, and a company minus one platoon. - Taura. Co A and one platoon of D Co, attached to the 304th Inf Regt - CP and two platoons - Rollingshain with one platoon at Schonborn. B Co, attached to the 417th Inf Regt - Hartmannsdorf. C Co, attached to the 385th Inf Regt - Limbach. Svc Co at Topseifersdorf.

The 1st Plt of A Co remained at the CP location. The 2nd Plt relieved the 3rd Plt in Schonborn at 1000. The 3rd Plt returned to the CP. A light tank platoon was detached at 1600 and returned to their company. Cpl Carver, slightly wounded earlier, was evacuated. B Co, attached to the 417th Inf Regt, assembled in their area for cleaning of tanks and equipment. Capt Leighton was relieved from command and transferred to Military Government. C Co, attached to the 385th Inf Regt, remained in Limbach. The first echelon and Co A continued maintenance work on vehicles. The 2nd Plt of D Co remained in Rollingshain without receiving a mission, was relieved from alert and returned to their company in Taura.

The weather was rain changing into sleet and hail with heavy overcast breaking off and on. It cleared considerably late in the period with fast moving clouds. Visibility was fair to good. Combat efficiency was excellent and the morale of the troops high.

23 Apr. 1945

According to a report from the 76th Inf Div, the enemy generally was east of our line, 500 yards north of Seifersbach, 1,000 yards north of Merzdorf, south along the eastern bank of the Zschopau River to the autobahn. They were also 300 yards east of the southern part of Merzdorf, southwest along the eastern side of the autobahn to 1,000 yards north of Neunkirchheim. There was no change in enemy units.

Eighty (80) enemy soldiers were in Pfaffenheim. They remained quietly on defensive improving positions with one small group observed digging in. No artillery or air activity was reported. A civilian stated a US jeep was ambushed at Sildar at 1724. One squadron digging in the vicinity of the airfield was observed about 1200. A civilian also reported an underground cave two kms long north of Frankenberg that was formerly used for training. An enemy recon plane with pilot and female companion landed in the vicinity of Gera at 1000. Total POWs taken during the period - 87.

Poison for the asking: The 2ⁿᵈ Evacuation Hospital reported four cases of alcohol poisoning. Two of the enemy had already died, and one was dying. According to the victims. One had been given a drink by a Russian refugee while others had traded "K" rations to a Polish refugee for the liquor.

The 304ᵗʰ Inf Regt's 1ˢᵗ Bn maintained defensive positions along the regimental front. The 2ⁿᵈ Bn was in Regimental Res. Cos E and two platoons of Co G guarded hospitals, supply and warehouse installations in Burstädt and Markersdorf. They also maintained contact with the 6ᵗʰ Armored Div on the left. One squad of Co G relieved elements of the armored division guarding the bridge in the vicinity of Corittzhain. The 3ʳᵈ Bn patrolled through regimental area and to the front.

The 385ᵗʰ Inf Regt's 1ˢᵗ Bn defensive positions and patrolled the regimental's right flank. The 2ⁿᵈ Bn continued to maintain law and order in Gera, Eisenberg, and Jena. The 3ʳᵈ Bn maintained defensive positions on the regimental front.

The 417ᵗʰ Inf Regt's 1ˢᵗ Bn continued to maintain defensive positions patrolled to the front. The 2ⁿᵈ Bn did the same. The 3ʳᵈ Bn was in regimental reserve to be committed only on division's orders.

Bn Hqs, Hqs. Co, and D Co of the 749ᵗʰ Tank Bn were still in Taura. A Co's CP and two platoons were still in Rollingshain with one platoon in Schonborn. They were still attached to the 304ᵗʰ Inf Regt. Co B, attached to the 417ᵗʰ Inf Regt was still in Hartmannsdorf. Co C, still attached to the 385ᵗʰ Inf Regt and Svc Co were still located in their respective locations, Limbach and Topseifersdorf.

A Co, along with the 304ᵗʰ remained in position throughout the period with no enemy activity. Co B, attached to the 417ᵗʰ remained in bivouac, also without enemy activity. Co C, attached to the 385ᵗʰ remained in bivouac in Limbach and carried on first echelon maintenance. One platoon of D Co had been attached to A Co for operations and returned to D Co's assembly area in Taura at 0700.

The following message was received from the 76ᵗʰ Inf Div: "It is important that enemy railway rolling stock be captured in working condition due to a shortage of this type of equipment. Units in the forward areas will not – repeat, will not - bomb or shell locomotives or rolling stock being used by the enemy but will seize it intact."

Lt Schiff was relieved of the command of Hqs Co and assigned to Hqs and Hqs Co. Capt Nowlin assumed command of Hqs Co. 1st Lt Rolston was relieved from his assignment to Hqs Co and assigned to B Co where he assumed command.

The weather consisted of rain and heavy overcast skies early in the period changing to scattered clouds and later clear in the period. Visibility was good. Combat efficiency was excellent. Morale of the troops continued to be high.

24 Apr. 1945

There as no change in the enemy front lines or enemy units in contact was reported by the 76th Inf Div. A displaced person reported that as of yesterday, roadblocks at entrances to Leukersdorf, Seifersdorf and Adorf were in place. A civilian reported 200 to 300 troops in squadron-sized groups were in houses in Silgmar. A factory in Limbach contained MGs, bombsights, plane blisters, and pistols. The enemy maintained defensive positions and opposed our patrols with small arms fire. One of our patrols was ambushed by friendly fire.

Ten airbursts of undetermined caliber came from the western edge of Mittweida at 1340. One enemy plane came over Rollingshain at 0005 hours. One FW190 flew southeast over the area at 1215. Twenty-five to thirty troops were observed pulling back to Chemnitz at 1640.

A civilian, at 1840, reported possible counterattack in the vicinity of Auerswalde during the night. One of our patrols was pinned down by small arms fire in the vicinity of Seifersbach at 1100.

Total POWs taken for the period - 536. All of them were from units "in contact" were deserters. They disposed of their weapons as follows: One squadron of five threw weapons and ammunition into a lake below high-tension wire between Rottluff and the super highway, others in Zschopau River in the vicinity of Frankenberg or in the sand pits in the vicinity of Merzdorf. One squadron brought all their weapons including one MG to our outpost and stacked arms before surrendering.

The 6th Co., 3rd GAF Replacement Bn, strength of about 90 men with 6 light machine guns and 45 bazookas relieved an unidentified Home Guard unit in the area on the 22nd. Thirty men of the 4th Vet Replacement Co with six MGs were located in the vicinity of Merzdorf the same day and about 50 men of the same battalion in the vicinity of Sachsenburg. Volksturm in Frankenberg was said to have been dissolved and the town was free of enemy troops.

The 304th Inf Regt's 1st Bn continued maintaining defensive positions. The 2nd Bn was in regimental reserve. Co E and two platoons of Co G continued to guard hospitals, warehouses, and supply trains in the vicinity of Burstädt and Markersdorf. The 3rd Bn patrolled vigorously to the front and through the regimental area. The regiment was prepared to defend a new line.

The 385th Inf Regt's 1st Bn continued maintaining defensive positions on the front and regimental's right flank. Co C relieved elements of the 4th Armored Div for guard duty in the vicinity of Meerane, Crillitschau and Glauchau. The 2nd Bn maintained law and order in the same areas of Gera, Eisenberg, and Jena. The 3rd Bn continued to maintain defensive positions along the regimental front.

The 417th Inf Regt's 1st Bn continued to maintain defensive positions and patrolled vigorously to the line. The 2nd Bn continued to maintain defensive position and also patrolled to the line. The 3rd Bn was in regimental reserve and was prepared to defend the new line.

The following info was taken from Message #1 received at 1930 at Hqs:

"Russian forces were expected to begin their advance on the Dresden-Chemnitz Road at noon this date.

The 76th Inf Div would withdraw beginning at once within the sector to a position generally along the line.

Inf Regts with present attachments would withdraw today through the 25th of Apr within assigned sectors to a position generally along the line in respective sectors shown. They would continue missions assigned in OD #18 within assigned areas of responsibility. The 1st Bn of the 417th Inf would revert to reserve during the night in the vicinity of Muhlau.

All other troops would follow verbal orders issued. The 2nd Bn of the 417th Inf Regt would make adjustments of defensive positions to conform to the new line during the night. The 3rd Bn would occupy a defensive sector, also during the night.

Small patrols were to patrol the line to protect defensive positions and/or to gain contact with the Russians.

Fire observed missions were to be only on definitely identified hostile targets.

A report of detailed dispositions for rearward positions was to be done.

The Div's CP would open at Limbach and close at Burstädt this date, with the hour to be announced.

The front line is also designated as the U.S.S.R. . "NO BOMB LINE".

Front line troops would construct adequate foxholes for protection against bombing. Patrols would be alerted to the danger of bombing in the patrol zone."

Location of the 749th Tank Bn troops had the Bn Hqs, Hqs Co, and D Co at Taura. Co A, attached to the 304th Inf Regt's CP and two platoons at Rollingshain and one platoon at Schonborn. Co B, attached to the 417th Inf Regt, was at Hartmannsdorf. Co C, attached to the 385th Inf Regt, was in Limbach and Svc Co, at Topseifersdorf.

The 304th Inf Regt with Co A attached, had the 1st Plt relieve the 3rd Plt at Schonborn about 1100. The 3rd Plt moved at 1700 to Ottendorf, arriving at 1800. Orders were received to move to the ridge west of Krumbach and fire on Merzdorf and Bensdorf. They fired approximately 125 rounds of HE and AP and 10,000 rounds of 30 caliber MG destroying 14 houses, strong points of the enemy. The 2nd and 3rd Plts moved at 1800 from Rollingshain and arrived at Wermsdorf at 1930. The 1st Plt returned to Ottendorf and moved to Rollingshain, arriving at 2330.

The 417th Inf Regt with Co B attached arrived in the assembly area of Hartmannsdorf performing maintenance on all vehicles. They received one new 76mm tank.

The 385th Inf Regt with C Co attached performed maintenance and radio work on all vehicles. At 1800 the company marched from Limbach to Hottenstein without incident.

The Svc Co left the bivouac area at Topseifersdorf at 1800 and proceeded to the new bivouac area arriving at 1930, a distance of approximately 14 miles. All companies were alerted at 2000 for employment against a counterattack.

The weather was cool and cloudy, heavy overcast, and rain. Visibility was fair. Combat efficient was excellent and morale of the troops, high.

25 Apr. 1945

A report from the 76th Inf Div reported there was no change in the enemy's front lines. They were generally east of the line at Garitzhain, Burstädt, eastern edge of Wittgendorf, eastern edge of Bonna, Rabenstein, and the western edge off Nutzung. There was no change in enemy units.

The enemy remained on the defensive opposing our patrols with small arms fire. One group attempted an unsuccessful ambush. Artillery fire with 15 to 20 rounds was reported falling in Grosa. One unidentified plane flew south at 1320. Fifteen enemy attempted an unsuccessful ambush of three enlisted men at 1805 with seven of the enemy killed. Total POWs taken during this period - 337.

An AT platoon leader, a lieutenant from the 79th Div, was shot by a German nurse in Bublingen, 13 miles southeast of Düsseldorf, while riding down the street in a jeep. The area had been previously cleared of enemy soldiers.

As per Message #4 dated this date, In the event of contact with the Russians, this Headquarters desires the following info:

"Identification and size of unit contacted.

Does this unit have communication with the next higher Hqs? If so, what type of communication?

Time and place of contact."

As per message #3 this date:

"At 0330 hours two Nazi agents evaded guards posted at the Corps Artillery Air Field and were able to sabotage several APOs. to the extent of smashing instrument panels and damaging gas tanks before they were discovered. When the guards noticed the saboteurs, they fired upon them but the latter escaped.

Each organizing commander will bring this incident to the attention of all troops of his command and will continue to take positive steps to insure that no such incident can occur at any installation for which he is responsible."

As per Message #2 this date:

"Red Cross convoys carrying POW relief supplies are operating in enemy territory. Vehicles are painted white with red cross, driven by Swiss, guarded by Germans. Such vehicles, when captured, will be inspected to ascertain contents, identifying personnel.

If relief mission is evident, such vehicles together with all personnel and supplies will be given safe conduct back to their operating base. If doubt exists after inspection, this Hqs will be immediately notified and vehicle retained under guard until further instructions are issued."

The 304th Inf Regt's 1st Bn was in reserve in the vicinity of Langen in the Banierdersheim District. The 2nd Bn occupied positions in defense of the new line. The 385th Inf's 1st Bn, minus one platoon, maintained defensive positions along the line. Co C maintained law and order in the vicinity of Gera, Eisenberg, and Jena. Co F guarded the bridges over the Mulde River and the regimental sector. The 3rd Bn maintained defensive positions along the line with regiment continuing to patrol the line. The 417th Inf Regt's 1st Bn reverted to Regimental Res in the vicinity of Muhlau and guarded bridges. One squadron guarded a warehouse in this town. The 2nd Bn strengthened the defensive position for the new line and continually patrolled and supplied recon.

They used a sound track as a psychological weapon. Several enemy surrendered. The 3rd Bn moved from Regimental Res to provide defense of the new line. One platoon of Co K was relieved from guarding the line. One squadron of Co I guarded a warehouse in the vicinity of Hartmannsdorf. They maintained continuous recon and patrolled to the line.

Location of the 749th Tank Bn troops showed the Bn Hqs and Hqs Co as well as the Svc Co was in Limbach. A Co, attached to the 304th Inf Regt was in Wermsdorf. B Co, attached to the 417th Inf Regt was in Hartmannsdorf. C Co, attached to the 385th Inf Regt was in Hohenstein. D Co was in Div Res at Limbach.

Bn Hqs and Co received orders to move to Limbach at 1515 so they moved from Taura at 1645 closing in at Limbach at 1815. The 1st Plt of Co A, attached to the 304th, left Rollingshain at 1030, relieving the 3rd Plt at Schonborn at 1100. The 3rd Plt returned to the town vacated by the 1st Plt. The 1st Plt moved to Ottendorf, leaving at 1700 and arrived at 1800. Orders were received to move to the ridge west of Krumbach and fire on Merzdorf and Siemsdorf. The 2nd and 3rd Plts moved from Rollingshain at 1830, arriving at Wermsdorf at 1930. The 1st Plt returned to Ottendorf at 1930, moved to Wermsdorf via Rollingshain, leaving at 2130 and arriving at 0330 hours. B Co, attached to the 417th, remained in position throughout the period with no activity. C Co, attached to the 385th moved from Limbach at 1800 and closed into Hohenstein at 1830. D Co moved from Taura at 1700 and closed into Limbach at 1815, traveling approximately eight miles.

The weather was warm and clear with scattered moving clouds. Visibility was good. Combat efficiency was excellent as was the morale of the troops.

26 Apr. 1945

The 76th Inf Div reported no change in the enemy's front lines or in contact with other units. French and Polish POWs report approximately 15 SS mad 15 troops in Auerswalde with an unknown number of enemy soldiers in Mittweida and Taura as of the 24th. A Russian POW stated approximately 50 SS and an undetermined number of vehicles were on the east side of Wittgendorf and 10 SS troops in Markersdorf with two light machine guns and infantry weapons as of this date.

One 20mm AA gun and an estimated 29,000 rounds of ammunition were in the vicinity of Hohenstein, they also reported. The enemy reoccupied positions vacated by our troops, including Auerswalde, Mittweida, Taura, Markersdorf, and Wittgendorf. There was a firefight in Taura at about 1600. Enemy troops moved into Auerswalde and approximately 30 SS were trucked into Taura at 1700. A large enemy force in the vicinity of Taura ambushed one of our patrols at 2000.

Russian POWs reported SS troops re-entered Mittweida at 1330. Our artillery knocked out an enemy MG at 1531. A jeep was observed pulling under a tree to escape plane observation at 1630. Large groups of civilians moved towards Burstädt from Chemnitz between 1900 and 1930. Sounds of a steam engine were heard at 0015. Russian POWs stated that a US appointed the SS seized Burgermeister in Wittgendorf at 1215. Four 210mm pieces, two in good condition with powder charges and miscellaneous equipment was found. Total enemy POWs taken during the period – 110.

Roadblocks on the perimeter of Chemnitz consisted of overturned street cards, and guarded by three or four men with Panzerfausts. No AT guns were observed defending the roadblocks. One hundred fifty (150) SS troops were dug in guarding small bridges. The Zeisig Forest was mined. The city police of Chemnitz were recently given SS pay books and committed with a strength of about 700 men. The 3rd GAF Replacement Bn has either been renamed or formed a part of Kampf Regt Ebersdorf. MajGen Pietsch (enemy) was said to be in command of Chemnitz defenses.

The Fuhrer Escort Div: This is a Panzer Div and was reported to be the strongest and best equipped in the German army before its recent commitment in the east. According to POW statements, the 1st Panzer Bn now has 13 Mark V tanks and the 2nd Panzer Bn has four 75mm assault guns. The division was originally the Fuehrer Escort Brigade, and as such, took part in the Ardennes offensive December 1944. It was upgraded to Panzer Div in Jan 1945 by the addition of a Panzer Artillery Regt of the 120th Panzer Engineer Bn. Flak Regt, an assault gun battalion and an AT battalion. Hermann Goering was said to have withdrawn to Munich. In addition, the Panzer Grenadier Regt was strengthened with two motorized battalions of the SS Leibstandarts Adolf Hitler. Personnel of the division was considered to be the best available consisting of comparatively young soldiers, led by fanatical officers.

BrigGen Remer, CO, a major until 20 July 1944, was reported to have committed suicide. The division was known as Fegersdosch Div, implying it to be a shock or breakthrough division.

As per Message #5 this date:

"As the Russian armies approach our front, there will be a natural tendency to identify as Russian any aircraft or German, whose silhouette or markings are in doubt. This may lead us to unjustly attribute to the Russians any careless or hostile act by such aircraft or tank.

It is directed that any reports relating to hostile acts by Russian aircraft or armored vehicles be carefully investigated and confirmed at organizational level before being pass to this Hqs."

The 1st Bn of the 304th Inf Regt was in reserve in the vicinity of Langen. They maintained vehicles and equipment; they also trained and oriented new personnel. They also patrolled the rear area. The 2nd Bn maintained defensive positions. The 3rd Bn was in reserve in the vicinity of Penig. They guarded the bridges in the regimental area, maintained vehicles and equipment, and trained and oriented new personnel. Along the line the 385th Inf Regt's 1st Bn minus one platoon, maintained defensive positions. Co C maintained law and order in Glauchau, Meerane, and Crimmitschau. They patrolled to the line and conducted training. The 2nd Bn assembled in Gera, maintained law and order there pending relief. Co F guarded the bridges over the Mulde River in regimental sector and conducted training for those not engaged tactically. The 3rd Bn maintained defensive positions along the line and patrolled the line. They, too, conducted training for those not tactically engaged. The 417th's 1st Bn was in regimental reserve in the vicinity of Muhlau. They also guarded the bridges over the Mulde River. One squadron of Co C guarded a warehouse in the vicinity of Muhlau. The 2nd Bn maintained defensive positions and patrolled to the patrol line. The 3rd Bn maintained defensive positions, patrolled to the line, guarded a train, and two warehouses in the vicinity of Hartmannsdorf.

The 749th Tank Bn's locations of the troops were as follows: Bn Hqs, Hqs Co. and Svc Co were in Limbach; Co A, attached to the 304th, had the CP and two platoons at Wermsdorf with one platoon in Burstädt. B Co, attached to the 417th, was in Hartmannsdorf, Co C, attached to the 385th, was in Hohenstein. Co D was in Div Res in Limbach.

The 1st and 2nd Plts of Co A, attached to the 304th, remained at the CP location. The 3rd Plt moved from Wermsdorf to Burstädt at 1000. They had left at 1600 with the first section moved with the infantry via Taura to Garnsdorf support the patrol. The 2nd section moved south of Burstädt along the railroad to guard ammunition and gas. Both sections returned at 030 hours to Burstädt. The remainder of the battalion remained in bivouac areas during the period with no other action. Instructions issued to the CO of the 301st Engineer Bn and received at this Hqs this date. They were to make necessary arrangements with the regimental commanders concerned for rehearsal of counterattack plans with their respective areas. They were also to coordinate counterattack plans with the CG, Div artillery and submit completed plans without delay. They were also to continue present missions and be prepared to assembly on four hours notice at the division's vicinity of Limbach to repel penetration in force by enemy in sectors of the 417th and 385th Inf Regts.

The weather was warm and clear with clouds. Visibility was good. Combat efficiency was excellent. Morale of the troops was also excellent.

27 Apr. 1945

There was no change in the enemy's front lines or in their units with whom our forces had contact, according to the 76th Inf Div. An estimated 300 troops armed with 20mm AA guns, small arms, and automatic weapons were in the vicinity of Lugau. They remained quietly on the defensive with some activity heard in the vicinity of Dorna; motors and horse drawn vehicles were heard in the vicinity of Chemnitz. No air or artillery fire was reported.

A white flare in the vicinity of Kaneler and two green flares in the same location were seen at 2235. Our artillery fired enemy activity in the woods near Borna on at 0115 hours. Total POWs taken during the period - 222.

SUBVERSIVE ORGANIZATIONS: Every effort will be made to secure maximum info on werewolves and other subversive organizations. Info will be forwarded to this headquarters with the least practicable delay.

SKORZENY TACTICS AGAIN: GAF and another POW indicated the enemy was preparing another Skorzeny operation behind our lines. On the basis of info obtained from the POW, especially trained personnel were to be dropped behind our lines from small aircraft, cub type plane, with the mission of attacking personages in important OPs and other military installations. With the enemy steadily being compressed into the final throes of last-stand warfare, it must constantly be kept in mind that in his desperation, he would be capable of resorting to any extremist activities. They would be wholly of a desperado nature and directly have no effect on major tactical operations. However, by such attacks, the enemy could commit spite murders and costly acts of sabotage. It is therefore strongly urged that all units be aggressively alert of this danger, particularly in rear areas, and that every precaution be taken to maintain unceasingly watchful guards at all CPs and other important military installations.

The 1511 GHQ Fortress Artillery Bn with about 300 men, eleven 122mm guns were observed in Tanneberg on 19 Apr destined for the Erzgebirge Mountains after having come from the Rune district. Fuehrer Begleit Div had three regiments (Armored

Regt, Inf Regt., and Anti-Aircraft Regt.) The infantry had about 150 men, Armored Regiment's 1st Bn had 10 Mark V tanks, about 50 other motorized vehicles, and about 400 men. The 2nd Bn had six assault guns (75mm long barreled guns on Mark III chassis), and about 200 men. Enemy personnel were dug in along the eastern edge of the woods west of Langen. The Volkssturm (Home Guards) Chemnitz has four companies, about 100 men each in army uniform. The 1st Co was located in the vicinity of Borna on 25 Apr. Thirty-five (35) SS personnel were also observed in Ottendorf on the same date.

The 304th Inf Regt's 1st Bn was in reserve in the vicinity of Langen. They maintained motors and equipment, trained and oriented personnel. Also, they patrolled the rear area. The 2nd Bn maintained defensive positions. The 3rd Bn was in reserve in the vicinity of Penig. They guarded bridges in the regimental area, patrolled to the line, maintained motors and equipment, trained and oriented personnel not tactically engaged.

The 385th Inf's 1st Bn, minus one platoon, maintained defensive positions and patrolled to the line.

Co C maintained law and order in Glauchau, Crimmitschau, and Meerane. The 2nd Bn assembled in the vicinity of Gera, pending relief. They trained personnel not tactically engaged. The 3rd Bn maintained defensive positions, patrolled to the line and trained personnel not tactically engaged.

The 417th Inf's 1st Bn was in regimental reserve in the vicinity of Muhlau. They guarded bridges across the Mulde River. One squadron of Co C guarded a warehouse near the river. The 2nd Bn maintained defensive positions, patrolled to the line. The 3rd Bn maintained defensive positions, patrolled to the patrol line, guarded train and two warehouses in the vicinity of Hartmannsdorf.

Location of the troops of the 749th Tank Bn was the same as the previous day.

Co A, attached to the 304th Inf Regt, had the 1st and 3rd Plts remain at the CP in Wermsdorf without any enemy activity. The 2nd Plt left Burstädt at 1300 and proceeded to the railroad southwest of Diesendorf via Taura, and arrived at their objective at 1345. An ammunition train consisting of approximately 30 cars was guarded by a few SS troops and was destroyed. An ordnance officer rode in a tank with the purpose of setting ammunition on fire but tanks fired one round in each car, destroying all the ammunition. Tanks returned to Burstädt at 1430. The remainder of the battalion remained in position with no activity during the period. Companies conducted training schedules as submitted in accordance with master training schedule from this headquarters with a copy submitted to division.

The weather was warm and clear with scattered moving clouds. Visibility was excellent. Combat Efficiency was excellent as was the morale of the troops.

28 Apr. 1945

According to the 76th Inf Div a civilian stated 20 troops and some vehicles were in Madersdorf. POWS stated KG Leitschulde, organized in Leisnig on 14 Apr were mostly from personnel of the 108th Inf Replacement Bn and had moved to Sieselwitz on 24 Apr. KG consisted of five companies, strength approximately 600 men with 25 light machine guns. A radio parts factory and possible a V-1 platoon was in Volkenberg. The enemy remained unaggressive with a few flares reported in Chemnitz. An estimated 20 to 25 rounds of artillery fell in the vicinity of Borna and an unknown number of white phosphorous shells fell in Rabenstein. Two red flares were seen in Limbach at 2230. Four to five white flares fell in Chemnitz at 1200. Total POWs taken during the period - 235.

The 304th Inf Regt's 1st Bn was in reserve in the vicinity of Langen. They maintained material, trained and oriented personnel. They also patrolled the rear area. The 2nd Bn was in reserve in the vicinity of Penzig. They guarded bridges in the regimental area, patrolled to the patrol line, maintained material, trained and oriented personnel not engaged tactically.

The 385th Inf Regt's 1st Bn, minus one platoon, maintained defensive positions. Co C maintained law and order in Glauchau, Crimmitschau, and Meerane. They patrolled, trained and oriented personnel not engaged tactically. The 2nd Bn, minus one platoon, was assembled in the vicinity of Gera pending relief. Co F guarded bridges over the Mulde River in the 385th Inf's zone. They trained and oriented personnel not engaged tactically. The 3rd Bn maintained defensive positions, and patrolled to the front.

The 417th Inf Regt's 1st Bn was in regimental reserve in the vicinity of Muhlau. The 2nd Bn maintained defensive positions and patrolled to the front line. The 3rd Bn maintained defensive positions and patrolled to the front line. They also guarded a train and two warehouses in Hartmannsdorf.

As per Secret Message #1 this date: Reference US Forces artillery fire in relation to Soviet Air Forces bomb line (present limiting line as published in Message #1, this Hqs, dated 28 Apr, south from intersection with division's northern boundary to the railroad, thence a line along the railroad to a point in Chemnitz, thence a straight line. Observed fire only may be placed on clearly defined hostile targets north of the boundary between the 76th and 89th Inf Divs and east of the Soviet bomb line. No restrictions on type artillery fire for targets in areas south of boundary between the 76th and 89th Inf Divs, and west of the Soviet bomb line.

As per Secret Message #2 this date: The following is quoted from a letter from the CG, 12th Army Group, for the info and guidance of all concerned:

1. "Due to repeated reports from Army units that our planes, some with enemy markings, are bombing and strafing friendly troops and installations, the 9th Air Force has conducted a complete investigation of all incidents reported since 24 Dec 1944. As a result of these investigations, the following points have been brought out.

a. No American aircraft shot down by friendly AAA was found to be operated by German pilots. There was not any evidence whatever disclosed which would indicate that the German Air Force had used captured American airplanes operationally not that American type airplanes with German markings had flown over the front lines. Such reports were due to faulty recognition and attempts by some ground personnel to identify airplanes by distinctive markings. It is impossible from the ground to identify airborne airplanes by distinctive markings.

b. There were three incidents where friendly aircraft believed to be operated by the enemy or with enemy markings were shot down by friendly ground fire. In each case, the aircraft were found to have had Allied markings and were piloted by American pilots, one of whom was killed. Two of these pilots were interrogated and found to be operating out of their prescribed areas due to navigational errors.

2. It is concluded from the above that the Germans are not using American type aircraft in attacks against ordnance trucks and that attacks by American planes are made against ordnance trucks because of navigational errors or failure to properly identify ordnance trucks. Vehicles will use all available identification panels in order to lessen the chances of attack by friendly planes."

The 749th Tank Bn had their troops located as previously with the CP and two platoons of Co A in Wermsdorf.

All companies remained in position with no activity during the period. They all conducted training schedules as submitted in accordance with the master training schedule. D Co with one platoon was to be alerted for possible employment with the 301st Engineer Bn with details of mission and hour to be announced. They received overlay and according counterattack plans were drawn up by the engineer battalion. Co C's Capt McProuty was evacuated to the hospital. Lt Winkler assumed command of Co C.

The weather was warm, heavily overcast with rather high clouds and rain throughout the period. Visibility was fair. Combat efficiency was excellent; morale excellent.

29 Apr. 1945

The 76th Inf Div reported no change in the enemy front lines and no change in their units. A bicycle patrol of nine men covered the area between Mittweida to the vicinity of Burstädt every day at 1100 and 1900. An SS motorized patrol from Mittweida to Markersdorf, Garnsdorf, Dratsdorf, and Chemnitz is observed daily at 1500. No enemy activity was reported. A POW deserter, however, stated daily bicycle to motorized patrols operate between Mittweida and Chemnitz. Total POWs taken during the period - 149. The Alarm Co in Schönau was reportedly formed from personnel of the 173rd Artillery Bn and arrived from Pilsner to Chemnitz on 16 Apr. They were in position along the super highway in the vicinity Schönau with 140 men, rifles and bazookas as of yesterday. One Plt was sent bicycles on recon of the super highway southwest of Chemnitz to get info about our front lines; after recon, they were to reassemble. POWs saw no German troops or supporting vehicles between Geyer and the front lines. The 4th Co of KG Pusch formed mainly from personnel of the 4th Field Kitchen Replacement Co H in Chemnitz has about 120 men with eight light machine guns along the super highway in the vicinity of Schönau on 27 Apr.

The 1st Bn of the 304th Inf Regt was in reserve in the vicinity of Langen. They patrolled the railroad areas. The 2nd Bn maintained defensive positions, guarded hospital at Burstädt. The 3rd Bn, in Penig, guarded bridges in the regimental area and patrolled to the patrol line.

The 385th Inf's 1st Bn, minus one platoon, maintained defensive positions. Co C maintained law and order in Glauchau, Crimmitschau, and Meerane. Co E relieved Co C to take over their maintenance of law and order. The 2nd Bn was relieved from maintaining law and order in Gera and assembled in the vicinity of Hohenstein. The 3rd Bn maintained defensive positions and patrolled to the front line.

The 417th Inf Regt was in regimental reserve in the vicinity of Muhlau; they guarded bridges across the Mulde River. One squadron of Co C guarded a warehouse at Muhlau. The 2nd Bn maintained defensive positions and patrolled. The 3rd Bn maintained defensive positions, guarded train, and guarded two warehouses at Hartmannsdorf.

There was no change in location of the troops of the 749th Tank Bn.

The entire sector was quiet throughout the period with no activity with the enemy.

All companies conducted training as outlined in the training schedule. A Co's 1ˢᵗ Plt relieved the 2ⁿᵈ Plt in Burstädt at 1200; the 3ʳᵈ Plt remained in position. D Co alerted one platoon in connection with counterattack plans of the 301ˢᵗ Engineer Bn.

The weather was cool, bright with slight clouds. Visibility was excellent. Combat efficiency - excellent; morale excellent.

30 Apr. 1945

According to the 76ᵗʰ Inf Div there was no change in enemy front lines or enemy units in contact. A POW stated that 20 enemy were committed as AT commandos along the eastern side of the autobahn to our front and were armed with two Panzerfausts per man, several semi-automatic rifles and rifles. The enemy remained unaggressive. A small group of 30 enemy was observed digging and 50 to 100 entering the woods. Vehicular activity was heard in the vicinity of Borna and Silgmar. Artillery fire was negligible with three wounds of white phosphorous. A plane was shot down by small arms fire at 0700. A civilian reported three SS cut telephone wire in Wittgendorf. Total POWs taken during the period - 91.

SABOTAGE: Six cases of liquor poisoning was reported during the period resulting in the death of four and serious illness of two. Three obtained the liquor in Weissenfels and it was reported to have been colorless, with an odor like airplane "dope"; the effect was delayed, as the men did not become ill until two days after having consumed it.

TRANSLATION OF CAPTURED DOCUMENT: "Der Fuehrer Orders "The situation on the western front is unfavorable to us because of the enemy's superiority in manpower, material and ammunition. Despite this, or rather because of it, we have to keep our energy up to key pitch. Only attacks against the enemy's flanks and disruption and cutting of his line of command guarantee success. Success in battle consists of constant attacks on the enemy in conjunction with partisan warfare. The main point in these attacks is to force the enemy with cunning guile to position his troops which are spread all over the country, in greater strength in those areas where he cannot afford to do so. Our own attacks are therefore not to be directed against the enemy's strong points but against his weak points - flanks, rear, line of command - if possible in his administrative areas. Infiltration of our own attacking troops through the enemy lines is therefore of supreme importance. We have to adopt the same method that was shown and taught to us by the Russians in the years 1942-1944. Our men have to infiltrate through the lines by ones or in small groups, supplied with sufficient ammunition, patrol and other material, and must attack only if they reach the rear areas where they can achieve complete surprise against the most sensitive points.

This order will naturally be applied to any major operation. These new orders for officers and NCOs will be transmitted immediately to all troops of the Army in the West." (Signed ADOLF HITLER)

Army Group Blumentritt: "This important order has to be made known immediately by all possible means (in writing, by telephone, or orally) down to the last man." (Signed BLUMENTRITT, General.)

The 1st Bn of the 304th Inf Regt remained in reserve in the vicinity of Langen and patrolled railroad areas. The 2nd Bn maintained defensive positions, guarded the hospital at Burstädt. The 3rd Bn remained in reserve in Penig. They guarded bridges in the regimental area and patrolled to the front line.

The 385th Inf Regt's 1st Bn maintained defensive positions and patrolled. The 2nd Bn, minus one platoon, remained in the assembly area in the vicinity of Hohenstein. Co E maintained law and order in Meerane, Crimmitschau, and Glauchau. Co F guarded the bridges over the Mulde River. The 3rd Bn maintained defensive positions and patrolled to the front.

The 417th Inf Regt's 1st Bn remained in Regimental Res in the vicinity of Muhlau and guarded bridges across the Mulde River. One squadron of Co C guarded a warehouse at the town of Muhlau. The 2nd Bn maintained defensive positions, and patrolled to the line. The 3rd Bn maintained operations defending the line. They also conducted training for those not tactically engaged.

The location of the troops of the 749th Tank Bn remained the same as previously. The entire sector was quiet throughout the period with no enemy activity for the companies. The battalion call words were changed effective 0600 this date. The new call words were as follows: Hqs and Svc Cos - HUDSON; A Co - AUBURN; B Co - BANTAM; C Co - CORD; D Co - DOUGH. The Assault Gun and Mortar Plts' radios will be set on headquarter channel, changing to the company channel when they work.

The weather was cold and windy with fast moving clouds. Visibility was good. Combat efficiency was excellent; morale also was excellent.

1 MAY THROUGH
9 MAY 1945

1 May 1945

The report from the 76th Inf Div the enemy front lines were generally east of the line of Goritz in Burstädt, the eastern edge of Wittgendorf, the eastern edges of Borna and Habenstein, and the western edge of Nutzung. Enemy units in contact were the KG Gruse, 1st and 2nd Cos of the 10th Recon Replacement Bn. Also in contact was the 2nd Co of the 4th Replacement Bn, the 1st and 2nd Cos of the 3rd Nebelwerfer Replacement Bn and elements of the 413th Armored Inf, the Inf Replacement Bn and the 3rd Air Force Replacement Bn from the GK Thomas.

A civilian stated that troops were in Rathaus and Taura and in many were entrenched in Littweim. Our patrols operating to the patrol line encountered no enemy; however, the enemy does occupy Rathaus and Taura. Air activity was negligible with two unidentified planes reported over the division's sector; no artillery fire was reported.

One enemy truck moved northeast in Rollingmain at 1730. Six enemy soldiers in civilian clothes and a vehicle with a white star identification were captured at 0200 hours. It was reported that KG Zeisig was formed from stragglers and convalescents. The strength was estimated to be about 400 men and 20 LMBs. About 200 enemy were located along the super highway and 100 men were at Neunkirchheim.

One POW stated the KG was under command of KG Gruse (CO Oberst Gruse). This KG is said to be in tactical command of all units in line along the super highway. Estimated strength was 2,000 men. KG has five light tanks and two assault guns located in the woods northeast of Olderan. Oberst Gruse was said to be in contact with Hauptman Probst, acting CG, or remnants of Furher Begleit Div. There was a meeting on 29 Apr to reach an agreement whether to surrender both KGs as a whole to US forces or to build one large KG to be committed against the Russians. There was a straggling collecting point at Ebersdorf and 50 SS at Auerswalde.

More Sabotage: Guards on the autobahn bridge comprised of two men dressed as civilians at 0230 hours on 25 Apr as they were preparing to blow the bridge. Upon examination of the piers it was found each pier had 26 holes, 13 of which were filled with explosive, sealed and camouflaged with a light coat of cement mortar making the holes very difficult to distinguish. The explosive was in the form of crushed rock and would easily pass as such. Samples examined by the 1st US Army was found to be of the same type as had been previously been found as filling in Topf mines.

The 1st Bn of the 304th Inf Regt was in reserve in the vicinity of Langen and performed maintenance on material, guarded the hospitals in Meerane and Crimmitschau. The troops also trained and oriented personnel and patrolled the railroad areas. The 2nd Bn maintained defensive positions and guarded the hospital at Burstädt. The 3rd Bn was in reserve in the vicinity of Penig. They guarded bridges in the regimental area, patrolled to the patrol line, performed maintenance on material, and trained and oriented troops.

The 1st Bn of the 385th Inf Regt maintained defensive positions, trained and oriented troops. The 2nd Bn, minus one platoon, was in the assembly area in the vicinity of Hohenstein. Co E maintained law and order in Meerane, Crimmitschau, and Glauchau. Co F guarded bridges over the Mulde River and relieved the 3rd Bn at 1445. Co I relieved Co E and also maintained law and order in Meerane, Crimmitschau, and Glauchau. Co K relieved Co F and guarded the bridges across the Mulde River. Training was conducted for troops not engaged tactically.

The 1st Bn of the 417th Inf Regt was in regimental reserve in the vicinity of Muhlau. They also guarded bridges across the Mulde River. One squadron of Co C continued to guard warehouses at Muhlau.

The Armed Forces of the 749th Tank Bn were attached as follows: Cos A and C were attached to the 417th Inf Regt, Co C attached to the 385th Inf Regt, and Co D was in reserve in the vicinity of Lambrecht. Bn Hqs, Hqs Co, and the Svc Co with two platoons were at Wermsdorf.

Limited training was conducted for those not tactically engaged and performed maintenance on equipment. Law and order continued to be conducted in Glauchau, Meerane, and Crimmitschau.

The entire sector was quiet throughout. All companies conducted training as outlined in training manual.

The weather was cold with visibility fair to good. Combat efficiency was excellent as was the morale of the troops.

2 May 1945

The 76th Inf Div reported the enemy front lines showed no change and the same enemy units in contact showed no change.

Three liberated POWs reported about seven enemy gun carriers. Two hundred (200) Volksturm (Home Guards) entered Chemnitz along with gendarmes from nearly all towns east and north of the town. There were obstacles along the entire length of Michelstrasse as of 29 Apr. They also stated there were approximately 10 tanks in the vicinity believed to be in the woods west of Martna Vald as of 30 Apr. Approximately 20 motorcycles and also an undetermined number of motor vehicles left towards Freiburg. There were 50 motor vehicles with 20 SS armed with Panzerfausts moving toward Dresden yesterday. Activity was negligible consisting of sniper fire with increased flare activity during the period. One unidentified plane was reported over the civilian sector that flew over Burstädt at 2205.

Ten SS with MGs, mortar,` and AA weapons were fired upon by our troops at 1930. Possible mortar positions in the vicinity of Borna were fired at 2200 and we received fire from the northwestern edge of Wittgendorf at 2210. Three white flares were observed in the vicinity of Chemnitz at 2330. Small arms fire was received from Osprung about 2300. Red, white, and two green flares were observed in the vicinity of Luchau at 2245.

Liberated POWs also `reported enemy women, approximately 35 years of age, would go through our lines to get info. They would arrive in Chemnitz in uniform, change to civilian clothes and go through the lines at about 0900 daily and return four hours later. Troops reported performing the same function.

BEWARE OF THE NAZIS. A 20-year-old German came to CIC Hqs offering any and all assistance against the Nazis. He claimed to have been a prisoner in a concentration camp for a year and wanted to get even. After interrogation his story fell apart. He was searched carefully and in his shoes were two certificates of fellow soldiers acknowledging the fact that the Nazi hater had personally accounted for two tanks, the latest on 11 Apr. He admitted then he was trying to conceal the fact he was a soldier so he could go home, 11 kms away. He would then work for us as he saw fit, and in the event he was "contacted" by the Nazi underground, he could show the certificate of soldiering to prove he was working against us. The rapid and aggressive advance of CCR prevented his getting a 3rd tank for which he would have been awarded a 15-day furlough (5th Armored Div.)

Enemy personnel in the railroad areas is an extract from a report from Corps Security Commander: "We continue to hear stories to the effect American units are telling people to get into civilian clothing, get off the highway, go home, and cause no trouble. The people concerned are trying to do this with the utmost determination. We have apprehended a large number that had already traveled 50 to 100 kms without having been stopped more than once or twice, then being allowed to proceed. One POW with a Solduch mine in his possession stated he was stopped three times by Americans at posts on the highway. Each time he told them he was a civilian, and they did not ask to see his papers, so he did not show them."

All German soldiers in uniform or civilian clothes must be taken into custody and evacuated through POW channels. Former members of the German armed forces who have been discharged since 6 June 1944 should be arrested and turned over to CIC for investigation. Any civilian found more than six kms from his home or out of his house after curfew is guilt of violating restrictions imposed by the military government unless he has an official pass in English and German signed by the aforesaid. He should be turned over to the nearest military government for detachment for trial.

Enemy agents at large: Proof continues to mount that the enemy has left behind an extensive network of espionage agents. Within the past five days VII Corp CIC has apprehended and obtained confessions from four such agents. Two possessed radio sets. Such operations are a constant menace not only as relayers of technical intelligence but as a potential info and directing service for all forms of subversive and guerrilla activity. Security precautions cannot be too painstaking (69th Inf Div Agents in Russian uniforms.) Enemy agent in civilian clothes surrendered in the vicinity of Erlau. One agent was wearing Russian trousers beneath his civilian clothes. He admitted he was an agent and revealed he was to start on a mission the night of 1 May with two companions - a Russian and a Hitler Youth. They were to wear Russian uniforms, carry pistols, and hand grenades. The mission was to contact our troops, pass as Russians, and try to get info. On the way back they were to sabotage our equipment and troops. All troops should be suspicious of attempts to obtain info of our dispositions and plans. Such persons should be sent under guard to the closest CIC detachment for screening. The Frauleins, too. Five girls, between the ages of 15 and 18, were arrested 30 Apr. Two were caught red-handed cutting wire. The other three were suspected of plotting against our front line positions. This information came from the 89th Inf Div.

The 304th Inf's 1st Bn was in reserve in the vicinity of Meerane and Rollingmain. They guarded hospitals in Meerane but were relieved from guarding hospitals in Crimmitschau. The 2nd Bn maintained defensive positions in Burstädt. The 3rd Bn remained in reserve in Penig as well as guarded bridges in regimental area. They also patrolled, conducted maintenance of material, trained and oriented troops. The 385th Inf Regt's 1st Bn maintained defensive positions and patrolled.

The 417th Inf Regt's 1st Bn was in regimental reserve in Muhlau. They guarded bridges across the Mulde River. All other activities remain the same as the previous day.

As per Field Message #5 this date, read as follows:

"German" soldiers in civilian clothes have been recently taken from towns in the division's area. The assumption may be made that enemy soldiers have infiltrated into our lines for one purpose or another and will continue to do so as long as areas to our front remain uncleared.

Commencing without delay organizations assigned areas of responsibility by this directive will initially clear all towns of enemy soldiers within respective areas assigned and will be prepared to comb some areas again on division's "orders".

COs of the 749ᵗʰ Tank Bn and the 691ˢᵗ TD Bn, and the 76ᵗʰ Artillery Div, will make available such personnel as are available to the CO, 778ᵗʰ AAA AW Bn to assist in the clearing. The CO of the 301ˢᵗ Engineer Bn will similarly furnish personnel to the CO of the 76ᵗʰ Recon Troops to clear another area.

All companies of the 749ᵗʰ Tank Bn were in the same locations as the previous day.

The 3ʳᵈ Plt of A Co relieved the 1ˢᵗ Plt in Burstädt at 1300. The 2ⁿᵈ Plt remained at the CP location. There was no other activity throughout the period for the battalion. All companies conducted training as outlined in the training schedule.

The weather was cold, slightly windy, and cloudy. Visibility was fair. Combat efficiency and morale - both excellent.

3 May 1945

The 6ᵗʰ Inf Div's general situation revealed no change in the enemy's front lines and no change in enemy units. Our troops were in Wermsdorf. The enemy remained unaggressive with scattered action in the division's sector. Considerable flare activity was reported.

A band of 30 boys and men who are operating the pushcarts was equipped with dynamite and other sabotage materials. It is possible other groups may use carts to haul their supplies and simulate being refugees. SS members\ and, Waffers SS members are reported to have blood markings tattooed on the upper left arm about one inch below the armpit. Information received from the 1ˢᵗ Army indicates; however, that since Jan 1945, attempts have been made by many to remove them by burning or by use of a silver nitrate pencil. It is believed it is impossible to remove the tattoo marks without leaving scars. In many cases where operations have presumably faded, large infected areas have been observed. Any POW found to have scars that might indicate that tattoo marks have been removed will be considered a possible member of the SS and will be treated accordingly until such time as interrogation either proves or disproves these suspicions.

Never too young: Two boys, one 15 and the other 6, approached a battalion mess hall and attempted to throw a hand grenade into the building.

The older lost control after pulling the pin dropped the grenade and the boy ran. Both were caught in the explosions; both were wounded but the youngster escaped. The 15-year-old had another grenade in his pocket and both were of American make.

Another incident: One of our patrols apprehended several civilians carrying TNT. They stated their mission was to blow up a factory.

The division continued defending the patrol line, conducted training for those not tactically engaged. Several male civilians were screened.

The location of troops of the 749th Tank Bn remains unchanged.

All platoons of the company remained in their respective positions. The company screened Wermsdorf for possible enemy soldiers and lethal weapons. Six POWs were taken. The 1st Plt of Co D was ordered to report to the 778th Air Bn Group at 0900. They received instructions and proceeded to Crimmitschau where they screened civilians for German soldiers. They completed two districts of the town and returned to the commanding group at 1730. The remainder of the battalion remained in bivouac areas.

The weather was cold and cloudy; it rained and sleeted throughout the period. Visibility was fair. Combat efficiency and morale of the troops remained excellent.

4 May 1945

According to the 76th Inf Div general situation, there was no change in the enemy's front lines as well as no change in enemy units.

Liberated POWs stated Freibach was heavily defended and many troops were in the woods to the north. The enemy remained unaggressive with 65 deserting to the front line units and many more apprehended in railroad areas. Flares were continually active, especially in the vicinities of Borna and Chemnitz. Three planes flew over the civilian sector including one ME262. One round of white phosphorous fell near the autobahn three miles east of Limbach. An unidentified plane cut its motor at 0335 hours. One ME262 flew over the area near Siegstadt and a possible tank was observed three miles southeast of Chemnitz.

Other liberated POWs stated 50 staff personnel were in Chemnitz. The 1st Army reported a unit called commando Villerstock was activated 10 days ago with about 50 small aircraft and 100 pilots in the vicinity southwest of Munich. Their mission was to destroy railroads and bridges in the same areas. They carried explosives and were instructed to go back home after completing the mission. There was a request for any info concerning this unit.

POWs also stated Chemnitz had two companies, about 150 men each with bazookas and a few MGs. That regiment had been organized about 27 Apr.

Fuhrer Escort Div: Four hundred (400) men under Maj Schnapauf escaped a Russian pocket. All personnel were reformed into KG Schnapauf. Remnants of the division attached to the Fuhrer Escort Div was on the front as separate regiment of which there were about 100 men (motorized) and had escaped a Russian, arrived in the vicinity of Zerau yesterday. The CO was Oberst Erhardt.

The division continued defensive missions and defended the front line. Training was conducted for those not tactically engaged, performed maintenance, maintained law and order in Glauchau, Meerane, and Crimmitschau. They guarded bridges over the Mulde River and screened male civilians.

The location of troops of the 749th Tank Bn remained the same as previously.

The 2nd Plt of Co E relieved the 3rd Plt in Burstädt at 1200. The 1st Plt remained in Wermsdorf. One officer and 16 enlisted men of Co D left the Co CP at 0800 to continue their mission with the 778th Bn in screening the town of Crimmitschau and returned at 1830.

The weather was cold, cloudy with fair visibility. Excellent morale of the troops and combat efficiency remained.

5 May 1945

According to the 76th Inf Div there was no change in the enemy's front lines or enemy units in contact.

A liberated POW stated there were two roadblocks on the road through Habenstein, an estimated 300m distance between outposts and deep trenches on the east side of the stadium. Civilians stated 6-12 man group patrolled Wittgendorf at night by 3 to 8 men, a motorized group, and Taura. Another liberated POW stated troops moved east out of Hilbersdorf about 0200 hours and through Nieder Wiesa at 2100. The enemy was unaggressive with a small group observed digging in. Flare activity was moderate in the division's sector.

Many POWs were apprehended as a result of screening operations. A civilian reported 22 US and 30 British POWs were in a factory in Geyer. There was small arms fire west of Chemnitz at 1956. Total POWs for the period - 492. Effective immediately only observed artillery fire will be placed on targets beyond the front line.

The 749th Tank Bn situation remained the same with the troops in the same location.

All Plts of Co A remained in their respective positions. The 2nd Plt assisted the 304th

Inf Regt in removing enemy and equipment from Taura from 1300 to 1500. One officer and 16 enlisted men of B Co continued in screening civilians for general soldiers in the town of Crimmitschau; they left the company at 0800 and returned at 1945.

The weather was cool, solidly overcast, with rain during the entire period. Visibility was fair. Combat efficiency and morale of the troops remained excellent.

6 May 1945

The enemy remained quietly on the defensive with one group observed digging in. Remnants of the 2ⁿᵈ Bn, 1ˢᵗ Armored Artillery Regt, surrendered to our troops last evening. Flare activity was decreased with just a few reported in the division's sector. Enemy aircraft was over the area but no attacks were reported. Seventy-five (75) French POWs were released this morning by the enemy because of food shortage. Unknown artillery and caliber fell in Grednitz from 0905 to 1000. Four enemy soldiers in a vehicle from Chemnitz were captured after entering US lines by mistake at 1200.

The division continued to defend the patrol line and conduct training for those not engaged tactically. Maintenance on material was performed; bridges, hospitals, and other installations in the division's sector were guarded. The mission of screening male civilians was completed. The troops were notified that H hour for the 89ᵗʰ Inf Div would be 0700 early tomorrow. VIII Corps would advance the right flank; the 76ᵗʰ Inf Div would continue their present missions. There was unrestricted artillery fire on areas in the zone of the VIII Corps west of the Grednitz - Prague line. Every precaution will be taken to prevent firing on Soviet forces that may be operating in the zone of VIII Corps' advance.

The location of the troops of the 749ᵗʰ Tank Bn remained unchanged.

The 1ˢᵗ Plt of A Co relieved the 2ⁿᵈ Plt in Burstädt. The 3ʳᵈ Plt remained at the CP location. Two Tanks of C Co moved to a point near Chemnitz for the purpose of arranging negotiations for the return of American prisoners but due to extremely poor visibility, no contact could be made and tanks returned to the company area. One officer and 16 enlisted men left the Co CP at 1000 to finish details on screening of Germans in Crimmitschau and returned to the CP at 1430.

The following message was received via telephone at 1925 from the 76ᵗʰ Inf Div: "Effective 1800 this date, the VII and VIII Corps as presently constituted pass operational control to the Ninth US Army; assignment and attachment of units to the Ninth Army and complete control of the area occupied by these corps will be effective

1800. You will continue in your present mission."

The weather was cold and rainy. Visibility was fair to poor. Combat efficiency and morale also remained excellent.

7 May 1945

There was no change in the enemy's front lines or units in contact according to the 76th Inf Bn. No aggressive enemy activity was reported during the period. Individuals and small groups continued to desert to front line troops. Five vehicles and a possible tank moved from Claussnetz to Laupersdorf. Four vehicles returned to Claussnitz at approximately 1500. Total POWs for the period: 349.

POWs of the 92nd Armored Artillery Regt stated the division pulled back from the eastern front without heavy losses and arrived in the vicinity of Klotzsche 28 Apr. Components of the division was the 21st Armored Regt, 59th and 112th Armored Inf Regts, 92nd Armored Artillery Regt with strength as of 3 May estimated to be approximately 8,000 men, about 100 tanks, mostly Mark Vs and Mark VIIs. An auxiliary regiment moved from Chemnitz to the vicinity of Langerfeld yesterday. Kamp Regt Ebersdorf had about 120 men with 6 light machine guns and 50 bazookas from the 2nd Co as of yesterday.

VIII Corps passed to Operational Control of the 9th US Army and hostilities were to cease.

Results of the period: Our troops continued with the same activities as noted yesterday including guarding bridges, hospitals and other installations in the division's sector.

Regarding the 749th Tank Bn: Hqs & Hqs Co and the Svc Co were in Limbach, A Co, assigned to the 304th Inf Regt was there as well. B Co, attached to the 417th Inf Regt was in Hartmannsdord with C Co being attached to the 385th Inf Regt in Hohenstein. D Co was also in Limbach. This is the749th's 273rd day in combat.

As per Message #2 this date: "Co A, 6th Armored reports Russians moving south on main highway. Will enter our lines at 1250." As per Message #27:

"A representative of the German High Command signed the unconditional surrender of all German land, sea and air forces in Europe to the Allied Expeditionary Forces (AEF) and simultaneously to the Soviet High Command at 1041, Central European time, 7 May, under which all forces will cease active operations at 0011 hours 9 May 1945.

Effective immediately all offensive operations by AEF will cease and troops will remain in present positions. Those involved in occupational duties will continue. Due to difficulties of communication there may be some delay in similar orders reaching enemy troops, so full defensive precautions will be taken.

No. Repeat - No release will be made to the press pending an announcement by the heads of the three governments. Present missions will be continued until further orders."

The troops of the 749th Tank Bn remained as previously.

All companies conducted training. There was no enemy action during the period. Effective 1800 this date, troops were operationally under the control of the 9th US Army. Recon was being made for billeting. D Co was at Gera where ordnance inspection of combat vehicles would take place tomorrow.

Weather was cold with rain, clearing early in the period. Visibility was fair to excellent. Combat efficiency and morale of the troops continued to be excellent.

8 May 1945

The 76th Inf Div reports there is no enemy front line and no enemy units in contact. There was slight air activity with no attacks reported during the period. Large groups continued to desert to the front line troops. With the unconditional surrender of Germany of all land, sea and air forces, the enemy capabilities are decidedly restricted. Nevertheless, a few fanatical diehards, determined to cause as much damage as possible to our troops, are at large in territory already occupied. Sabotage and sniping remain a constant threat to security. With German companies in a state of chaos there may still be small groups capable of resisting who have not year heard of the surrender. At 0800 a JU88 was believed to have been shot down by our AA. One FW190 was reported flying very low east to west. There was a large fire at Altendorf at 2124.

The division continued to defend limiting line, conducted training, performed maintenance, guarded bridges, hospitals, and other installations in the division's sector.

Elements of the Russian Army were contacted at 0700.

Locations of the troops of the 749th Tank Bn remain unchanged with the exception of Co D that was now in Gera.

The 3rd Plt of Co A relieved the 1st Plt in Burstädt at 1300. The 2nd Plt remained at the CP location. D Co left the bivouac area at Limbach at 0600 and traveled to Langenburg arriving at 0930 having traveled approximately 40 miles; Langenburg was where ordnance inspection was done of all combat vehicles of all companies would take place.

Advance billeting party was sent to Russdorf, Chursdorf, and Langenburg in preparation for movement in the next period.

The weather was warm and clear with good visibility. Combat efficiency and morale of the troops was once again excellent.

9 May 1945

The 76th Inf Div report: Twelve (12) planes flew over the division's sector from 1800 to 2000. No attacks were reported. Hundreds of enemy military were continuing to surrender to our troops. One enemy plane landed at 2000. Six planes flew at 2400; two ME109s flew over at 1000. One FW190 flew at 1403. Two jet-propelled planes flew over north at 1940. An enemy pilot attempted to cross a bridge on foot in Langenburg and was mortally wounded after shooting one of our guards when called upon to halt. This occurred at 0006 hours.

Armed Forces: The 749th Tank Bn was relieved from attachment to the Inf Regts. B Co was at Gera for ordnance inspection.

Training was conducted for those not engaged in security of administration. The following instructions will go in effect immediately:

"No civilians will be permitted to cross our lines.

No American troops, except by proper authority, will be permitted to cross our lines from west to east.

All attempts by American military personnel to cross our lines from west to east without proper authority will be reported immediately to this Hqs giving names of such personnel and units to which they belong.

Permission for American Military Personnel to cross our lines from west to east will only be granted in exceptional cases and then only upon authorization of this Hqs.

American Military Personnel without proper authority (pass) will be detained but their name, organization and mission or business requiring crossing of lines will be determined and reported to this Hqs. For personnel in uniform of friendly or hostile nations will pass through our lines as provided by current instruction and for dispositions as such instructions prescribes."

The location of the 749th Tank Bn showed Bn Hqs & Hqs Co in Russdorf, A, B, and Co Cos s well as the Svc Co to be in Langen Chursdorf. D Co was in Gera.

Opoerations for the period: All companies conducted training in accordance with training schedules. CESSATION OF ALL HOSTILITIES IN EUROPE TOOK

EFFECT OFFICIALLY AT 0001 THIS DATE.

"VE DAY" marked the 311th day in combat for the 749th Tank Bn. D Co with light tanks were undergoing ordnance check at Gera. Companies were relieved from attachment to regiments of the 76th Div and reverted to Bn control as of 9 May 1945. A Co was relieved from attachment to the 304th Regt; B Co relieved fromf attachment to 417th Regt; C Co relieved from attachment to the 385th Regt and the battalion moved to a new bivouac area. Bn CP and Hqs Co left Limbach at 0900 hrs and arrived in Ruyssdorf at 0930 hours. A Co left Wernsdorf at 0900 hrs and arrived in Langen Chursdorf at 1130 hours. B Co left Hartmannsdort at 1300 hrs and arrived in Langen Chursdorf at 1430 hours. C Co left Hohenstein at 0900 hors and arrived in Langen Chursdorf at 0930 hrs. Svc Co left Limbach at 1045 hrs and arrived in Langen Chursdorf at 1115 hours.

The weather and visibility was warm, clear with good visibility. Combat efficiency and morale were excellent.

UPDATE

I was notified on July 15, 2011, that my sister Mildred Humphries, widow of Ernest Humphries, had passed away and was asked by their son, Dr. Dennis Humphries, to come to her funeral. I did. It was a lovely service. I met one of my nephew, Dennis's sons, Jeff. Jeff and his family resided in the small community of North Pole, Alaska and he invited me to come meet his family. I left on July 18, 2012, and returned home on July 31, 2012.

POW REPORT

The following consoilidated POW report for the 749th Tank Battalioin covering the period from 3 July 1944 to 9 May 1945 is:

COMPANY	ASSISTED IN CAPTURE	CAPTURED
"A" Co	19,000	2,700
"B" Co	19,450	3,500
"C" Co	20,150	26,680
"D" Co	14,000	1,300
Hqs Co	1,000	200
TOTAL	73,600	34,380

ROSTER OF KEY PERSONNEL 749TH TANK BATTALION

20 JUNE - 1 OCTOBER 1944

ROSTER OF KEY PERSONNEL

749th TANK BATTALION
20 June - 1 October 1944

Liaison Officer	1st Lt. Alton H. Askins
Hqs. Co. Commander	1st Lt. Harold W. Shiff
A Company Commander	Capt. Ancel L. McNeely
B Company Commander	1st Lt. Ralph A. Leighton, Jr.
C Company Commander	1st Lt. Joseph R. McProuty
D Company Commander	1st Lt. Eugene K. Snyder
Service Company Commander	1st Lt. Archibald L. Wilhelm
Medical Detachment Commander and Battalion Surgeon	Capt. Joseph M. Mele

AWARDS AND DECORATIONS
AND UNITS TO WHICH THEY WEREASSIGNED
AT TIME OF INJURY

DISTINGUISHED SERVICE CROSS
2nd Lt. William W. Moore, B Company, 25 Mar. 1945 (POSTHUMOUSLY)

SILVER STAR
Capt. James J. Woods, Jr., D Company, 1 Nov. 1944, 79TH Inf Div
2nd Lt. John E. Lemberg, A Company, 1 Nov. 1944, 79th Inf Div
2nd Lt. Roy N. Grigsby, C Company, 1 Nov. 1944, 79th Inf Div
Sgt. B. R. Mulley, C Company, 1 Nov. 1944, 79th Inf Div
Sgt. Raymond Lee, B Company, 10 Nov. 1944, 79th Inf Div

S/Sgt. Quentin J. Hayden, D Company, 25 Dec. 1944, 79th Inf Div

Capt. James F. Redford, B Company, 21 Jan. 1949, 44th Inf Div (POSTHUMOUSLY)
2nd Lt. James B. Malloy, A Company, 29 Jan. 1945, 44th Inf Div
Pfc Leonard D. Szarowicz, B Company, 21 Feb. 1945, 44th Inf Div
S/Sgt. Harold E. Bush, B Company, 23 Mar. 1945, 70th Inf Div

2nd Lt. Fredrick H. Person, C Company, 2 May 1945, 70th Inf Div

BRONZE STAR

BRONZE STAR

Capt. James F. Bedford, D Company, 20 Nov. 1944, 79th Inf Div

1st Lt. Joseph R. McProuty, D Company, 20 Nov. 1944, 44th Inf Div

1st Lt. Ralph A. Leighton, Jr., D Company, 20 Nov. 1944, 44th Inf Div

2nd Lt. William Norbaly, D Company, 20 Nov. 1944, 44th Inf Div

2nd James Webben, A Company, 13 Nov. 1944, 44th Inf Div

2nd Lt. David C. Herring, III, A Company, 13 Nov. 1944, 44th Inf Div

S/Sgt. James Bobbett, A Company, 1 Nov. 1944, 79th Inf Div

S/Sgt. Merlin A. Hansen, A Company, 1 Nov. 1944, 79th Inf Div

S/Sgt. James D. Malley, A Company, 20 Nov. 1944, 79th Inf Div

Sgt. Allen J. Parks, A Company, 1 Nov. 1944, 79th Inf Div

Sgt. Lawrence J. Wilson, B Company, 2 Nov. 1944, 79th Inf Div

T/4 Edwin F. Hansman, D Company, 20 Nov. 1944, 44th Inf Div

Pfc Joseph P. Carroll, D Company, 20 Nov. 1944, 44th Inf Div

Pfc John J. Reardon, D Company, 20 Nov. 1944, 44th Inf Div

Capt. Robert A. Swenson, Hq. Company, 29 Jan. 1945, 44th Inf Div

Capt. Euclid K. Willis, Hq. Company, 3 Jan. 1945, 44th Inf Div

1st Lt. James M. Holston, Hq. Company, 29 Jan. 1945, 44th Inf Div

Sgt. John A. Mernin, A Company, 29 Jan. 1945, 44th Inf Div

T/4 Willard E. Burns, B Company, 4 Jan. 1945, 79th Inf Div

Cpl. Isidore C. Ruggerio, B Company, 12 Jan. 1945, 79th Inf Div

Cpl. Russell C. Whistler, B Company, 16 Jan. 1945, 44th Inf Div

T/5 Norman B. Charron, A Company, 29 Jan. 1945, 44th Inf Div

T/5 Francis W. Krause, B Company, 4 Jan. 1945, 79th Inf Div

T/5 Elmcr H. Will, B Company, 4 Jan. 1945, 79th Inf Div

Pfc Albert S. MacDowell, A Company, 29 Jan. 1945, 44th Inf Div

Pfc Harold G. Nehring, A Company, 29 Jan. 1945, 44th Inf Div

Lt. Col. Hollan Fann, Hq. Co., 26 Feb. 1945, 79th Inf Div

Capt. Alton D. Wilson, Hq. 26 Feb. 1945, 44th Inf Div

M/Sgt. Harvey J. Vaughan, Jr., Hq. Co., 2 Feb. 1945, 44th Inf Div

T/Sgt. Jack Morris, Hq. Co., 2 Feb. 1945, 44th Inf Div

T/Sgt. Robert J. Pringle, Hq. Co., 2 Feb. 1945, 44th Inf Div

Sgt. Jack P. Goodman, A Company, 20 Feb. 1945, 44th Inf Div

Sgt. Richard B. Jackson, A Company, 2 Feb. 1945, 44th Inf Div
Sgt. William A. McLemore, A Company, 6 Feb. 1945, 44th Inf Div
Sgt. John W. Tribbey, J r., B Company, 20 Feb. 1945, 44th Inf Div
Cpl. Anthony Osso, A Company, 2 Feb. 1945, 44th Inf Div

T/5 Eldon Y. Armstrong, C Company, 11 Feb. 1945, 44th Inf Div
T/5 Floyd T. Droege, A Company, 2 Feb. 1945, 44th Inf Div
Pfc Alton E. Bruno, C Company, 13 Feb. 1945, 44th Inf Div

S/Sgt. Harold E. Bush, B Company, 1 Mar. 1945, 44th Inf Div
Sgt. William H. McFadden, B Company, 11 Mar. 1945, 44th Inf Div
Sgt. Kurt P. H. Pfortner, B Company, 23 Mar. 1945, 70th Inf Div
Sgt. August P. Vogele, C Company, 1 Mar. 1945, 44th Inf Div
T/4 John O. Kaiser, C Company, 17 Mar. 1945, 70th Inf Div
T/4 John L. Kile, B Company, 11 Mar. 1945, 44th Inf Div
Cpl. Vincent L. Dwyer, C Company, 17 Mar. 1945, 70th Inf Div
T/5 Romain W. Weaver, B Company, 11 Mar. 1945, 44th Inf Div
Pfc John C. Carlo, C Company, 17 Mar. 1945, 70th Inf Div
Pfc Francis J. Cuffaro, B Company, 16 Mar. 1945, 70th Inf Div
S/Sgt. Hans Monson, C Company, 8 Mar. 1945, 749th Tank Bn
Sgt. Charles W. Botimer, III, A Company, 24 Mar. 1945, 9th Evac. Hospital
Sgt. Heinz K. W. Harting, C Company, 8 Mar. 1945, 749th Tank Bn
Sgt. Russel C. Whistler, B Company, 10 Mar. 1945, 2nd General Hospital
T/4 Frank M. Galbreath, "V" Company, 8 Mar. 1945, 749th Tank Bn
T/4 John F. Zuend, C Company, 8 Mar. 1945, 749th Tank Bn
Cpl. Thomas J. Cook, C Company, 8 Mar. 1945, 749th Tank Bn
T/5 Carl Eck, C Company, 1 Mar. 1945, 21st Station Hospital
Pfc Archie Cherne, A Company, 8 Mar. 1945, 749th Tank Bn
Pfc Anthony DiCarlo, C Company, 8 Mar. 1945, 749th Tank Bn
Pfc Gilbert Lopez, A Company, 8 Mar. 1945, 749th Tank Bn
Pfc Eugene E. Medley, A Company, 8 Mar. 1945, 749th Tank Bn
Pfc Rex H. Wilkening, A Company, 8 Mar. 1945, 749th Tank Bn
Pvt. Edwin B. Boder, A Company, 10 Mar. 1945, 2nd General Hospital
Capt. Joseph M. Mele, Medical Detachment, 5 May 1945, 76th Inf Div

OAK LEAF CLUSTERS TO BRONZE STAR

Capt. Dudley F. Coney, C Company, 26 Dec. 1944, 44th Inf Div

Capt. Ancel L. McNeely, A Company, 26 Dec. 1944, 44th Inf Div

1st Lt. Bertram Kaufman, B Company, 30 Dec. 1944, 44th Inf Div

2nd Lt. Julius D. Hersh, Hq & Hq Co., 27 Dec. 1944, 79th Inf Div

2nd Lt. Loren G. Rosencrantz, B Company, 30 Dec. 1944, 79th Inf Div

S/Sgt. Edward J. Cichocki, D Company, 8 Dec. 1944, 44th Inf Div

S/Sgt. Frederick D. Eck, B Company, 30 Dec. 1944, 79th Inf Div

Sgt. J. W. Brakebill, B Company, 30 Dec. 1944, 79th Inf Div

Sgt. Edward J. Gallerie, D Company, 25 Dec. 1944, 44th Inf Div

T/4 Jack P. Goodman, A Company, 30 Dec. 1944, 44th Inf Div

Pvt. James J. Byrnes, Service Company, 13 Dec. 1944, 44th Inf Div

T/Sgt. John J. Dibble, B Company, 4 Jan.1945, 79th Inf Div

T/5 James Livolsi, B Company, 4 Jan. 1945, 79th Inf Div

Cpl. John E. Jones, A Company, 8 Feb. 1945, 44th Inf Div

Sgt. Ernest Humphries, C Company, 17 Mar. 1945, 70th Inf Div (my brother in law)

PURPLE HEART

1ˢᵗ Lt. Dudley F. Coney, C Company, 21 Nov. 1944, 9ᵗʰ Evac. Hospital
1ˢᵗ Lt. Bertram Kaufman, B Company, 2 Nov. 1944, 44ᵗʰ Inf Div
2ⁿᵈ St. John A. McCrea, C Company, 23 Nov. 1944, 51ˢᵗ Evac. Hospital
S/Sgt. Quentin J. Hayden, D Company, 21 Nov. 1944, 79ᵗʰ Inf Div
Sgt. George A. Baker, D Company, 29 Nov. 1944, 9ᵗʰ Evac. Hospital
Sgt. Cecil Dilsworth, A Company, 19 Nov. 1944, 46ᵗʰ Evac. Hospital
Cpl. Harvey W. Cripe, Hq. Co., 19 Nov.1944, 9ᵗʰ Evac. Hospital
Cpl. Frank A. Gentile, C Company, 21 Nov. 1944, 79ᵗʰ Inf Div
Cpl. Theodore Pappas, A Company, 21 Nov. 1944, 51ˢᵗ Evac. Hospital
T/5 Louis J. Sullivan, A Company, 21 Nov. 1944, 79ᵗʰ Inf Div
Pfc Howard F. Cullen, A Company, 21 Nov. 1944, 79ᵗʰ Inf Div
Pfc Tommy D. Smith, B Company, 2 Nov. 1944, 79ᵗʰ Inf Div

Sgt. Robert W. Hummer, B Company, 2 Dec. 1944, 749ᵗʰ Tank Bn
Pfc Michael J. Popich, A Company, 2 Dec. 1944, 749ᵗʰ Tank Bn
Pfc John C. Reydel, Jr., D Company, 5 Dec. 1944, 23ʳᵈ Station Hospital
Pvt. Ervin C. Jarvis, D Company, 18 Dec. 1944, 749ᵗʰ Tank Bn
Pvt. Alfred Niejadlik, C Company, 2 Dec. 1944, 749ᵗʰ Tank Bn
Pvt. George Sapounas, Service Co., 18 Dec. 1944, 749ᵗʰ Tank Bn
Pvt. Harold D. Sutter, D Company, 1 Dec. 1944, 749ᵗʰ Tank Bn
Pvt. Charles C. Wilson, C Company, 2 Dec. 1944, 749ᵗʰ Tank Bn

S/Sgt. Harold E. Bush, B Company, 18 Jan. 1945, 749ᵗʰ Tank Bn
S/Sgt. Elmer H. Tombre, D Company, 7 Jan. 1945, 749ᵗʰ Tank Bn
Sgt. Percy G. Jenkins, Jr., D Company, 18 Jan. 1945, 749ᵗʰ Tank Bn
Sgt. Fred W. Pelcher, D Company, 18 Jan. 1945, 749ᵗʰ Tank Bn
Sgt. Lawrence J. Wilson, D Company, 18 Jan. 1945, 749ᵗʰ Tank Bn
T/4 Edwin F. Hansman, D Company, 18 Jan. 1945, 749ᵗʰ Tank Bn
Cpl. John E. Johns, A Company, 18 Jan. 1945, 749ᵗʰ Tank Bn
T/5 Robert J. Christie, A Company, 18 Jan. 1945, 749ᵗʰ Tank Bn
T/5 Frank Pumillo, C Company, 18 Jan. 1945, 749ᵗʰ Tank Bn
T/5 Fred Renz, B Company, 7 Jan. 1945, 749ᵗʰ Tank Bn
Pfc Alroy Chaffee, D Company, 18 Jan. 1945, 749ᵗʰ Tank Bn
Pfc Vernon L. Covington, C Company, 7 Jan. 1945, 749ᵗʰ Tank Bn

Pfc Andrew B. Douglas, Service Company, 7 Jan. 1945, 749th Tank Bn
Pfc Lawrence H. Farman, B Company, 18 Jan. 1945, 749th Tank Bn
Pfc Henry L. Smith, B Company, 11 Jan. 1945, 27th Evac. Hospital
Pvt. Seymour Fried, Service Company, 7 Jan. 1945, 749th Tank Bn
Pvt. Robert T. North, Hq. Company, 18 Jan.1945, 749th Tank Bn
2nd Lt. Fredrick H. Person, C Company, 27 Feb. 1945, 749th Tank Bn
S/Sgt. Elvis H. Lewis, B Company, 27 Feb. 1945, 749th Tank Bn
S/Sgt. Michael J. Mosca, A Company, 27 Feb. 1945, 749th Tank Bn
Sgt. Albert Blackburn, Hq. Company, 27 Feb. 1945, 749th Tank Bn
Sgt. Richard B. Jackson, A Company, 27 Feb. 1945, 749th Tank Bn
Sgt. Kurt P. H. Pfortner, B Company, 27 Feb. 1945, 749th Tank Bn
Sgt. John W. Womack, C Company, 27 Feb. 1945, 749th Tank Bn
T/4 Ottis E. Keown, C Company, 27 Feb. 1945, 749th Tank Bn
T/5 Carl R. Defriece, C Company, 27 Feb. 1945, 749th Tank Bn
T/5 Stanley Mijal, C Company, 27 Feb. 1945, 749th Tank Bn
Pfc William Singer, Service Company, 27 Feb. 1945, 749th Tank Bn
Pvt. Walter F. Smith, B Company, 27 Feb. 1945, 749th Tank Bn

S/Sgt. Michael J. Mosca, A Company, 2 Apr. 1945, 2nd General Hospital

BRONZE OAK LEAF CLUSTERS TO PURPLE HEART

S/Sgt. James P. Merritt, B Company,	9 Nov. 1944, 79th Inf Div
Sgt. Clifford H. Clements, C Company,	15 Nov. 1944, 79th Inf Div
Pfc Tommy D. Smith, B Company,	2 Nov. 1944, 79th Inf Div
Capt. James J. Woods, Jr., B Company,	15 Dec. 1944, 3rd General Hospital
Sgt. Clifford H. Clements, C Company,	2 Dec. 1944, 749th Tank Bn
T/5 Louis J. Sullivan, A Company,	7 Jan. 1945, 749th Tank Bn
Capt. Robert A. Swenson, Hq. Co.,	27 Feb. 1945, 749th Tank Bn

CHANGE IN KEY PERSONNEL SOMETIME IN NOVEMBER 1944

CHANGE IN KEY PERSONNEL
SOMETIME IN NOVEMBER 1944

Battalion Commander	Major Hollan Fann
Executive Officer and S-3	Major Paul E. Davison
S-4	Capt. Alton D. Wilson
S-2	Capt. Robert A. Swenson
S-1	1st Lt. Archibald L. Wilhelm
Motor Maintenance Officer	Capt. Euclid K. Willis
Communication Officer	1st Lt. Willatf I. Newlin
Liaison Officer	1st Lt. Alton N. Askins
Headquarters Commander	Capt. John A. Long (Hospital)
	1 Nov. to 29 Nov. 1944
	1st Lt. Harold W. Schiff - 30 Nov.
A Company Commander	1st Lt. Ancel L. McNeely (Hospital)
	1 Nov. to 29 Nov. 1944
	1st Lt. Jeffrey D. Conway - 30 Nov.
B Company Commander	Capt. James F. Redford
C Company Commander	1st Lt. Dudley F. Coney (Hospital)
	1 Nov. to 19 Nov. 1944
	1st Lt. Joseph R. McProuty

Nov. to 30 Nov. 1944

Service Company Commander	Capt. Lee D. Greatchus
Medical Detachment Commander and Battalion Surgeon	Capt. Joseph M. Mele

CHANGE IN KEY PERSONNEL SOMETIME IN DECEMBER 1944

CHANGE IN KEY PERSONNEL   SOMETIME IN DECEMBER 1944

Battalion Commander	**Lt. Col. Holland Fann**
Executive Officer and S-3	**Major Paul E. Davison**
S-4	**Capt. Alton D. Wilson**
S-2	**Capt. Robert A. Swenson**
S-1	**1st Lt. Archibald L. Wilhelm**
Motor Maintenance Officer	**Capt. Euclid K. Willis**
Communication Officer	**Capt. Willard I. Nowlin**
Liaison Officer	**1st Lt. Alton H. Askins**
Headquarters Company Commander	**1st Lt. Harold W. Schiff**
A Company Commander	**1st Lt. Jeffrey D. Conway**

B Company Commander   Capt. James F. Redford
    1 Dec. - 11 Dec. 1944
    Capt. James J. Woods, Jr.
    11 Dec. - 31 Dec. 1944

C Company Commander	**1st Lt. Joseph R. McProuty**
D Company Commander	**1st Lt. Eugene K. Snyder**
Service Company Commander	Capt. Lee D. Greatchus
Medical Detachment Commander	
and Battalion Surgeon	Capt. Joseph M. Mele

CHANGE IN KEY PERSONNEL SOMETIME IN JANUARY 1945

CHANGE IN KEY PERSONNEL   SOMETIME IN JANUARY 1945

Battalion Commander	Lt. Col. Holland Fann
Executive Officer	Major Paul E. Davison
S-3	Capt. Euclid K. Willis
Assistant S-3	Capt. James J. Woods, Jr.
S-4	Capt. Alton D. Wilson
S-2	Capt. Robert A. Swenson
S-1	2nd Lt. Julius D. Hersh
Motor Maintenance Officer	Capt. Leo D. Greatchus
Communications Officer	Capt. Willard I. Nowlin
Liaison Officer	1st Lt. Alton Askins
Hq. Company Commander	1st Lt. Harold Schiff
A Company Commander	Capt. Ancel L. McNeely
B Company Commander	1st Lt. Ralph A. Leighton, Jr.
C Company Commander	1st Lt. Joseph R. McProuty
D Company Commander	1st Lt. Eugene K. Snyder
Service Company Commander	1st Lt. Archibald L. Wilhelm
Medical Detachment Commander and Battalion Surgeon	Capt. Joseph M. Mele

CHANGE IN KEY PERSONNEL SOMETIME IN MARCH 1945

CHANGE IN KEY PERSONNEL
SOMETIME IN JANUARY 1945

Battalion Commander	Lt. Col. Holland Fann
Executive Officer	Major Paul E. Davison
S-3	Capt. Euclid K. Willis
Assistant S-3	Capt. James J. Woods, Jr.
S-4	Capt. Alton D. Wilson
S-2	Capt. Robert A. Swenson
S-1	2nd Lt. Julius D. Hersh
Motor Maintenance Officer	Capt. Leo D. Greatchus
Communications Officer	Capt. Willard I. Nowlin
Liaison Officer	1st Lt. Alton Askins
Hq. Company Commander	1st Lt. Harold Schiff
A Company Commander	Capt. Ancel L. McNeely
B Company Commander	1st Lt. Ralph A. Leighton, Jr.
C Company Commander	1st Lt. Joseph R. McProuty
D Company Commander	1st Lt. Eugene K. Snyder
Service Company Commander	1st Lt. Archibald L. Wilhelm
Medical Detachment Commander and Battalion Surgeon	Capt. Joseph M. Mele

CHANGE IN KEY PERSONNEL SOMETIME IN APRIL 1945

CHANGE IN KEY PERSONNEL   SOMETIME IN APRIL 1945

Battalion Commander	Lt. Col. Hollan Fann
Executive Officer	Major Paul E. Davison
S-3	Capt. Euclid Willis
Assistant S-3	Capt. James J. Woods, Jr.
S-4	Capt. Alton D. Wilson
S-2	Capt. Robert A. Swenson
S-1	1st Lt. Julius D. Hersh
Motor Maintenance Officer	Capt. Lee D. Greatchus
Liaison Officer	1st Lt. Alton H. Askins
Hq. Company Commander	1st Lt. Harold Schiff 1 Apr - 22 Apr. 1945 Capt. Willard I. Nowlin 23 Apr. - 30 Apr. 1945
A Company Commander	1st Lt. Jeffrey D. Conway
B Company Commander	Capt. Ralph A.Leighton, Jr. 1 Apr. - 22 Apr. 1945 1st Lt. James R. Holston 23 Apr. - 30 Apr. 1945
C Company Commander	Capt. Joseph R. McProuty
D Company Commander	Capt. Eugene Snyder
Service Company Commander	Capt. Archibald W. Wilhelm
Medical Detachment Commander and Battalion Surgeon	Capt. Joseph M. Mele 1 Apr. - 19 Apr. 1945 Capt. William F. French 20 Apr. - 30 Apr. 1945

ROUTE OF ADVANCE PERIOD COVERING JULY 1944 TO 31 MAY 1945

NORTHERN FRANCE TO BELGIUM
Peronne
Cambrai
Denain
St. Amand
Planard (Belgium border - 2 Sept. 1944
Rumegies (on Belgium border)

BELGIUM BORDER TO EASTERN FRANCE
St. Amand
Valenciennes
Cambrai
Perenne
Man
Guiscard
Coucy le Chautes
Saissons
Rheims - 7 Sept. 1944
Vertus
Fere-Champenoise[1]
Sommeseus
Arcis
Lesmont
Brienne le Chateau[2]
Joinville - liberated 8 Sept. 1944
Neuf Chateau
Mirecourt
Charmes - liberated 11 Sept. 1944
Morivillier
Gerberviller
Xermanenil
Fraimbois

1   Champoenoise is an adjective coming from Champagne where champagne is produced, smaller than Brittany.

2   Brienne, a part of France, is a name like Brittany, only smaller.

Chaudefontaine
Lunéville - liberated 19 Sept. 1944 - Crossed the LeMeurthe River on 22 Sept.
Fort de Paroy - cleared 10 Oct. 1944

EASTERN FRANCE TO ALSACE-LORRAINE
Croismare
Marainviller - 13 Oct. 1944
Embermédil - 21 Oct. 1944
Leintrey
Avricourt
Rechicourt
St. George
Remeling
Sarrebourg - liberated 20 Nov. 1944
Lixheim - 23 Nov. 1944
Eschbourg and Dossenheim Pass - secured 23 Nov. 1944
Saverne Gap - participated in breakthrough
Drulingen
Diemeringen - 7 Dec. 1944
Montbronn - 13 Dec. 1944
Hambach - 22 Dec. 1944
Sarralbe - 30 Dec. 1944
Sarre-Union
Vittersbourg - 13 Jan. 1945
Sarraltroff - 9 Mar. 1945
Diemeringen - 15 Mar. 1945
Montbronn - 18 Mar. 1945
Bitche - 19 Mar. 1945

GERMANY
Pirmasens
Sarnstall - 23 Mar. 1945
Gross Fischlingen - 24 Mar. 1945
Neustadt

Kreigsfeld

Mainz - 30 Mar. 1945

Frankfurt

Bad Homburg-Nouhm

Laubach

Ulrichstein - 31 Mar. 1945

Romrod

Alsfeld

Hainrode - 1 Apr. 1945

Rotenburg-Bebra

Rockensuss - 3 Apr. 1945

Sontra

Eschwege - 8 Apr. 1945

Wanfried

Mülhausen

Lancensalza

Grafentonna - 10 Apr. 1945

Nermsdorf - 12 Apr. 1945

Neumark

Bonau - 13 Apr. 1945

Osterfeld

Zeitz

Wintersdorf - 15 Apr. 1945

Altenburg

Topfseifersdorf - 16 Apr. 1945

Burstädt

Taura - 18 Apr. 1945

Limbach - 24 Apr. 1945

Russdorf - 8 May 1945 CESSATION OF ALL HOSTILITIES IN
EUROPE - VE DAY

Langenburg - 11 May 1945

BIBLIOGRAPHY

Blum, Howard, Wanted! The Search for Nazis in America, The New York Times Book Col, 1977

Blumanson, Martin, Kasserine Pass, PDJ Books, 1961

Bradford, George, Great Tank Battles of WWII – A Combat Diary of the Second World War, Arco Publishing Company, Inc., 1970

Breuer, William B., Unexplained Mysteries of World War II, John Wiley & Sons, Inc., 1997

Burns, Ken, The War – An Intimate History, 1941-1945, the movie produced by Ken Burns, 200___

Carse, Robert, A Cold Corner of Hell – The Story of the Murmansk Convoys 1941-45, Doubleday & Company, Inc., 1969

Cooper, Matthew, The German Army – 1933-1945-Its Political and Military Failure, Bonanza Books, 1979

Doubler, Michael D., Closing With The Enemy – How GI's Fought the War in Europe, University Press of Kansas, 1994

Eisenhower, Dwight D., At Ease, Stories I tell to Friends, Doubleday & Company, 1967

Farrington, Karen, WWII Ground, Sea & Air Battles, Abbeydale Press, 1995
Front Page, A Collection of Historical Headlines from the Los Angeles Times, 1881 – 1989, Harry N. Abrams, Inc., Publishers, New York, 1981

Garrett, Richard, P.O.W., David & Charles, 1981

Gavin, James M., On to Berlin, Battles of an Airborne Commander, 1943-1946, The Viking Press, 1978

Hogg, Ian, Tank Killing – AT Warfare by Men and Machines, Sarpedon, 1996

Hotz, Robert Lee, The Human Face of War, Los Angeles Times Magazine, October 29, 2000

Houston, Donald E., Hell on Wheels, Presidio Press, 1977

Miller, David, Submarine Disasters, The Lyons Press, 2006

Mocksey, Major K.J., Panzer Division, TheMailed Fist, Ballantine Books, Inc., 1968

Newark, Tim, Turning the Tide of War – 50 Battles that Changed the Course of Modern History, Octopus Publishing Group, Ltd., 2001

Nichols, David, Ernie's War, Random House, 1986

Page One, Major Events 1920-1987 as Presented in the New York Times, 1987, Times Books

Patton, Jr., General George S., War as I Knew It – A BattleMemoirs of "Blood 'n Guts", Bantam Books, 1979

Porter, Clifford F., Soldiers' Art from the 9st Infantry Division in Italy, 1944-1945, 91st Infantry Division (Training Division) and the Center of Military History, 2004

Powell, Colin, My American Journey, Random House, 1995

Schneider, Wolfgang, Panzer Tactics, German Small-Unit Armor Tactics in World War II, J. J. Fedorowicz Publishing, Inc., 2000

Schwarzkopf, General H. Norman, The Autobiography…It Doesn't Take A Hero, Bantom Books, 1992

Shirer, William L., The Rise and Fall of the Third Reich, A History of Nazi Germany, `Fawcett Publications, Inc., 1959

Stein, R. Conrad, The Story of the Battle of the Bulge, Children's Press, 1977
Time Books, Absolute Victory – America's Greatest Generation and Their World War II Triumph, Time, Inc., 2005

Tobin, James, ErniePyle's War – America's Eyewitness to World War II, Univeristy Press of Kansas, 1997

Tompkins, John S., The Weapons of World War III – The Long Road Back From the Bomb, Doubleday & Company, Inc., 1966

Von Lang, Jochen, The Secretary Martin Bormann: The Man Who Manipulated Hitler, Random House, 1979

Vonnegut, Jr., Kurt, Slaughter-House Five, Delacorte Press, 1968

Ward, Geoffrey C., The War – An Intimate History, 1941 – 1945, Alfred A. Knopf, 2007

Weingartner, James J., Hitler's Guard – Inside the Fuhrer's Personal SS Force, Berkley Books, 1974

Werbell, Frederick E. and Thurston Clarke, Lost Hero – The Mystery of Raoul Wallenberg, McGraw-Hill Book Co., 1982

Winston, Robert A., Dive Bomber, Naval Institute Press, 1939

Winston, Robert A. Fighting Squadron, Naval Institute Press, 1946

World War II – The German Front: Prelude to War, The Nazi Strike, The Secret Life of Hitler, and Nuremberg Trials – DVD, 2006

Yeide, Harry, The Tank Killers, Casemate, 2004

Yeide, Harry, Steel Victory – The Heroic Story of America's Independent Tank Battalions at War in Europe, Random House, 2005

TANK BATTALION MAPS AND MISSIONS

From the Author - About These Maps

Maps were very important, as each day the officer of the battalion would tell the troops where they were to hit next, particularly if one of the groups they were protecting was in "hot water" so to speak. Those groups also informed the tank battalion members where there were a lot of Germans or snipers. At some point on occasion the Germans left especially when the tank battalions and other soldiers were close to the German border. It was at certain points when the troops arrived where they were headed and found an empty house, that house generally became the Headquarters for the officers.

The maps occasionally showed where the areas were full of trees or near a river or lake. The Battle of the Bulge was the worst as our men arrived there in the dead of winter without winter clothing whereas the Germans wore white uniforms and it was sometimes difficult to tell if they were actually the enemy or townspeople. I've been where the Battle of the Bulge was fought and one can still see the damage done to the area, especially the trees. Many of the townspeople, particularly in the small communities were against Hitler and provided food and such to our troops.

I've also been to where one of the POW camps was located. The nearest town was only 6 miles away and when the Americans freed the camp, the mayor of the town was brought to see what had been happening as he claimed he didn't know there was a POW camp there. When he was returned home, he killed his entire family and committed suicide. The buildings where the POWs were kept, had been demolished; but the ovens, and carts for carrying the prisoners to the ovens were still there. I saw the room where the medical horrors were performed, etc. Relics such as gold teeth, skulls, bones, etc. were upstairs and I didn't have the nerve to go there; now I wish I had put the thoughts behind me and go anyway.

NEW INFO—

One thing I didn't mention when the mayor of the town was brought to the camp is that he had to have known as the odor was terrible. It even made some of our troops ill. The name of the town is Weimar and the name of the prison camp is Buckenwald pronounced Bu Ken Val. It is categorized as the second worst camp, exceeded only by Auschwitz. It was liberated by the American Third Army on 11 April 1945, the day before President F. D. Roosevelt's death.

Until 1951, the Russian used it as a concentration camp for enemies of East Germany.

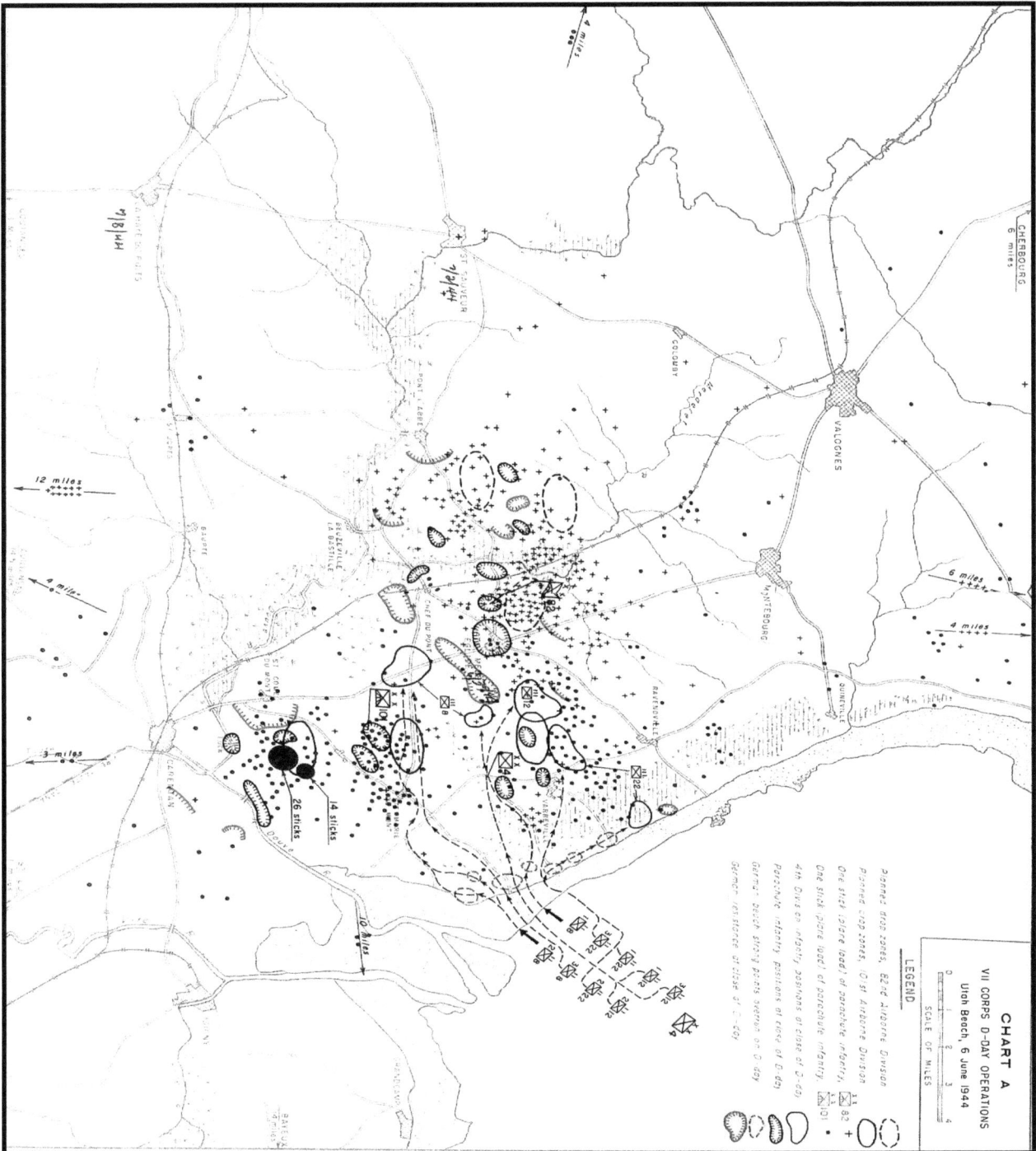

Chart A- VII Corps D- Day Operations Utah Beach June 6, 1944

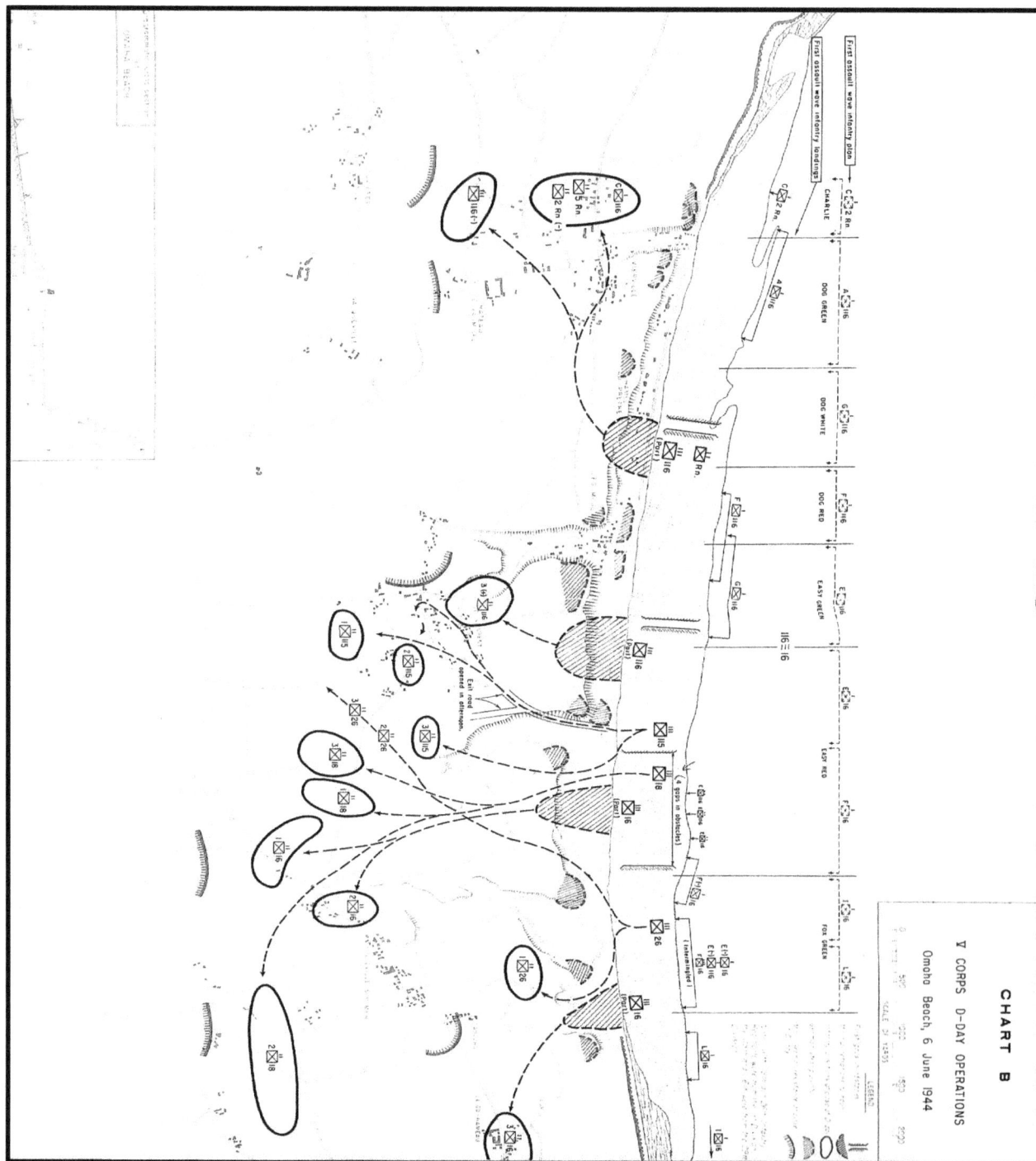

Chart B- V Corps D- Day Operations Omaha Beach June 6, 1944

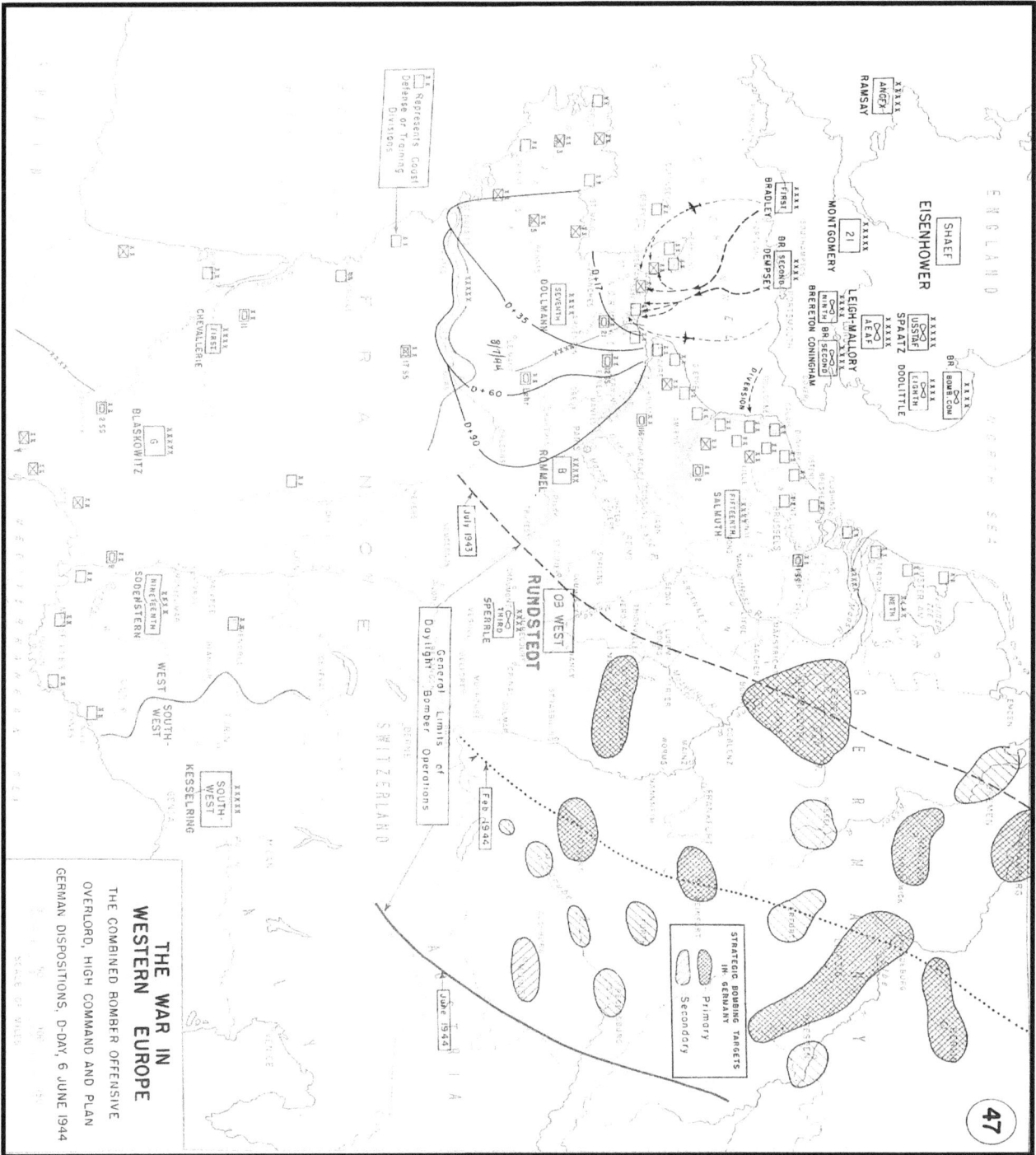

The War in Western Europe   Combined Bomber Deffensive   D-Day   June 6 1944

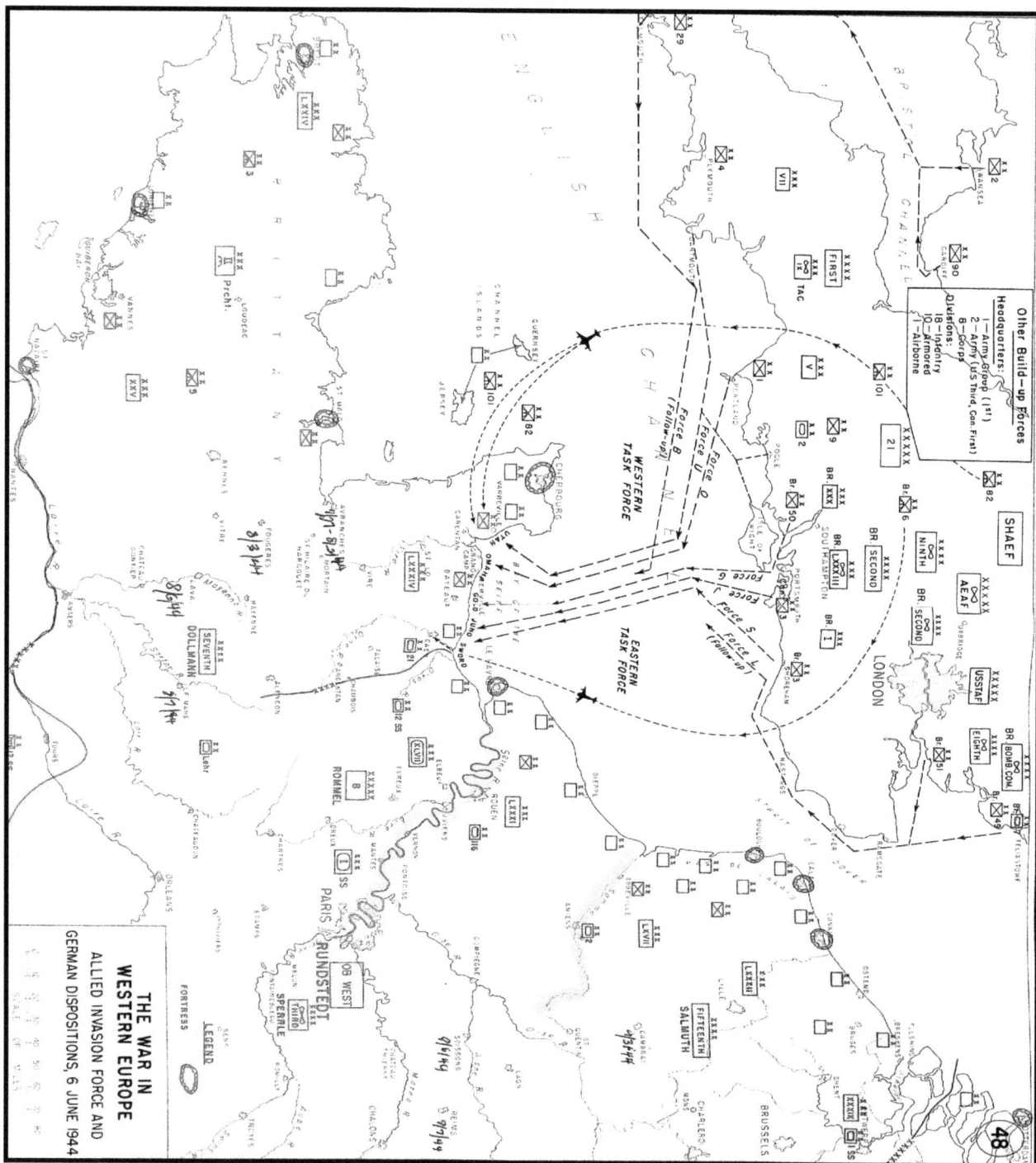

The War in Western Europe   Allied Invasion Force and German Disposition
D-Day   June 6 1944

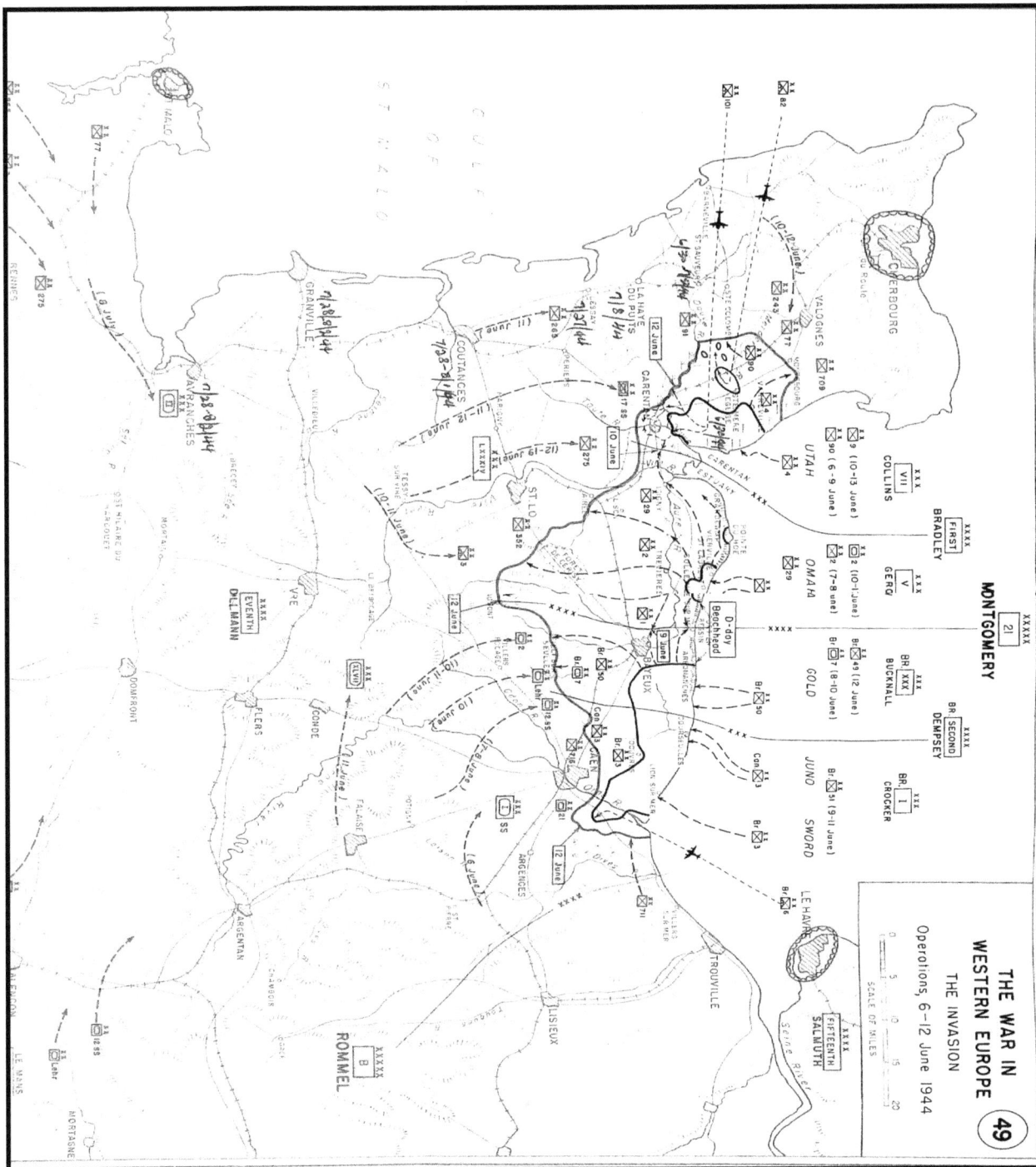

The War in Western Europe   The Invasion   June 6-12 1944

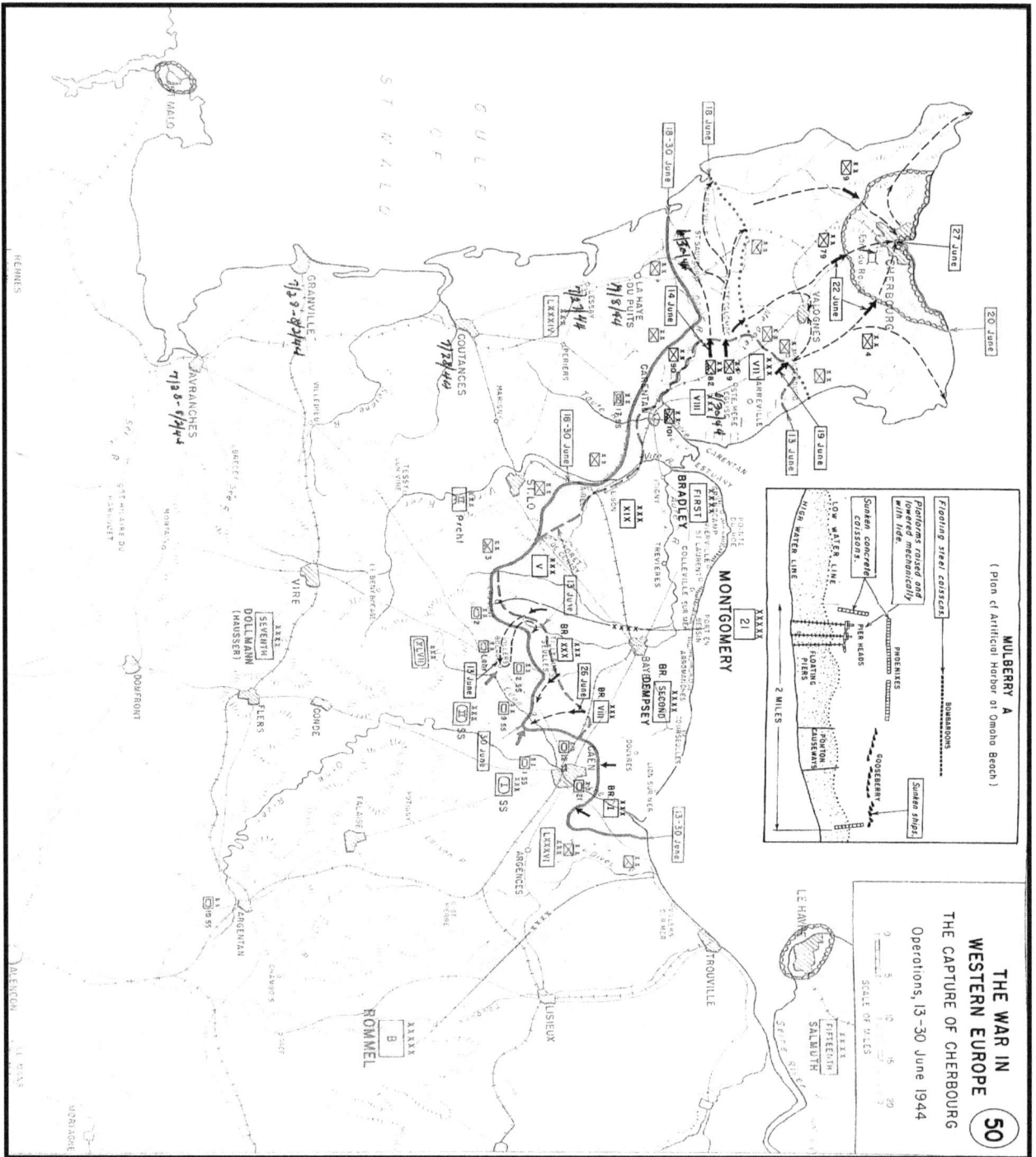

The War in Western Europe   The Capture of Cherbourg   June 13-30 1944

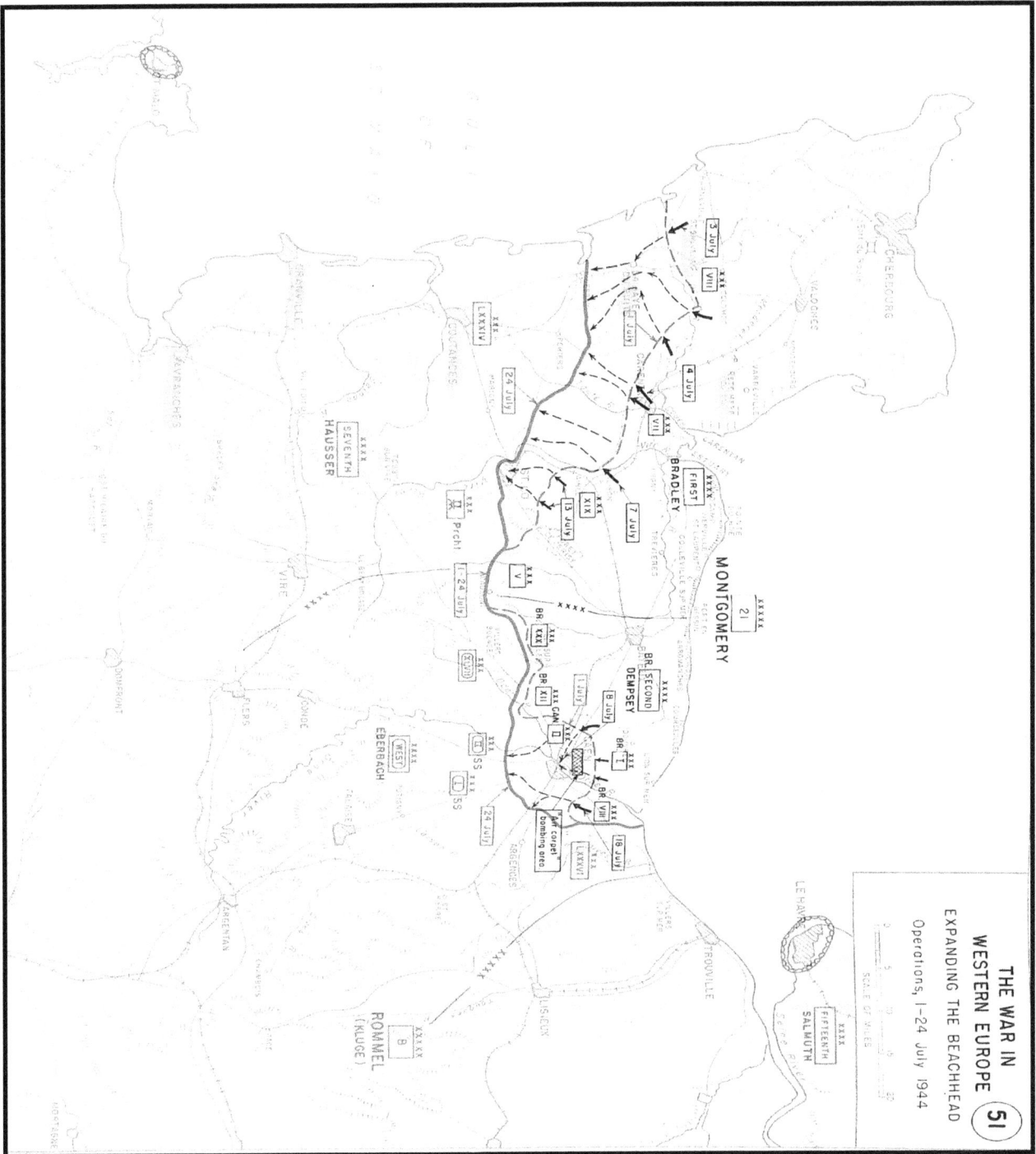

The War in Western Europe   Expanding the Beachhead   July 1-24 1944

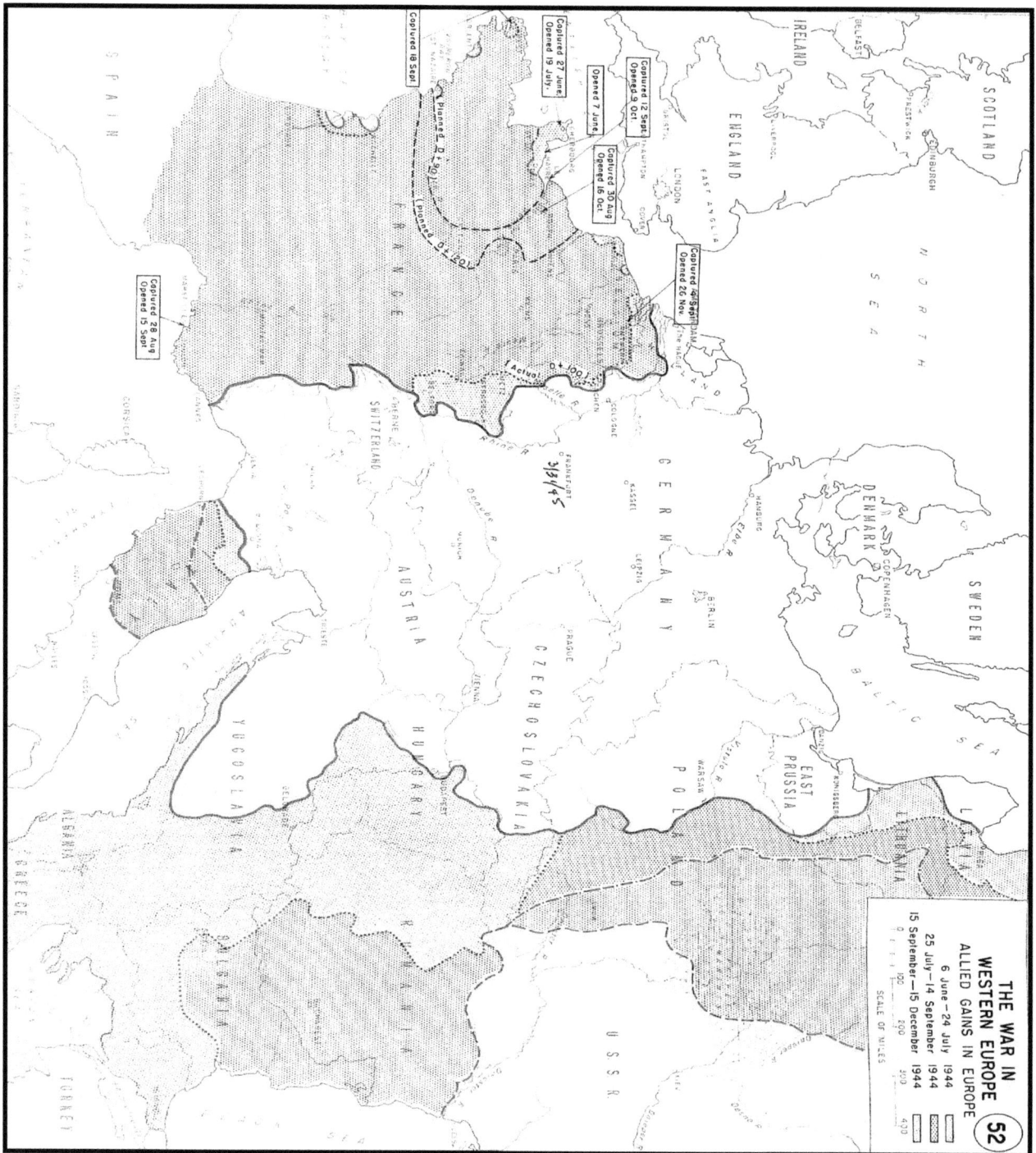

The War in Western Europe   Allied Gains In Europe   June various dates 1944

The War in Western Europe   The St. Lo Breakthrough   July 25-31 1944

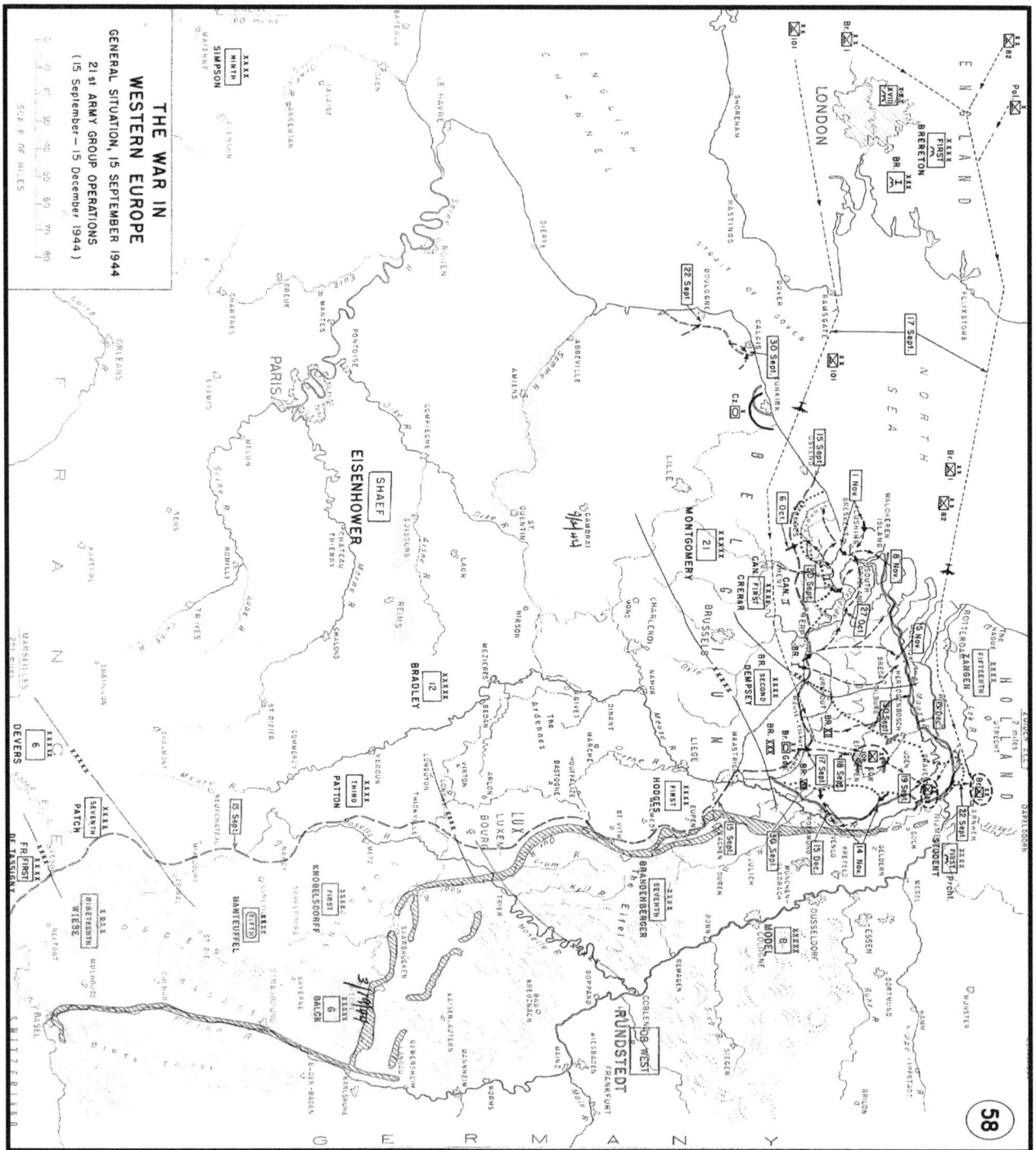

THE WAR IN
WESTERN EUROPE
GENERAL SITUATION, 15 SEPTEMBER 1944
21st ARMY GROUP OPERATIONS
(15 September – 15 December 1944)

The War in Western Europe   General Situation   September 15 1944

The War in Western Europe The Ardennes Campaign December 16-25 1944

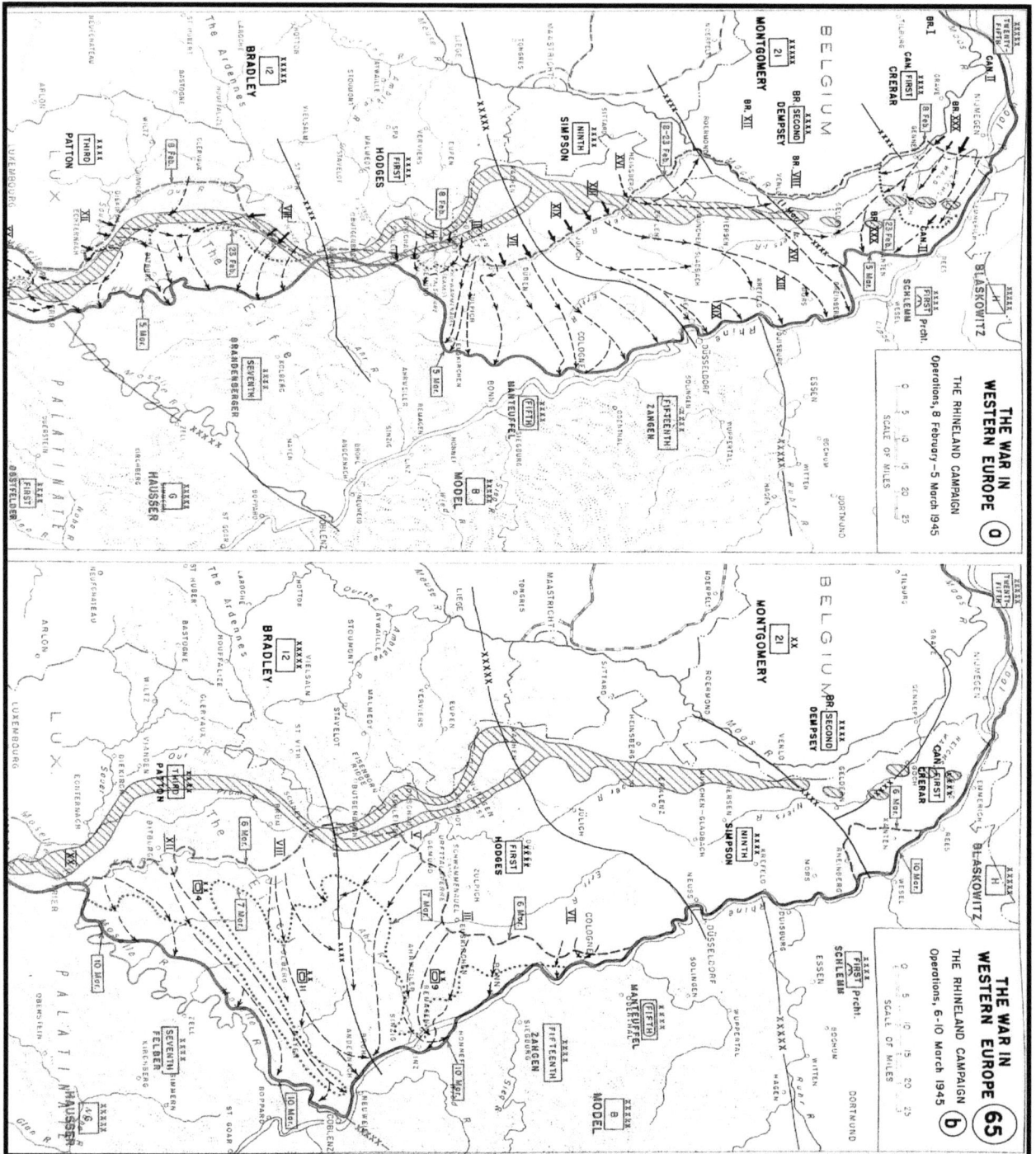

The War in Western Europe   The Rhineland Campaign   6-10 March 1945

The War in Western Europe Summary- The Rhineland Campaign 21 March 1945

THE WAR IN
WESTERN EUROPE
CROSSING THE RHINE

Operations, 22–28 March 1945

The War in Western Europe   Crossing the Rhine   22-28 March 1945

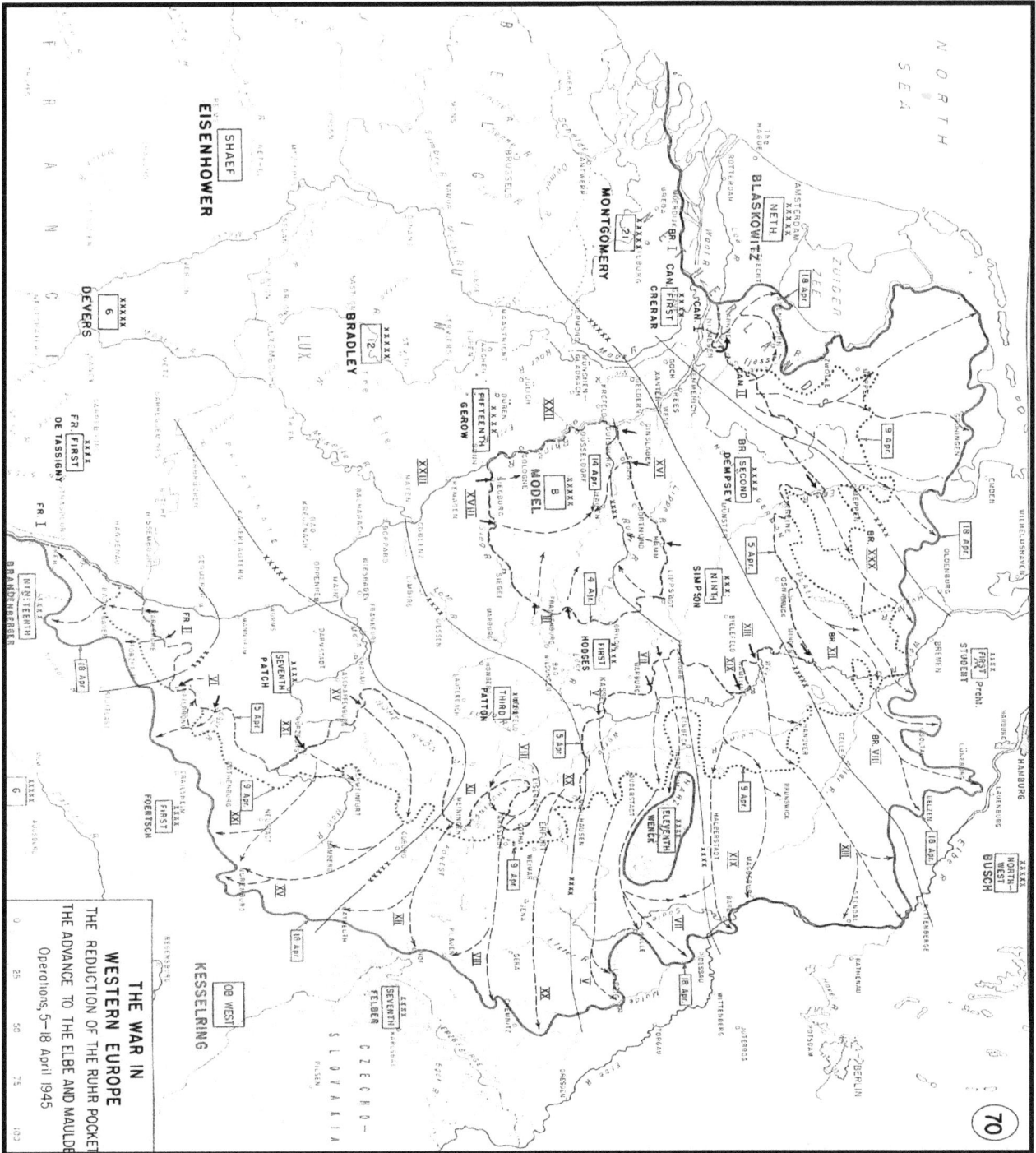

The War in Western Europe The Advance to the Elbe and Maulder 5-18 April 1945

The War in Western Europe   Encircling the Ruhr   29 March- 4 April 1945

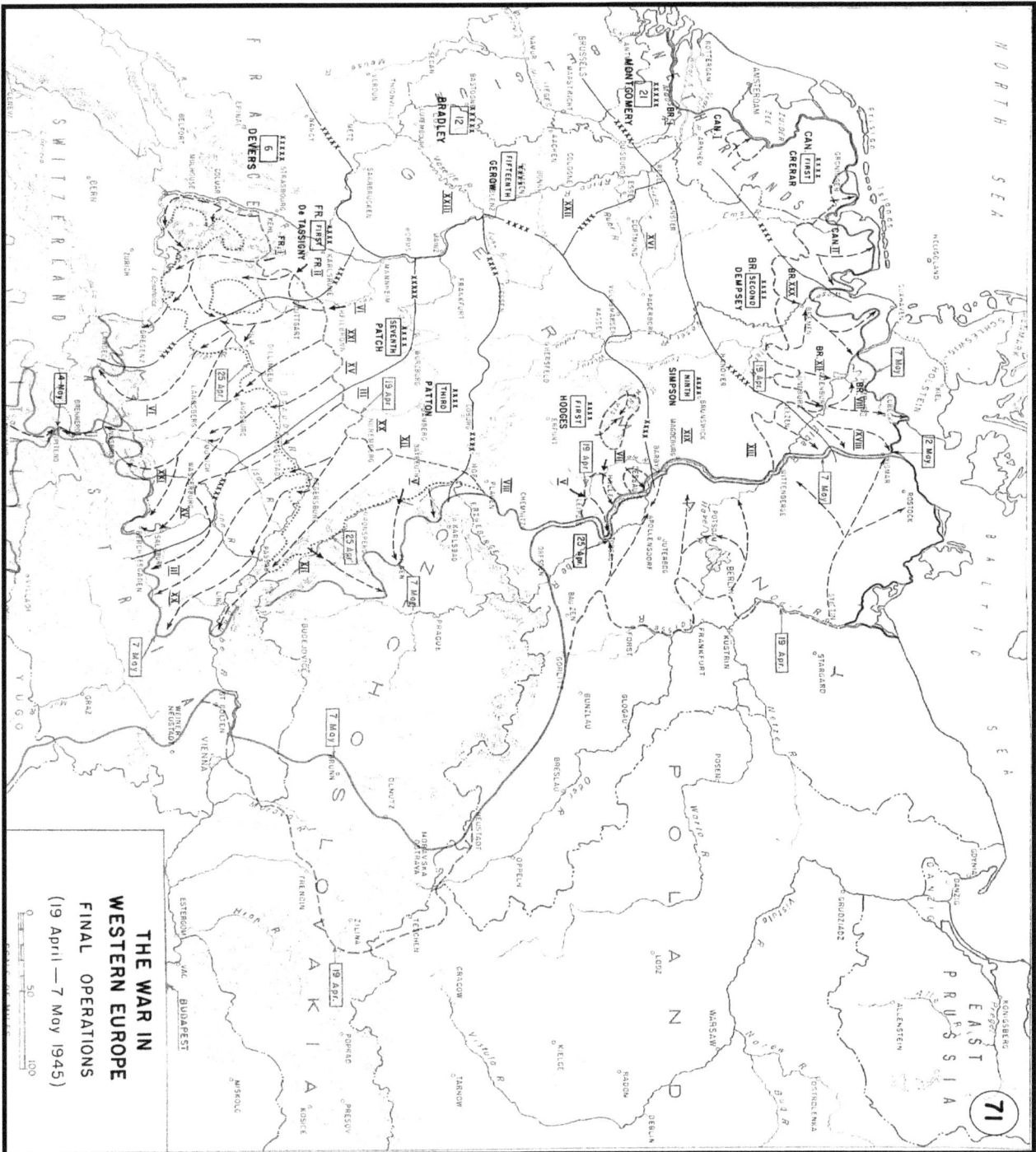

THE WAR IN
WESTERN EUROPE
FINAL OPERATIONS
(19 April — 7 May 1945)

71

The War in Western Europe   Final Operations   19 April - 7 May 1945

GLOSSARY

1st Lt	First Lieutenant
2nd Lt	Second Lieutenant
AG	Assault gun
AP	Anti-personnel
AT	Anti-tank
Bn	Battalion
Bn Adj	Battalion Adjutant
Capt	Captain
Cav	Cavalry
CoCO	Company Commander
CP	Command Post
Cpl	Corporal
CT	Combat team
CWO	Chief Warrant Officer
Div	Division
ExO	Executive Officer
FA	Field Artillery
FO	Field Order
GRP	Group
HE	High explosive
Hqs & Hqs Co	Headquarters & Headquarters Company
Inf	Infantry
IP	Initial Point
KIA	Killed in Action
Kms	Kilometers
LO	Line Officer
LSTs	Landing Ship Transports
LtCol	Lieutenant Colonel
Maj	Major
Med Det	Medical Detachment
MG	Machine gun
MIA	Missing in Action
MLR	Main line of resistance
MP	Military Police

OP	Observation Post
OpL	Operation Plan
Pfc	Private First Class
Plt	Platoon
POD	Place of Departure
POW	Prisoner of War
Pvt	Private
Recon	Reconnaissance
Regt	Regiment
Res	Reserve(s)
S/Sgt	Staff Sargeant
Sgt	Sargeant
SP	Self-propelled
Ste	Saint
Svc Co	Service Company
T/5	Technician 5
TAC	Tactical Air Command
TD	Tank destroyer
US	United States
WIA	Wounded in Action
WP	White phosphorus shells

AUTHOR BIOGRAPHY

History was always my favorite subject. I was 2 months shy of my 7ᵗʰ birthday when World War II began with the United States becoming involved. I remember the troop trains, the ladies no longer being able to purchase the silk stockings as they were being used to make parachutes the troops would need. I remember the ration books we had to use to purchase gas and other necessary items. I remember the "butter" not being butter but lard but to make it look more like butter we put in yellow coloring. Being brought up on a farm, my father either donated or sold cows, pigs, an occasional horse, and some chickens to the military.

This book took me some time research locating my brother-in-law's tank battalion's history and other tank survivors and relatives those who died.

I am a Women's Army Corps veteran (Korean Conflict) having taken Basic Training at Fort Lee, Virginia and my base afterwards was Fort McClellan, Alabama, both of which are now closed.

At age 71 I was honored to go on the Ride for the Wall from Magalia, California to Washington, D.C. in honor of all veterans but especially the Vietnam vets as many of them did not get a welcome home. I'd make the trip again in a heartbeat as it was wonderful, inspiring, met lots of interesting people along the way, ex-military men and women, if there is such a thing as "ex-military," because what one learns in basic, one never forgets, and seeing some of this wonderful country.

This is an excellent source of some of our military history and great for history buffs. You have to read this book!

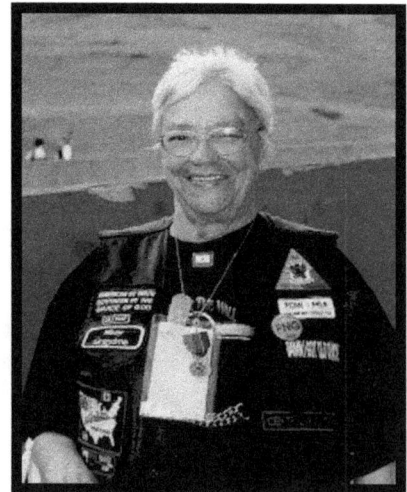

Thank you and God Bless America.

B. J. Bryan